ARRESTING CINEMA

SURVEILLANCE IN HONG KONG FILM

KAREN FANG

STANFORD UNIVERSITY PRESS

STANFORD, CALIFORNIA

Stanford University Press
Stanford, California

© 2017 by the Board of Trustees of the Leland Stanford Junior University.
All rights reserved.

Printed in the United States of America on acid-free, archival-quality paper

Library of Congress Cataloging-in-Publication Data available upon request.

ISBN 978-0-8047-9891-4 (cloth)
ISBN 978-1-5036-0070-6 (paperback)
ISBN 978-1-5036-0075-1 (electronic)

Cover image: Film still from *Back Yard Adventures* (1955), a Cantonese remake of
Hitchcock's *Rear Window.*

Typeset by Motto Publishing Services in 10/14 Palatino

For Elliot and Benjamin (my best work)

CONTENTS

From *Rear Window, Modern Times,* and *Man with a Movie Camera,* to *Blow-Up, The Conversation,* and *The Truman Show,* some of world cinema's best-known and most critically acclaimed films are about surveillance. Surveillance films extend over a wide range of genres and include movies as diverse as *The Matrix, The Lives of Others, Caché,* and even low-budget, pulpy films like the *Paranormal Activity* horror franchise or breakthrough independent films like *sex, lies, and videotape.* One of the main things that these films have in common is that they usually portray social, spatial, and data monitoring as intrusive, perverse, repressive, and violent. This critical and highly suspicious view of surveillance has only consolidated as a result of digital technology and the highly contested debates about security and civil liberties in the post-9/11 world. Well into the twenty-first century, controversies regarding data mining, biometrics, mandatory ID cards, and other technologies and practices have caused modern society to grow more cautious about the varied and pervasive forms that subject us to surveillance. Within this context, cinematic representation can function as a compelling mirror of the ubiquitous instances of screen- and camera-mediated monitoring by which many of us live our daily lives.

Arresting Cinema adds to this extensive critical and popular dialogue by exploring Hong Kong film both as a necessary contribution to an otherwise predominantly Western-centered discourse and as the source of a unique view of surveillance ethics and aesthetics. Hong Kong cinema has been long known for its prolific production and enviable local and regional success; during its height in the mid-1970s through the early 1990s, the industry exported films throughout Asia, and the market was almost unique in that its consumption of locally made product exceeded that of Hollywood imports. But Hong Kong cinema should also be noted for its intelligent and often unexpected take on world film's important surveillance themes. In Hong Kong film, surveillance themes can surface in unique and unconventional genres, such as gambling and comedy, and often in contexts that depict those themes with a tolerance or enthusiasm unprecedented in Hollywood-dominated treatments. Yet, rather than dismiss these differences between Hong Kong and Hollywood cinema as symptomatic of essential and orientalist differences between East and West, we should take a closer look at the territory's history, especially the cinema's acumen at blending imported Hollywood conventions with Chinese cultural traditions, which demonstrate Hong Kong's direct engagement with global surveillance culture. As shown by recent high-profile events, such as the 2014 "Umbrella" protests by local democratic activists and the temporary stay in Hong Kong the preceding year of American domestic spying whistleblower Edward Snowden, Hong Kong has long fostered a complex tradition of surveillance critique whose history, while idiosyncratic, nevertheless has great relevance for the world at large.

This book is guided by two overarching themes. One is the relationship of surveillance to spectacle, not only the way that cinematic images engage surveillance theory and practice but also the disparate concepts and aesthetics that "surveillance" and "spectacle" imply. Although much of the recent scholarship on surveillance imagery in cinema tends to characterize these terms as related, this was not always the case. Michel Foucault, for example, famously opposes surveillance to spectacle in *Discipline and Punish*, and Laura Mulvey, in her equally seminal essay "Visual Pleasure and the Narrative Cinema," sketches a similar opposition, contrasting a Hitchcockian cinema of narrative investigation with a Sternbergian aesthetic in which image trumps all. Yet Hong Kong film, with its inveterate surveillance plots and imagery knitted into kinetic action and its famously eye-popping film idiom, combines both aesthetics. Like D. A. Miller's influential literary account of how surveillance behaviors become naturalized into an artistic and narrative mode, Hong Kong film history shows how surveillance became an integral component of the cinema's emblematic genres and visual attributes.¹ Indeed, with regard to the film medium in particular, Hong Kong's dynamic cinema traditions present a rich and intriguing archive to contrast with the spectacular surveillance traditions widely noted in Western film.

This formal interest in surveillance spectacle also relates to my second overarching theme: Hong Kong film's challenge to Chinese soft power. Originally coined to conceptualize American foreign policy after the Cold War, "soft power" is now a major topic in studies of Chinese and Sinophone film and culture, which since the mid-2000s have used the term to describe China's aspirations to the global influence once associated with American hegemony.² Surveillance has always been an implicit factor in soft power, given the concept's Cold War origins and especially its current revival with Chinese ascendancy, but when realized in film, the issue of soft power further underscores the aesthetic and thematic differences between Hong Kong images of surveillance and more overtly spectacular cinema emanating from China's surveillance state. Thus, while cinematic manifestations of Chinese soft power can be found in the recent revival of traditional *wuxia* martial arts films; the crowd-pleasing blockbuster films of Feng Xiaogang, the "Chinese Spielberg"; or even Zhang Yimou's orchestration of the 2008 Beijing Olympics, this book's focus on Hong Kong film reveals an alternative aesthetic. This aesthetic's unique treatment of surveillance behaviors contrasts with the hard political intent behind Chinese soft power. Its comparative subtlety and occasionally subversive undertones pose an alternative mode of Sinophone soft power that paradoxically emanates from a position of political disempowerment.

Like many fans of Hong Kong film, my love for the city is almost impossible to disentangle from my fascination with its cinema, but given my interest in surveillance, this popular conflation of city with cinema is particularly justified by the centrality of screen and camera mediation in both entities. No one who visits or lives in Hong Kong can fail to recognize the ubiquitous closed-circuit television (CCTV) monitors and security cameras throughout the city, imparting an inevitable familiarity to the sense of seeing the city—and oneself—on-screen. Yet, as this book shows, this explicitly cinematic surveillance imagery is but the tip of the iceberg in a massive official and de facto surveillance complex that includes the territory's omnipresent private watchmen and security guards, unusually strong regulations and informal practices regarding human monitoring, a wealthy and remarkably powerful municipal government, and one of the world's largest and most empowered urban police forces. Local cinema mirrors these structural attributes in some of the genres most commonly identified with Hong Kong film, but what is particularly intriguing about both Hong Kong cinema and the city itself is that they have fostered those developments to the point that they exist largely unremarked. Thus, while it is common for London to be described as the "most surveilled city in the world," Hong Kong provides an important counter and comparison to that claim. If the assertive and tellingly awed tones by which London is described betray a perverse kind of pride, Hong Kong's equally extensive surveillance society deserves similar notice—and is all the more intriguing because it has developed almost without notice.

ACKNOWLEDGMENTS AND A NOTE ON TRANSLATION AND USAGE

This project has benefited from many important supporters and readers. I am indebted to Sam Ho, Hosam Aboul-Ela, and Margot Backus for their support and readings in the project's earliest stages. Stephanie DeBoer, Michael Shapiro, and other anonymous press readers provided invaluable expertise in bringing the project to completion. Alex Cheung; Roger Lee; and Michael, Peggoty, and Seewai Hui shared industry insights and thoughts about their own careers. Paul Fonoroff, Barbara Fei, and Zunzi graciously granted permission to reproduce images, and Philip Chan even sourced the image in Figure 3.3 himself. Along with his rich professional history and connections from the Royal Hong Kong Police, David Hodson generously shared his personal archive of clippings and memorabilia. At Radio Television Hong Kong Janet Mak spoke to me about her two and half decades at the helm of *Police Report* and *Police Magazine*. Kristof Van den Troost first informed me about *Backyard Adventures* and answered questions about censorship; Cindy Chan provided much-needed context and access to difficult-to-find movies; and Howard Choy facilitated in a variety of issues of translation, editorial preparation, and local contacts. At the Hong Kong Film Archive, Diana Miu and Francisco Lo extended patient and resourceful support. Portions of this project have been presented at Hong Kong Polytechnic, Lingnan University, the Chinese University of Hong Kong, and the University of Hong Kong; I am grateful to King-fai Tam, Mark Hampton, Jeffrey Martin, and others for inviting me to these institutions and to the audiences for their comments. Duy Lap Nguyen provided invaluable suggestions in the final stages of writing, and Eszter Simor kindly assisted the final manuscript preparation. Throughout the press process, I could not imagine a more responsive, professional, and supportive editor than Jenny Gavacs. Costs arising from the final manuscript preparation were supported by the University of Houston College of Liberal Arts and Sciences, and much of this research and writing was conducted with the generous support of the Houstoun Endowment at the University of Houston Department of English.

Finally, a brief note on translation and usage. For reasons of concision and in keeping with Hong Kong film's international distribution, this book references material through its most commonly used English versions. Film titles and screen dialogue are referenced according to English-language marketing and subtitles; individuals are referenced by commonly used English transliterations; and Sinophone figures and film genres are referenced according to their most common discursive rendering (e.g., Stephen Chow, *wuxia*, and kung fu). Cantonese Romanization follows the Jyutping system, and in cases where Cantonese and Mandarin are equally used, both renderings are provided. When relevant, deviations or expanded information is included in the notes, and a glossary of Chinese film titles, persons, and terms (including alternative film titles used in Taiwan) is appended.

I am grateful to Timmy Chen Chih-Ting for assistance with translation and Chinese-language research. Mistakes or errors anywhere in the manuscript, however, of course are my own.

INTRODUCTION

A RACE OF PEEPING TOMS?
"REAR WINDOW ETHICS" IN HONG KONG

SURVEILLANCE, HERE LOOSELY DEFINED as any technology or practice engaged in social, spatial, and data monitoring, is a ubiquitous aspect of world cinema, simultaneously influencing the medium's visual aesthetics and providing a compelling subject of narrative representation. Along with its attendant manifestations, such as voyeurism, eavesdropping, policing, predictive behavior, risk assessment, financial and actuarial speculation, surveillance has been a recurring aspect of landmark films from the inception of the art form. Indeed, the cinematic exploration of surveillance ethics and aesthetics that Tom Gunning finds in early films such as *The Arrest of a Pickpocket* (1895), *A Subject for the Rogue's Gallery* (1904), *Falsely Accused* (1908), and *Le pickpocket mystifié* (1911) has, if anything, only intensified in the post-9/11 climate of global security concerns and controversies regarding mass electronic data mining.[1] Thus, in recent years, media scholars such as Catherine Zimmer, Sébastien Léfait, and Garrett Stewart have each separately identified "surveillance cinema" as a distinct subgenre or trend in contemporary film.[2] Building on earlier work by Norman Denzin, John Turner, and Thomas Levin, their critical analyses of movies ranging from Fritz Lang's Expressionist *M* (1931) to Hollywood sci-fi spectacles such as *Déjà Vu* (Tony Scott, 2006) and *Source Code* (Duncan Jones, 2011) fashion a de facto canon of world surveillance film.[3]

Nonetheless, the movies analyzed by those studies are almost without exception filmed and set in the Western world, leaving the racial, cultural, and geographic homogeneity of that film tradition largely unnoticed and unexamined.[4] Although this hemispheric bias no doubt reflects Hollywood's hegemony—and that of Western culture in general—it is also outdated in light of today's global instantaneity and the ascendant power of Eastern and Pacific Rim countries such as China and India. Asian cinema's exclusion from these studies is particularly regrettable given the region's rich cinematic traditions and the distinct and various ways that surveillance manifests across colonial, Communist, and non-Western spaces. For a glimpse of how intimately and insightfully surveillance may be engaged by a nonmainstream or non-Hollywood movie set outside the Global North, one has only to look at *The Battle of Algiers*, the now-classic 1966 film about the Algerian revolution. Shot on location in the Casbah by a collaboration of local activists and Italian neorealist filmmakers, the movie is credited with helping catalyze resistance to French colonization during its initial release, and in recent years it has enjoyed renewed significance as American military and foreign policy strategists recommend the film as a case study in techniques of guerrilla warfare and control of civic unrest.[5]

Like *The Battle of Algiers*, Hong Kong cinema also originates in a society steeped in the intersection of colonial influence with local ethnic culture, and its cinematic representations of surveillance deserve consideration even if only on the basis of its status as one of the world's most successful film industries. Many moviegoers are already familiar with *Infernal Affairs*, the 2002 local blockbuster about a cat-and-mouse game between an undercover cop working a long-term assignment in a gang and the gang mole inside the police force who is ordered to find him. If Western audiences had not already heard about the Hong Kong film as a result of its regional success, the movie became globally recognizable several years later when it was remade as *The Departed*, Martin Scorsese's 2006 movie that won the Oscar for Best Picture. Although the ease with which the Hong Kong film was adapted into a major Hollywood feature might suggest the former as a genre exercise devoid of specifically local attributes, Hong Kong historian and cultural studies scholar Law Wing-sang points out that *Infernal Affairs* belongs to a long tradition of undercover-cop movies crucial to Hong Kong film and cultural identity.[6] This affinity between global culture and the motifs of covert operations prevalent in Hong Kong cinema demonstrates the insights of a regional, East Asian, putatively non-Western, colonial, and postcolonial cinema in contributing to Western-dominated surveillance discourse. Both eminently local and profoundly exportable, *Infernal Affairs* exemplifies Hong Kong surveillance cinema's salience for its distinctly local tradition of Hong Kong undercover-cop movies and the way that seemingly unique local product intervenes in more globally familiar, Western-dominated surveillance culture.

REAR WINDOW ETHICS

In fact, *Infernal Affairs* is hardly the first instance of Hong Kong cinema's engagement with world surveillance cinema traditions, further revealing the complex ways in which it both engages and departs from dominant Western modes. In 1955, only a year after the release of Alfred Hitchcock's *Rear Window*, local theaters were also screening *Backyard Adventures*, a Hong Kong remake of the Hollywood film (Fig. I.1).[7] Best known as a rapidly assembled charity effort to raise funds for the family of comedian Yee Chau-shui, who had abruptly passed away, the movie also warrants attention because of its curious departures from world cinema's archetypal surveillance film. True to much Hong Kong cinema, *Backyard Adventures* may at first appear a derivative imitation, using the same Chinese title as used for *Rear Window*'s local exhibition and closely following *Rear Window*'s premise of a wheelchair-bound photographer who spends his convalescence peering at his neighbors across a mutual courtyard. It is so closely modeled on the Hollywood original that, at times, *Backyard Adventures* reproduces *Rear Window* with shot-for-shot fidelity (Fig. I.2). But where Hitchcock's film begins with the photographer's nurse and girlfriend criticizing his voyeurism, deploring his "rear window ethics" and the fact that "we're becoming a race of Peeping Toms," the Hong Kong film notably lacks any such anxiety. Instead, in pointed contrast to the movie's classic Hollywood precedent, *Backyard Adventures* shows the man's fiancée encouraging him to pass the time through voyeurism, even fetching him binoculars and taking the step of stimulating his viewing by pointing to individual windows and narrating imagined stories (Fig. I.3).

FIGURE I.1. Hong Kong's "rear window ethics" in *Backyard Adventures* (Liangyou Film Company, 1955).

FIGURE I.2. Remaking Hollywood, shot for shot: one of the many *Rear Window* reenactments in *Backyard Adventures* (Liangyou Film Company, 1955; Paramount Pictures, 1954).

FIGURE I.3. Visual pleasure and the narrative cinema: learning to enjoy watching in *Backyard Adventures* (Liangyou Film Company, 1955).

In fact, these striking visual and thematic differences between Hollywood's globally canonical surveillance film and its regional Hong Kong adaptation are only magnified as *Backyard Adventures* proceeds. While many other notable discrepancies arise—ranging from the latter film's reversal of Hitchcock's original stage blocking by having the love interest wheel the photographer *toward* the window (Fig. I.4), to the inclusion of completely unprecedented elements such as a group of half-naked fitness enthusiasts whose visual spectacle is surpassed only by a Chinese opera troupe that abruptly files in to perform—nowhere is the Hong Kong movie's idiosyncrasy more apparent than in its utter abandonment of the murder mystery that is the defining attribute of Hitchcock's film. Unlike the Hollywood movie, the Hong Kong film has no criminal discovery, as the photographer's inadvertently overhearing a nighttime scream is dismissed as an adverse reaction to medication, and even the killing of a troublesome dog (a plot

FIGURE I.4. Embracing the voyeurism that others resist: Hong Kong cinema inverts Hitchcock's stage blocking (Liangyou Film Company, 1955; Paramount Pictures, 1954).

detail consistent with the original film) is literally laughed off by the characters. Thus, much like the film's overall displacement of Hitchcockian thriller into a quintessentially Hong Kong instance of playful, multigeneric, rapidly produced pastiche, *Backyard Adventures* revels in unqualified enjoyment of visual observation, voyeurism, and surveillance never imagined in Hitchcock's canonical surveillance film.

MADE IN HONG KONG

Both *Infernal Affairs* and *Backyard Adventures* raise several questions that guide this book. What do these Hong Kong movies suggest about local surveillance culture, either within Hong Kong itself or in terms of the cinema's relationship to the surveillance themes that pervade so much world film? How are these cinematic images of surveillance shaped by Hong Kong's complex colonial and postcolonial history as well as its having a highly successful, regionally dominant film industry? And what does Hong Kong surveillance cinema contribute to the global discourse on surveillance that otherwise remains overly Western-centric?

To answer these questions, this book begins by interrogating some of the fundamental assumptions underlying critical studies of surveillance cinema. As academic disciplines, both film and surveillance studies tend to explore surveillance cinema as unmediated, relatively straightforward images of surveillance culture without sufficient consideration of either the global map in which these cinemas take place or the various ways in which local film traditions might shape different surveillance imagery. As a result, scholarly studies of surveillance cinema promulgate a geographically and culturally limited landscape of surveillance culture in which predominantly European and American movies corroborate the historical and speculative societies described by George Orwell, Aldous Huxley, and Michel Foucault. Although the images and narratives depicted in these classic works are primarily critical and negative, their geographic bias nevertheless contains a degree of self-congratulation. Because surveillance has long been characterized as a sign of social modernity and little acknowledgment is made of the difference between cinematic representation and actual human experience, the hemispheric bias in most surveillance film studies perpetuates a notion that surveillance is an attribute limited to Western modernity.

Within surveillance studies, for example, David Lyon's frequent references to American and European movies exemplify this one-sidedness. His many works are seeded with references to movies like *Gattaca, Minority Report,* and *The End of Violence;* as Lyon justly reasons, although "some people may have read social science or philosophical work on surveillance, a much larger audience will have seen a surveillance movie."[8] While these films offer compelling and accessible glimpses of surveillance themes and concepts and critical discussions of the films are often focused on esoteric legal and technical questions, Lyon's references downplay distinctions that might be specific to European and Hollywood film styles or the American, German, and New Zealand directors behind the films. In some ways this critical prioritizing of white bodies and English-language settings is not surprising, as it resembles the landscape of surveillance studies—and surveillance geopolitics—itself. Like UKUSA or "Five Eyes," the global intelligence network in which predominantly white, Western, English-speaking countries of Britain, Canada, New Zealand, and Australia cooperate with the United States in an information-sharing partnership that reinforces American hegemony, surveillance studies' uses of film perpetuate a geographic and cultural bias that aligns modernity primarily with Western culture.[9]

Film studies is not much different, despite the discipline's greater attention to the discrepancy between reality and representation and the role of film tradition in shaping or inspiring representation itself. Although film studies has long explored the distinct linguistic and cultural attributes of "national" cinema, critical writing about surveillance's reflexive properties—the implicit self-reference and media representation common in filmic representations of visual and auditory monitoring—resembles surveillance studies in that it also tends to overlook cultural difference. The oft-referenced essays by film scholars and theorists John Turner and Thomas Levin are cases in point. Building on observations about spectatorship and the cinematic apparatus made in seminal essays by Christian Metz or about movies like *Rear Window*, Turner and Levin claim that the proliferating time stamps, optical markers, screens within screens, and other visual and narrative attributes of 1980s and 1990s cinema mirror surveillance's dramatic expansion in the second half of the twentieth century. Yet the movies that both authors reference—which, in addition to other previously mentioned titles, include *WarGames* (John Badham, 1983), *Thelma & Louise* (Ridley Scott, 1991), *Sneakers* (Phil Robinson, 1992), *Menace II Society* (Hughes Brothers, 1993), *Enemy of the State* (Tony Scott, 1998), and *Timecode* (Mike Figgis, 2000)—are merely a more extensive version of the Western filmography typical of Lyon and other surveillance scholars. One has to wonder how these otherwise illuminating studies of cinematic surveillance would benefit from the inclusion of important and intriguing entries of world film such as *High and Low*, Akira Kurosawa's tautly engrossing 1963 procedural about the investigation of a kidnapping—and a genre movie arguably as engaged with epistemological questions as the director's other, more critically commanding film, *Rashomon*—or the more recent *Neighboring Sounds*, a 2012 Brazilian thriller about an affluent neighborhood that unknowingly employs a private security service staffed by the adult children of their exploited former servants.[10]

It is precisely this tension between surveillance cinema's reflexive conventions and its reflectionist properties as an ethnographic glimpse into surveillance culture itself that makes Hong Kong cinema a crucial resource, not just for Asian film specialists and scholars of world film and surveillance culture but indeed for anyone concerned about surveillance's mounting impact throughout the world. As many scholars have already demonstrated, Hong Kong has always had a complicated relationship with Hollywood and the global culture that it tradition-ally shapes.[11] In the specific case of surveillance cinema, this means that Hong Kong surveillance films such as *Backyard Adventures* and *Infernal Affairs* are unusually fruitful sites of global scrutiny, despite—or precisely because—their frequent engagement with better-known Hollywood surveillance imagery is informed both by local surveil-lance culture and by the cinema's aspirations to rival Hollywood itself. Although the current Hong Kong film industry, as a result of a pre-cipitous decline during the years leading up to Hong Kong's 1997 re-unification with China, no longer approximates the level of produc-tivity and regional dominance it once commanded, it is telling that surveillance-themed movies like *Infernal Affairs* continue to be a re-curring strain among the Hong Kong movies that sustain local box of-fice and that provide the means by which Hong Kong film influences global culture. Despite China's recent emergence as the world's larg-est film market—as well as its long-standing notoriety as an intensely surveilled state—it is politically subordinate but culturally important Hong Kong whose cinema presents insights for global surveillance culture.

GAMBLING FILMS AND TENEMENT MOVIES

Hong Kong surveillance cinema's richness is evident in the diverse motifs by which surveillance manifests itself, beyond the subgenre of undercover policing and covert-operation movies that Law Wing-sang calls "Hong Kong undercover." As Law himself notes, covert policing and undercover-cop plots are highly conventional formulas in global crime drama, but they have acquired particular significance in Hong Kong because the genre's theme of conflicting identities and serving two masters evokes the territory's unique political history as a former colony that transitioned to Chinese rule without ever having gained complete self-rule. These themes are readily apparent in *Man on the Brink*, a 1981 undercover-cop drama that is often cited as one of the first and most important examples of what would become known as the "Hong Kong New Wave" and continues through *City on Fire*, a 1987 noir that has been the subject of much critical and popular attention, both for its perceived allegorization of Hong Kong's impending 1997 reunification with China and its uncredited remaking by Hollywood filmmaker Quentin Tarantino in his early, critically acclaimed *Reservoir Dogs* (1992). Yet surveillance themes can also be detected in other less obvious Hong Kong film genres and traditions that are relatively unknown to world film but whose idiosyncratic and local treatments nevertheless have much to contribute to global surveillance discourse.

The *du pian/dou pin*, or gambling film, is one such alternative Hong Kong film genre distinguished for its striking and sophisticated surveillance imagery. Perhaps most commonly recognized through *God of Gamblers* (1989) and the many sequels, spin-offs, spoofs, and imitations that film spawned, the genre explores the stratagems and experiences of financial speculation and gaming. The gambling film has been a recurrent thread in local cinema since the early 1970s, when loosening censorship freed the industry to portray vice and widespread unemployment enhanced the appeal of the genre's stories of instant wealth.[12] Casino security, card counting, and the display or interrogation of poker faces are recurrent images within the films (Fig. I.5), evidencing gambling's obvious engagement with social, spatial, and data monitoring (also see Fig. 4.4). This narrative emphasis on surveillance typical of such movies as *Challenge of the Gamesters* and *Mahjong Heroes* (both 1981) or *Sup Sap Bup Dup* (1975, whose title is a colloquialism describing a bad roll of dice) is often stylistically reinforced by optical and cinematographic flourishes such as zoom, swish pan, point-of-view (POV) shots, split screens, aerial and under-the-table shots, and screens within screens. Although some of these visual gestures are typical of 1970s film style and not unique to gambling movies, it is telling that recent *dou pin* continue to revel in cinematographic display, prominently incorporating computer-generated imagery (CGI) in post-decline movies like *Poker King* (2009) and the *From Vegas to Macau* series (2014, 2015, 2016). So mutually imbricated is the genre in both the metaphoric and metonymic aspects of surveillance cinema that Hong Kong gambling films often conflate the surveillance skills that enable gambling success with the triumph of Hong Kong cinema itself. *The Casino* (1972), for example, is a tightly choreographed Shaw Brothers gambling film, notable for stylizations that may be attributable to John Woo, who long before his later fame as an action auteur served as the movie's assistant

FIGURE I.5. Gambling genre conventions: casino security in *God of Gamblers* and a poker face in *Games Gamblers Play* (Win's Movie Productions, 1989; Golden Harvest / Hui's Film Production Co., Ltd., 1974).

director. The film displays a cinematographic pleasure in gambling-motivated surveillance through the frequent, rapid tracking shots and zooms that convey the intense, vigilant gaze by which gamblers and spectators regard each other and the game. Indeed, in a literal "money" shot whereby the hero's winning dice throw is photographed through aerial POV, the movie literalizes Hong Kong's frequent conflation of surveillance and cinema by allying aleatory victory with the optical pleasures of local gambling movies.

Hong Kong gambling films are rife with such moments, attesting to both gambling's popularity in local culture and surveillance studies' theoretical interest in gambling as a site of both formal and informal monitoring.[13] It is commonly known, for example, that casinos and gaming industries are the first nonmilitary adopters of surveillance technology and practices, a fact that further highlights gambling movies as an index of both surveillance's penetration into domestic culture and the artistic aspiration implied by the cinematic trope. Yet while a Hollywood movie like Brian De Palma's 1998 casino movie, *Snake Eyes*, is often cited by film and surveillance scholars for its opening long take, Hong Kong's prolific, long-standing, and highly diversified tradition of gambling films had already begun exploring these affinities much earlier and more comprehensively than arguably any other site of world film.[14] The cinema's rich tradition of gambling movies should thus be appreciated not only as a symptom of local culture but also as an important site of surveillance commentary. By manifesting a gambling film tradition much earlier and more extensively than any other cinema in world film, local gambling movies position Hong Kong at the forefront of global surveillance trends.

The tenement film is another genre closely identified with Hong Kong film and cultural history whose imagery and narratives pose interesting contributions to global surveillance culture. The tradition depicts *ban jian fang* (*baan gaan fong*), the common local practice of subdividing rooms, installing multiple families within single-family homes, or otherwise improvising living space within places not intended for many residents. This practice first became common in Hong Kong during the 1950s, when housing stock in the small and rapidly growing territory proved increasingly incapable of keeping pace with postwar growth.[15] As a genre the tenement film relates to surveillance because voyeurism and eavesdropping are recurrent scenarios within such movies, suggesting it is an inevitable condition of Hong Kong life. One classic tenement movie, *The Dividing Wall* (1952), shows the escalating tensions that develop between two bachelors whose boarding house rooms share a flimsy partition (Fig. I.6). Also known as *The Happiness of Living Together*, the film interestingly emphasizes the benefits of surveillance, particularly the ad hoc family ties and mutual care that arise among unrelated people sharing close quarters. In 1961, American urban writer Jane Jacobs described such a phenomenon as "natural sur-

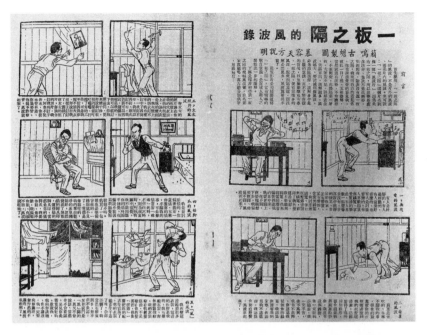

FIGURE I.6. Tenement-genre conventions: detail from promotional film program for *The Dividing Wall* (Loon-Ma Film Company, 1952; courtesy of Barbara Fei, Paul Fonoroff, and Hong Kong Film Archive).

veillance," a term that would later become important for policing and criminology, but, as occurred in Hong Kong's gambling film tradition, the peripheral cinema developed this notion with prescience and profusion.[16] For example, the later tenement movie *Rear Entrance* (1960)— although set amid more affluent bourgeois townhouses—shows a childless couple adopting a neglected girl they spy in their shared back alley, and the popular *Lucky Seven* comedy series (beginning 1970) depicts residents of a high-rise apartment pooling goods and services while a group of rooftop-dwelling bachelors revel in the Peeping Tom voyeurism that *Rear Window* approaches so gingerly.

So central, in fact, are tenement movies to Hong Kong surveillance cinema that classic examples of the genre rank among some of the most important films in Hong Kong cinema and cultural history. *In the Face of Demolition*, for example, is a 1953 film by the then new left-leaning local film company Union Film Enterprises. It concerns a close-knit group of working-class neighbors who pull together when their mod-

FIGURE I.7. A race of Peeping Toms: communitarian ethics, *In the Face of Demolition* (Union Film Enterprises, 1953).

est tenement is abruptly slated for redevelopment (Fig. I.7). The film is an icon of local film and popular culture, widely remembered for the "all for one, one for all!" slogan that its characters echo throughout the movie.[17] The motto became an anthem for progressive Hong Kong audiences, who saw in the film's compassionate portrait of working-class disempowerment an implied critique of the lack of social services that would be exposed by the disastrous Shek Kip Mei fire that occurred within a few weeks of the film's release.[18] Although it was certainly the fire (which created a housing crisis overnight) that is conventionally attributed as the event that triggered the government's subsequent creation of a public housing program, *In the Face of Demolition* constitutes an important document in local perception of surveillance and social control. The director (Lee Tit) and lead actor (Ng Chor-fan) are both known for fostering a socially progressive strain in Cantonese filmmaking. Influenced by the "Clean Film Movement," a mainland effort to improve society through the use and reform of local film culture, the two were key players in the founding of Union Film itself, which required affiliated talent to invest in the production and then distributed profits evenly, reproducing in its business practices the centralized oversight and submission to communitarian ethics announced by this classic tenement movie's motto.[19]

Similarly, the 1973 Shaw Brothers classic, *The House of 72 Tenants*, is another archetypal tenement film that shows the extent to which surveillance tropes are both indicative of local culture and instrumental in expressing cinematic aspirations.[20] Although best known for using its nostalgic period setting and Cantonese dialogue to inaugurate a new era of distinctly local, proudly indigenous Hong Kong film, the movie is also, more basically, a tenement film whose treatment of generic conventions includes natural surveillance.[21] Thus, *The House of 72 Tenants* depicts the intimacy and mutual support of a group of struggling tenement residents, particularly as they capitalize on the limited privacy and collective surveillance enabled by living in close quarters, to undermine their tyrannical landlady and the opportunistic policeman who assists her. For example, when the landlady attempts to frame one resident for theft, she is foiled because a neighbor spies her deceit from his conveniently placed, *Rear Window*–like apartment (Fig. I.8); when the woman beats her adopted daughter, the resident who inhabits a bunk suspended beneath her floor hears the girl's cries and bursts

FIGURE I.8. Apprehending criminality from a *Rear Window*–like apartment in *The House of 72 Tenants* (Celestial / Shaw Brothers, 1973). Note that the trumpet in the character's hands visually resembles the telephoto lens in *Rear Window* (see Figure I.1).

FIGURE I.9. "All for one, and one for all!" A neighbor comes to the rescue (by bursting through the floor) in *The House of 72 Tenants* (Celestial / Shaw Brothers, 1973).

through the floor to assist her (Fig. I.9); and in the film's climactic sequence the residents conspire to spirit the abused girl away from her mistress's clutches by pretending she has cholera—thereby relying on contemporary practices of quarantine and medical surveillance to ensure that the girl is successfully removed.

As does the gambling genre, Hong Kong tenement movies display an unusually positive relationship to surveillance, and the spectatorial pleasures the films advocate are also reflexively manifested in film style itself. In *The House of 72 Tenants*, for example, surveillance cinema's tendency to use visual and cinematographic devices to foreground its thematic and narrative motifs is most obvious in the many freeze frames that punctuate the film whenever a new character is being introduced or to underscore a punch line, particularly in scenes when the tenants' nemeses are foiled (Fig I.10).[22] Freeze frames are generally more common in Hong Kong than in Hollywood cinema, but in *The House of 72 Tenants*, their extravagant number is further enhanced by the movie's generic emphasis on surveillance, which conflates physical and criminological arrest in the freeze frames' visual prolonging of the moments in which illicit and unethical acts have been prevented and their perpetrators apprehended. Literal scenes of *J'accuse!*, *The House of 72 Tenants'* many freeze frames have obvious precedents in world film, whose contrast with Hollywood-style freeze frames further illustrates Hong Kong surveillance cinema's unique perspective.

FIGURE I.10. *J'accuse!* Visual and narrative arrest in freeze frames in *The House of 72 Tenants* (Celestial / Shaw Brothers, 1973).

Thus, while *The Great Train Robbery* and *Butch Cassidy and the Sundance Kid,* for example, both end with iconic freeze frames whose content and imagery reinforce a cinematographic identification with criminal apprehension, those famous Hollywood moments of climactic freeze frame align aggressive surveillance with establishment authority, in sharp contrast to the multiplicity, humor, and domesticated uses with which surveillance appears in a classic Hong Kong film such as *The House of 72 Tenants.*

"HONG KONG ON A BAD DAY"

Not all Hong Kong surveillance films are as tolerant as tenement and gambling movies, of course, but those genres' emphases on capitalism and urban crowding, as well as the allegories of ambiguous sovereignty typical of the "Hong Kong undercover" subgenre, prefigure a number of attributes central to modern surveillance. For decades, theorists and cultural critics have been observing a major shift in surveillance practice. The panoptic and traditionally formal or official sources of restriction and enclosure originally described by Orwell and Foucault have been displaced by a diffuse, decentralized, increasingly invisible and intangible but still constant monitoring arising from capitalist corporations and consumer behavior.[23] This post-panoptic "society of control" described by Gilles Deleuze is echoed in more recent accounts of

FIGURE I.11. Realizing Hollywood surveillance sci-fi: full-body transport scans in *Total Recall* (Carolco Pictures, 1990, left) and the Hong Kong airport (South China Morning Post, right).

"new surveillance," lateral surveillance, *sous*veillance, the "surveillant assemblage," the "sensor society," and the "soft cage," and, for cinema, it gives new context to prior cinematic images in which Hong Kong is identified as a place forecasting global surveillance trends.[24] In fact, Hollywood film—and Western surveillance culture more generally— already harbors several widely recognizable instances of Hong Kong's surveillance prescience. For example, in *Blade Runner*, Ridley Scott's 1982 adaptation of a short story by celebrated science-fiction author Philip K. Dick and a film partly financed by Hong Kong film magnate Sir Run Run Shaw, the movie's award-winning dystopian image of future Los Angeles was famously envisioned as a result of the director's instructions that it should look like "Hong Kong on a bad day."[25] Similarly, the recent (and much-contested) introduction of full-body magnetic resonance imaging technology in US and other global airports prompted recollections of a similar image from *Total Recall* (1990), another Hollywood sci-fi movie based upon a Philip K. Dick story. However, such technology was already commonplace in Asia more than a decade earlier, when the Hong Kong airport, in response to the 2003 severe acute respiratory syndrome (SARS) outbreak, became one of the first to impose thermal bioscanning as a mandatory condition for entering and leaving the territory (Fig. I.11).[26]

Aside from their obvious similarities as Hollywood adaptations of Philip K. Dick stories, what *Blade Runner* and *Total Recall* highlight through their mutual allusions to Hong Kong is the territory's primacy in emerging global surveillance culture. Drawing on Hong Kong's notoriety as one of the world's most densely crowded urban spaces and its conventionally more positive reputation as a prosperous and technologically advanced metropolis firmly embedded in global networks of air travel and multinational capital, these two Hollywood films corroborate Hong Kong cinema's own generic traditions by affirming modern surveillance society as an artifact of predominantly urban and capitalist conditions. Indeed, although *Blade Runner* and *Total Recall* are both special effects–laden sci-fi films typical of Hollywood surveillance that have little in common with contemporary Hong Kong cinema and particularly the distinct surveillance traditions that Hong Kong film fosters, it is telling that Steven Soderbergh's 2011 pandemic thriller, *Contagion*, intuitively seems to channel Hong Kong surveillance cinema by showing epidemiologists using casino footage to locate "patient zero" in a Hong Kong restaurant (Fig. I.12). Hong Kong is known to be a likely source of disease transmission because of its urban density, suspect sanitation standards, and high rate of air traffic. *Contagion* builds on that knowledge while also exhibiting the difference between Hollywood and Hong Kong surveillance. Inadvertently echoing Hong Kong gambling genres by incorporating casino surveillance footage as an element of cinematic spectacle, *Contagion* recalls

FIGURE I.12. Hong Kong starts a global pandemic in *Contagion* (Warner Bros., 2011). Note the digital camera's screen within screen, typical of surveillance cinema and in the movie later connected to casino footage to enable a response to the outbreak.

Blade Runner and *Total Recall* both by indicting Hong Kong as an origin point of global surveillance behaviors and by exhibiting a paranoia about ubiquitous, ineluctable surveillance far different from many of Hong Kong film's treatments of the same theme.

A RACE OF PEEPING TOMS?

The reasons for Hong Kong's centrality in global surveillance culture as well as its unique approach to the topic may at first seem cultural, an ethnographic or essentialist assumption of ethnic Asian difference. In *Rear Window*'s canny rhetoric this might be expressed as the idea that Hong Kong is "becoming a race of Peeping Toms." Indeed, existing scholarly studies of Hong Kong culture and society seem to corroborate this account. Although few area studies publications invoke surveillance as a specific topic of research, for more than half a century Hong Kong has been subject to critical inquiries from a variety of disciplines attempting to explain the territory's high levels of government intervention and low standards of privacy by referencing the idea that "Chinese lacks a word for privacy" and that "Chinese have developed ways of managing space, time and people that even the most extreme crowding does not lead to any particular increase in social stress."[27] Interestingly, much of this earlier work was conducted by colonial-era scholars who minimize distinctions between a generalized Chinese culture and history and the specific conditions of Hong Kong's urban, capitalist, colonial society. However, these assessments persist in more recent work by Hong Kong–born or –based scholars who have otherwise transformatively refocused local history and cultural studies around the particularities of the territory's hybrid political and cultural heritage and the phases of its economic development under colonial rule and subsequent Chinese sovereignty. Despite widely publicized ideas about Hong Kong's status as an exemplar of free-market capitalism and positive colonial noninterventionism, leading local historians, sociologists, and economists such as Lau Siu-kai, Ma Ngok, Leo Goodstadt, Elizabeth Sinn, and Steve Tsang all describe Hong Kong as a politically pragmatic population that willingly conforms to centralized forms of power in exchange for economic opportunity.[28] This notion gained widespread publicity in the 1990s when venerable Chinese sociologist, current government policy maker, and former president of the Chinese University of Hong Kong, Ambrose King Yeo-chi, wrote in a leading Hong Kong newsmagazine that despite decades of Western influence he "still cannot tell if Chinese culture has privacy in the western tradition."[29] And in some of the most explicit studies of local surveillance culture Hong Kong–born theorist Rey Chow, who has long drawn attention to Foucault's failure to adequately explore colonial and non-European sites, joins Aihwa Ong in claiming that Hong Kong residents, long accustomed to the peculiar regulations and disempowerments of colonial and postcolonial society, are exemplary modern subjects adept at negotiating conditions of control and monitoring to their own advantage.[30]

These notably nonjudgmental and even admiring tones by which commentators describe Hong Kong residents' peculiar tolerance for government intrusion and social control provide scholarly context to the unique surveillance perspective visible in local tenement, gambling, and undercover genres. While only Chow and Ong address local cinema in particular, such cultural and ethnographic scholarship implies that if Hong Kong surveillance cinema is insightful about modern surveillance culture, the reason lies in attributes distinct to Chinese culture or Hong Kong's hybrid colonial heritage more specifically. Missing, however, in this implicit description of Hong Kong as a "race of Peeping Toms" are the filmic conventions implicated through the cinematic lens, which have always been instrumental to surveillance cinema's value as a forum for exploring emerging surveillance trends. Film and surveillance studies alike, for example, invariably cite *Metropolis* and *Modern Times*, two early twentieth-century films whose dystopian representation of industrialization prefigured the use of CCTV monitoring several decades before the technology's creation and widespread use (see Fig. 1.5). As that example illustrates, films about surveillance are uniquely positioned to forecast future surveillance technologies and practices, both because of their explicit diegetic representation and cinema's subtler formal properties of intense visual observation and interpretive insight. Although Orwell also anticipated screen- and camera-enabled visual monitoring in his famous literary imagery of Big Brother's "telescreens," it is the Fordist-Taylorist emphasis on capitalist productivity in *Metropolis* and *Modern Times* that makes cinema and its prescient depictions of CCTV monitoring a more accurate forecast of current surveillance culture.

Hong Kong obviously belongs to this global CCTV discourse through the Hollywood references exemplified in *Contagion* and *Total Recall*, as well as the countless instances of screens within screens that proliferate throughout Hong Kong film of the same era. But what is most important about Hong Kong cinema's foreshadowing of contemporary surveillance trends are the diversification of cultural representation and the way attributes typical of the cinema itself structure these insights into global surveillance theory and practice. For example, in one widely cited study of Hong Kong film's historical success, Ding-Tzann Lii observes that the cinema was able to invert core-periphery hierarchies typical of media and cultural imperialism precisely because its colonial perspective made its cinema sensitive to minority perspectives. This encouraged local stars like Jackie Chan to develop plots and protagonists whose ethnic perspective and inclusive, non-specific ethnic, racial, or national attributes invert the white male privilege and exoticizing orientalism of more conventionally iconic Hollywood heroes such as Rocky, Rambo, James Bond, and Indiana Jones.[31] Although surveillance is not a specific topic for Lii and his analysis fails to acknowledge action's material and symbolic importance as the world's most lucrative film genre, Lii's essay is pertinent for surveillance cinema and world surveillance theory because it demonstrates how Hong Kong cinema's artistic and industrial alternatives to traditional Hollywood images of power attained their own power by trafficking in globally relevant images of alterity.[32]

Similarly, in their studies of Hong Kong cinema and media's penchant for remake and adaptation, Yiman Wang and Paul Lee have both emphasized the aspirational and power implications by which foreign media commodities are adapted for local consumers.[33] Although neither explores surveillance per se, like Lii both show how Hong Kong's prolific but comparatively lower-budget cinema and media foster an ethos in which remake and adaptation are not derivative, unimaginative products but ambitious creative expressions that invert or supplant the conventionally "imperial" appropriations that occur when hegemonic agencies co-opt foreign properties. This paradigm, which Wang calls a "subaltern remake," is precisely the conceit of *Backyard Adventures'* Hollywood adaptation, and although Wang emphasizes discipleship and teaching as common motifs of Hong Kong and Sinophone adaptations and remakes, *Backyard Adventures'* surveillance theme should also be recognized as one of world cinema's most familiar tropes for that premise. As evident in such famed intertextual genealogies as *Rear Window, Blow-Up* (1966), *The Conversation* (1974), and *Blow Out* (1981)—in which the later films address and revise aspects of the preceding—surveillance themes are also often vehicles by which a cinema or its filmmakers position themselves within a worldwide artistic field.[34]

In fact, *Blow Out's* director, Brian De Palma, is well known for using surveillance and voyeurism as motifs to reference influential films and filmmakers, but what is crucial for Hong Kong film about this Hollywood analogue is how it reinforces surveillance cinema's reflexive qualities. As in De Palma's work, Hong Kong film's recurrent surveillance motifs must be understood as expressions of the ambitions of this most inventive and resourceful of cinemas—with the difference, of course, that Hong Kong film develops this motif within a greater variety of genres, among a wider panoply of filmmakers, and across a considerable number of decades, arguably surpassing that of any other region of world film. The reasons for this intense identification with surveillance undoubtedly reflect aspects of Hong Kong's unique culture and history but cannot be divorced from cinematic conventions, particularly the tradition of aesthetic compensation by which Ackbar Abbas and Yiu-wai Chu both describe cinema's compelling but fundamentally ephemeral imagery as the perfect emblem of Hong Kong's ambivalent culture and political identity.[35] Although poignant, these circumstances further motivate the cinema's surveillance motifs, partly because the cinema shows what surveillance means among a population for whom intense social and government oversight are inescapable, but especially because surveillance's centrality within global film culture provides opportunities for Hong Kong cinema to position itself alongside the hegemonic powers conventionally privileged in canonical Hollywood and other Western surveillance cinema.

FROM *ACES GO PLACES* TO *LOVE AND THE CITY*

The first film in the hugely popular *Aces Go Places* franchise vividly illustrates the ingenious ways in which Hong Kong cinema's outsider,
low-budget, seemingly *naïf* qualities can foreshadow global surveillance trends.[36] Appearing early in 1982, six months before *Blade Runner,*
this first installment in what would become a six-episode series of spy
parodies and caper comedies features the transnational partnership
between a dashing local jewel thief (Cantopop star Sam Hui), a famed
Chinese American detective (US-educated comedy actor and director
Karl Maka), and a Hong Kong cop (Taiwan-born Sylvia Chang), who
are appointed by colonial authorities to investigate a diamond heist
by an internationally sought criminal mastermind.[37] Equal parts Pink
Panther imitation and James Bond spoof, the movie makes surveillance
both a trope of cinematic aspiration and an arena in which the agility
of an affluent but politically nonautonomous urban and capitalist society trumps more conventionally hegemonic global powers. The film
is a creation of then-upstart production company Cinema City, which,
like Union Film, was founded by a group of industry talents eager to
create an alternative to studio productions, but it differed significantly
in that Cinema City was a highly commercial operation. Thus, the film
is rife with intertextual references that simultaneously announce its
pretensions to Hollywood-style power while using parody to acknowledge its underdog or outsider position. Some of these allusions to the
Western surveillance canon are flagrantly parodic, such as "Kody-
jack," the bald, lollipop-loving Chinese American cop who clearly references a popular American television detective. The movie's villain
is an overweight, rasping fusion of the Godfather and the cat-stroking
Blofeld from the Bond films. But other moments in the film invoke surveillance more subtly and in ways that dramatically allegorize the
counterintuitive power and pleasure of Hong Kong surveillance film.
The very premise of the film's caper is established through an irrever-
ent send-up of "war-room" scene conventions, which in *Aces Go Places*
shows British, French, American, and Chinese military brass improb-
ably deferring to the Hong Kong police. Typical of the film's escapist
fantasy, this comic inversion of global hierarchy nevertheless is justified in the climactic scene that both presages contemporary technolog-

FIGURE I.13. David and Goliath in world surveillance cinema: Hong Kong–made miniatures face down an international villain in *Aces Go Places* (Cinema City, 1982).

ical and consumer trends toward miniature robotics and graphically symbolizes local subversiveness in a captivating stunt sequence in which the villain's phalanx of armored vehicles is defeated by a fleet of miniature, locally manufactured remote-controlled drones (Fig. I.13).[38]

The whimsical and comparatively low-tech play on Hollywood spectacle by *Aces Go Places* may be somewhat predetermined by the generic and production limitations resulting from Hong Kong's shallower-pocketed film industry, but it is precisely because of those conditions that the movie so effectively demonstrates modern surveillance society as a depoliticized, postnational consumer phenomenon rather than a subject of traditional official and institutional forms of power. Indeed, typical of Hong Kong surveillance culture and cinema, *Aces Go Places* converts surveillance into opportunity, benefit, and pleasure. A recurring gag throughout the movie portrays the impossibility of finding a secluded location in which to relay top-secret information within overcrowded and voyeuristic Hong Kong. Instead, the officer and his informant always find themselves overheard by unintentional but nevertheless willing eavesdroppers—a knowing joke about Hong Kong's dense urban spaces and also a characteristically ludic play on surveillance both consistent with the film's overall spy parody and symptomatic of Hong Kong's unique surveillance culture.

A similar, less tongue-in-cheek image of Hong Kong's surveillance society is rendered in the popular 1994 romance *Love and the City*, a formulaic yet utterly satisfying movie typical of Hong Kong film. The movie is occasionally referenced among film buffs as "A Moment of Romance 6," in knowing acknowledgment of its debts to a blockbuster 1990 film starring heartthrob actor and pop idol Andy Lau. Replicating a number of details from the original *A Moment of Romance*, *Love and the City* portrays the attraction between a wayward delinquent (played by heartthrob and pop star Leon Lai) and a gentle and well-connected young woman, who has the same name (Jo Jo) and is played by the same actress (Wu Chien-lien) as in the original film. And as might be expected of this unabashed remake, surveillance is a crucial motif that uses the trope both to acknowledge the film's position as a remake and to assert the new film's originality. This crucial thematic role of surveillance in the film manifests through a recurring emphasis on mobile telecommunications, whose appearance in *Love and the City* most obviously functions as a technological analogue for motorcycle scenes widely remembered from *A Moment of Romance* but also anticipates current awareness of mobile telecom as one of the modern world's most powerful sources of surveillance data. Throughout the film, characters constantly try to contact each other through pagers and by leaving messages with human-operated answering services, a common consumer service in precellular early 1990s Hong Kong.

At its most basic, this plot emphasis on telecom-facilitated contact is the film's creative variation of time-honored narrative mandates for romantic couples to endure challenges and "meet cute." It also reflects sociocultural aspects of contemporary Hong Kong in which large populations of low-skilled labor make such consumer services highly affordable and the limited privacy of most local housing encourages relentless peripateticism, during which individuals rely on telecommunications to remain accessible while restlessly circulating through urban space. Such fetishistic images of mobile telecommunications are a recurring aspect of Hong Kong film, both reflecting the fact that Hong Kong has one of the fastest and deepest rates of cellular penetration in the world and more specifically exhibiting a rich tradition of mobile telecom imagery within local cinema that antedates spine-tingling cell phone sequences in *Infernal Affairs*. Further evidence of surveillance's unusual importance within *Love and the City* is that the film's thematic and narrative emphasis on telecommunications is integral to the film's very reason for being. In a particularly overdetermined instance of surveillance motifs guiding Hong Kong cinema, *Love and the City*'s opening coincided with a huge advertising campaign by Hutchinson Telecom, then Hong Kong's leading telecommunications provider, which had hired Leon Lai to front an elaborate multimedia ad campaign, ultimately becoming the first in a legendary series of ad spots featuring local film and music stars promoting the company.[39]

Of course, with the exception of wartime propaganda, few movies are as directly imbricated in the surveillance practices they depict, but what is most interesting about *Love and the City*'s commercially motivated theme of telecom-assisted romance is how it anticipates and naturalizes the operations of mass electronic data mining that are now widely recognized as one of the most common means by which global citizens are subjected to social, spatial, and information monitoring. This prescient image of post-panoptic surveillance occurs in the film's climax, which centers on the young man's efforts to contact his beloved. Repeatedly leaving messages with the telephone messaging service, the man fails to reach the woman but inadvertently wins the sympathy of the many young female operators at the messaging service switchboard, who are charmed by his devotion and speculate about the romance (Fig I.14). Touched by his ardor, the operators act on their own initiative and against the rules of conduct prescribed by both company and civic ethics to help the young man. Asking if he "know[s] her home address or her workplace," the operators mobilize their own inquiry, reaching out over digital and fiber-optic networks to connect with their counterparts in a concentrated effort to locate the young woman. In a thriller or stalker film such queries might brew fear, but because the film is a romance, these legal and ethical violations are portrayed as heroic and are touchingly conveyed through a montage of voice-over and aerial shots that idealize telecommunications. Instead of a "system that has as its goal the complete elimination of electronic privacy worldwide"[40]—as some current surveillance critics indict metadata harvesting—this key scene in a Hong Kong surveillance film serves its commercial purpose by portraying telecom-enabled surveillance as a priceless assertion of human feeling. Ob-

FIGURE I.14. Metadata romance in *Love and the City* (Keyboard Ltd., 1994). Note the visual repetition of eavesdropping, transgressed barriers, and gossip visually reprised from the tenement film (compare with Figures I.6 and I.7).

viously motivated by the film's place in an orchestrated campaign of commercial synergy—and pointedly undermining Paul Virilio's influential claim regarding cinema's quasi-military affinity with violent surveillance[41]—the enchantingly romanticized depiction of technologically facilitated surveillance that infuses *Love and the City* also demonstrates how the diffuse and lateral gaze often positively depicted in Hong Kong film occasionally prefigures surveillance trends in the world at large.

ARRESTING CINEMA

To chart the individual and systemic ways by which Hong Kong surveillance cinema sheds light on surveillance culture and practice far beyond its own borders, this book undertakes a comparative analysis of Hong Kong and Hollywood films. The aim is to show Hong Kong cinema's frequent and detailed engagement with one of world film's most enduring motifs, documenting how the cinema's cultural context and positioning shape a uniquely local surveillance tradition that also has great insight for world surveillance culture. Like seminal studies of Hong Kong film by Ackbar Abbas and Stephen Teo, this study encompasses a wide variety of movies and genres from a longer historical scope than typically covered in most such studies; and in the model of Richard Slotkin, Dana Polan, and Siegfried Kracauer, I aim to show how a national or culturally distinct cinema can be understood through a single, governing motif that is both tied to prevailing cultural concerns and at the heart of many of the cinema's most distinctive visual and aesthetic attributes.[42] Chapter 1 begins by using the film oeuvre of beloved comedian and multitalented creative persona Michael Hui to show how the star's detailed, recurring, and singularly comic perspective on surveillance exemplifies attributes of Hong Kong surveillance cinema in general. Building on this sanguine and often optimistic view of surveillance and social monitoring typical of Hui's work, Chapter 2 revisits action and crime films from the years leading up to Hong Kong's 1997 reunification with China to show how surveillance was always at the center of both insights about and misunderstandings within critical approaches to Hong Kong film. Further dissecting critical understandings of Hong Kong cinematic geopolitics at the time of the handover, Chapter 3 focuses on a reunification-era variant of cop movies as well as the cinema's long identification with official policing to explore the productive collusions between entertainment media and the Hong Kong police. This sophisticated, often purposefully conventionalized corollary to well-known ties between local film and organized crime constitutes one of Hong Kong cinema's most visible intersections of cinematic production and political power. It also contextualizes the final chapter, which explores censorship and the changing motifs of surveillance and covert operations within a post-reunification, post-decline Hong Kong cinema that survives by capitalizing on the mainland's vast audience at the cost of the industry's willing accountability to Chinese state policy.

The capaciousness of surveillance as an interpretive site of Hong Kong film, however, is not comprehensive and necessarily entails some omissions. This absence is particularly obvious with regard to emblematic Hong Kong genres like the martial arts film traditions of *wuxia* and kung fu, whose relative inapplicability to the predominantly urban and explicitly modern focus of surveillance cinema is a key issue in Chapter 4, in which the current *wuxia* revival increasingly dominating Hong Kong-China coproductions paradoxically reaffirms the local resonance of *policiers*, cops and robbers, "shoot 'em ups," and undercover stories beloved in Hong Kong film. Similarly, this book's critical survey is limited to narrative cinema, including a remarkable percentage of remakes and adaptations, and places close readings of well-known Hong Kong and Hollywood movies amid a textured survey that references nearly two hundred Hong Kong and Sinophone films. Thus, attentive to Hong Kong film's prolific commerciality as well as the artistic aspirations embedded in its frequent surveillance motifs, for reasons of concision this book omits an equally intriguing surveillance tradition in art film, currently best known globally through video and installation luminaries such as Sophie Calle, Michael Snow, and Nam Jun Paik but also a key quality of the work of influential Hong Kong video artist Quentin Lee.[43]

In place, then, of an impossibly totalizing account of a cinema as deep and multifaceted as Hong Kong's, this book takes for its title a metaphoric description that aptly encapsulates surveillance's importance in both the cinema's unique stylistic attributes and its engagement with global discourses regarding surveillance cinema and modern culture and society at large. "Arresting" is an adjective often used for Hong Kong cinema, typically invoked to describe the industry's fast-paced and stunt-filled action; unconventional and discontinuous temporal editing; high-key lighting and florid palettes; occasionally outré humor and incongruous flourishes; and even the frantic, relentlessly eager-to-please nature of this profoundly commercial cinema.[44] Rarely noted, however, is how these attributes bespeak a complicated relationship between surveillance and spectacle, perhaps most obviously realized in the crime and police stories that crowd so much of Hong Kong's cinematic output. Indeed, even more revelatory is how surveillance underlies a variety of other less predictable genres, such as comedy or the Hong Kong–specific traditions of gambling and tenement movies, and how surveillance stylistically recurs in the proliferating freeze frames that some Western viewers find embarrassingly typical of Hong Kong film.

Although Hong Kong cinema is deeply engaged with world film traditions of conflating criminal and cinematographic arrest, the latter examples of generic variety and freeze frame suggest that its "arresting" cinematic aesthetics are not limited to moments of narrative indictment. Rather, they take on a pervasive logic integral to both the cinema's inimitable visual style and its unconventionally sanguine perspective on the surveillance experiences generally depicted elsewhere with great trepidation. This book is devoted to this less tangible, but no less powerful, field of insight available through Hong Kong film—the local product that, as Ackbar Abbas notes, stems from a "cultural space where the act of looking itself is both the most developed and most problematic act of all."[45] Taking Ridley Scott at his word by using locally produced film to explore what he might have meant by "Hong Kong on a bad day," *Arresting Cinema* is the first book to track Hong Kong film's myriad surveillance subgenres and imagery and to connect those motifs to both the cinema's visual innovations and its place in global surveillance discourse. Current knowledge about surveillance cinema and surveillance culture more generally will never be truly global without coming to terms with this most fascinating of world cinemas. Only by exploring Hong Kong cinema can we begin to shape a truly global understanding of the artistic and cultural issues within surveillance cinema that Hitchcock called "rear window ethics."

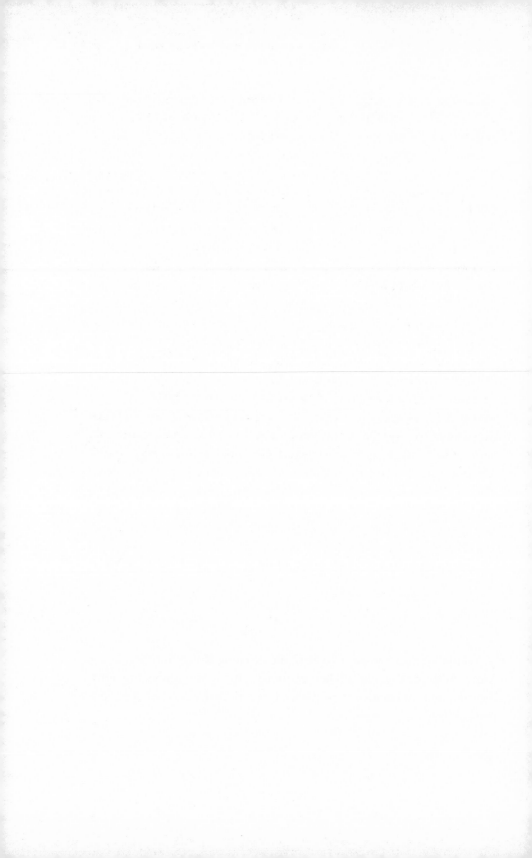

ONE

WATCHING THE WATCHMAN

MICHAEL HUI'S SURVEILLANCE COMEDIES

HONG KONG'S IDIOSYNCRATIC APPROACH to surveillance culture and film is apparent in the cinema's formative years as well as many of its leading figures and texts. The multitalented comedian Michael Hui, for example, whose directorial debut in 1974 succeeded *The House of 72 Tenants* at the top of local box office, is often cited alongside this film as a key factor in local cinema's emergence as a predominantly Cantonese-language film tradition made by, for, and about local Hong Kong culture. Although surveillance has never previously been noted as a defining aspect of the star's film oeuvre, such an affinity between this landmark movie and those of the iconic comedian invites questions about their thematic similarities.[1] Hui emerged as director, screenwriter, and star in five consecutive number-one surveillance films, including *Games Gamblers Play* (1974), *The Private Eyes* (1976), and *Security Unlimited* (1981). Like *The House of 72 Tenants*, these movies' explicit depiction of surveillance technologies and practices portrays surveillance as a constitutive attribute of Hong Kong culture and society. Additionally, Hui's home genre of comedy intensifies the lighthearted and affirmative surveillance imagery that *The House of 72 Tenants* presents more sentimentally. While a purely Hollywood-focused study of surveillance cinema such as Norman Denzin's *The Cinematic Society* claims that movies cannot portray surveillance with humor unless in the satiric manner of Rob Reiner's 1982 noir parody *Dead Men*

FIGURE 1.1. Hui's transnational celebrity and nonaction forms of global Hong Kong film: Spanish poster for *The Private Eyes* (1976, collection of author).

Don't Wear Plaid, Hui's films show Hong Kong cinema's sustained exception to Denzin's claim that surveillance and comedy are mutually exclusive.[2]

This paradoxical fusing of surveillance with comedy in Michael Hui's films cannot be overstated, and further augmenting the comedian's importance within local film and surveillance cinema in particular is the fact that at the height of his career, Hui was also popular in markets throughout Asia and even in Europe (Fig. 1.1). Although such international distribution is not unusual for Hong Kong film, it is striking because comedy's dependence on linguistic and cultural context typically obstructs its exportability.[3] That Hui—like Bruce Lee and Jackie Chan, his contemporaries at then leading new upstart film distributor Golden Harvest, where the comedian started his directorial career—was able to transcend his local market suggests that his films contain qualities that are not only specific to Hong Kong but also of great relevance to audiences beyond. As this chapter shows, in Hui's films, surveillance is further important as the universal attribute that unifies the star's movies and presumably helped make his films popular abroad. Indeed, as a distinct and recurring theme of the self-authored and self-directed films that Hui made after joining Golden Harvest, surveillance also becomes a vehicle of artistic and creative ambition and a motif by which Hong Kong cinema's unusually sanguine or affirmative perspective on surveillance is further demonstrated by Hui's own professional history.

Although it may seem unusual to devote an entire chapter to the film oeuvre of a single figure, this approach is legitimated by Michael Hui's centrality within the local industry and his films' engagement with the cinema's recurrent surveillance themes. His 1982 hit, *Security Unlimited*, provides a particularly vivid instance of both his surveillance themes and the peculiarly positive cast by which surveillance appears in his films and throughout Hong Kong film as a whole. At the time of its release, the film about a small private security detail was the highest-grossing local movie in Hong Kong history, and it is often credited with spawning a number of copycat comedies starring Michael's brothers, Sam Hui and Ricky Hui, that loosely resembled *Security Unlimited* in blending sight gags and spectacular gadgetry with plots of upward mobility. While these accounts justly highlight Hui's commercial influence and that of *Security Unlimited* in particular, by overlooking the significance of that film's specific surveillance subject, these accounts ignore the film's continuity with similar themes throughout his oeuvre and its contrast with the canon of world films on the same subject. By ignoring *Security Unlimited*'s explicit depiction of Hong Kong's participation in the massive expansion of privatized policing that Alison Wakefield, Clifford Shearing, and Phillip Stenning identify as a major attribute of First World economies throughout the 1980s and 1990s, more general understandings of Hui's influence miss his film's address to the same artistic and cultural topic previously portrayed in such canonical world surveillance films such as *The Conversation*.[4] It overlooks how Hui's signature comic genre presents a radically more sanguine approach to surveillance than that typically associated with such classic Western surveillance movies.

Later in this chapter, I will say more about how *Security Unlimited* and other Hui films' seemingly oxymoronic fusion of surveillance with comedy is founded on a pragmatic view of surveillance practices that presents Hui himself as its chief beneficiary. First relevant here, however, is how *Security Unlimited* and other Hui films mobilize both local and global surveillance cinema traditions to position a profoundly local movie as relevant to the world at large. *Security Unlimited*'s Chinese title, *Mo deng bao biao/Mo dang bou biu*, literally translates as "modern security guard" and merges an antiquated term for bodyguard (*bao biao/bou biu*) familiar from *wuxia* films with an English loan word commonly used in Chinese since the 1930s to denote a modernity specifically identified with Western culture.[5] Understanding the full extent of Hui's contribution to both local and global surveillance cinema mandates a similarly hybrid, multilayered approach, beginning with recognizing surveillance as a crucial element of the social realism for which his comic films have long been famed but also exploring how that recurrent motif merges local and global surveillance themes ultimately to promote the artist himself. As this chapter shows, although Hui's incongruously comic approach to surveillance may seem almost unique in world surveillance film, Hui's surveillance comedies figure the artist himself as the personification of the upwardly mobile benefits enabled by surveillance cooperation. Long before Stephen Chow and Ronald Cheng—two younger comedians also deeply identified with Hong Kong culture and entertainment—Hui positioned himself as a "Hong Kong everyman," and his singular, seemingly idiosyncratic tendency to use surveillance motifs to showcase himself exemplifies the lateral gaze that distinguishes Hong Kong surveillance cinema.

SURVEILLANCE AND HONG KONG'S EVERYMAN

Ironically, Hui's centrality within Hong Kong cinema history is a major reason why his sustained engagement with surveillance motifs has long gone unnoticed. Widely described as a "Hong Kong everyman," Hui is known for playing irascible, curmudgeonly characters whose cheap practicality but relentless schemes to get rich quick figure himself as an exemplar of existence within Hong Kong's fast-paced and fiercely capitalistic economy.[6] All of his movies are set in specific and highly detailed industrial and professional situations, such as food service, entertainment media, and other consumer and service industries, and as might be expected of such a Fordist or Taylorist ethos, surveillance is a recurring aspect of such environments. However, its very ubiquity throughout Hui's repeated depictions of laboring individuals trying to survive in Hong Kong's then rapidly accelerating economy can obscure that otherwise unifying motif. For example, one of the two other top-grossing films with which Hui debuted in the 1970s as director and screenwriter as well as star, *The Last Message* (1975), takes place within the notably Foucauldian setting of a mental hospital and follows two opportunistic employees as they try to discover the location of an inmate's hidden treasure by using an EEG machine to record the man's brain waves and interpreting them as Morse code. Although such a premise may not invoke surveillance in the overt manner of a gambling or detective film, *The Last Message* hinges on data gathering and the institutional and technological monitoring of individuals—themes that also characterize *The Contract* (1978), a satire of television programming that includes a running gag in which network executives gather in the company boardroom to confront poorly performing producers with data regarding their recent ratings. In further demonstration of the pervasive or even compulsive surveillance within Hui's imagery, the film also shows the executives taking bets on how long it takes the disgraced showrunners to throw themselves out the window and timing the event with stopwatches.

As *The Last Message* and *The Contract* show, surveillance is such a persistent and unifying aspect of Hui's oeuvre that it appears even in movies that are not as explicitly identified with the topic as *Games Gamblers Play, The Private Eyes,* and *Security Unlimited.* So central, in fact, are surveillance behaviors to Hui's incarnation of the Hong Kong everyman that the motif continues even in the comedian's films from the later 1980s and early 1990s, a period during which he had begun to retreat from multilevel creation. Like much Hong Kong film (and commercial film in general), Hui often repeats successful formulae, and his willingness to recycle effective gags is evident not only in his general socioeconomic focus but also specifically surveillance's frequency as a comic set piece. His films are full of moments in which characters are caught behind X-ray screens (*The Last Message, Mr. Coconut*); simulate telephone answering services (*Inspector Chocolate, Mr. Coconut*); and elude capture by hiding inside costumes, pretending to be statues, or otherwise hiding in plain sight (*The Contract, The Private Eyes, Security Unlimited, Front Page*). These sight gags and other surveillance-related jokes are but the tip of the iceberg in a deep and sustained comic investment in surveillance as a defining aspect of local society, as is apparent in some of his films' longer, favored set pieces.

The Private Eyes, for example, features Hui as a niggardly private detective who monitors his employees with the same intensity that he applies to his commissioned investigations, as he keeps a running a tab on his employees' debts and expenses. A similar joke recurs much later in *Hero of the Beggars* (1992), where Hui plays a mainland military captain adrift in Hong Kong who invokes the paternalist authority invested in his hierarchal authority to demand control of his underlings' wages, ultimately inciting a mutiny in which the subordinates organize against their superior. Similarly, *Inspector Chocolate* (1986) and *Chicken and Duck Talk* (1988) both include scenes where uniformed health and sanitation inspectors visiting restaurants or food purveyors come face-to-face with resourceful food-service workers who do everything in their power to obscure cockroaches and other consequences resulting from the shortcuts that optimize efficiency and enable affordable dining. Both a joke about the notoriously "dirty" nature of cheap Asian restaurants and an affectionate portrait of the bureaucratic institutions for oversight and enforcement that characterize prosperous modern Hong Kong, these repeated scenes of health and sanitation inspection in Hui's films exemplify the centrality of surveillance within his oeuvre as a whole.

As in *The House of 72 Tenants*, the film to which they are often compared, Hui's films depict surveillance as an inevitable attribute of Hong Kong social fabric, while also distinguishing themselves by exhibiting a realism and contemporaneity not present in the Shaw studio's period film. Hui's movies are set in bottling factories, hotel and restaurant kitchens, warehouses, and office back rooms, often shot on location, in a visual elaboration of the star's "everyman" quality that recalls the social realism of early Cantonese cinema while updating their content with explicitly modern scenarios. In a specifically autobiographical strain of Hui's detailed and realistic depiction of local surveillance culture, *The Contract* is just one of several movies set in media and entertainment industries whose depiction of audience testing and other forms of corporate data gathering is likely informed by the star's show business start in television. Similarly, in a more general instance of Hui's films depicting the variety of ways by which social, spatial, and data monitoring manifest in Hong Kong daily life, *The Magic Touch* (1992) depicts a deceptive and fraudulent fortune-teller under investigation by the Inland Revenue Department for underpayment of taxes. He earns his living not from any real gifts but through an elaborate con in which he culls personal data by exploiting his clients' habituation to the territory's ubiquitous watchmen and a municipal regulation requiring residents to bear and produce identification at all times.[7]

So central to Hui's oeuvre, in fact, are these pointedly local and self-consciously realistic depictions of surveillance that they are present literally from the beginning of his directorial career, as evident in the opening sequences to *Games Gamblers Play*. In this film, like *The House of 72 Tenants'* use of the tenement genre, Hui's use of the gambling genre takes up a local film tradition closely associated with monitoring but immediately announces his stylistic difference from its precursor through the precredit sequence. This starts with an exterior establishing shot of Hong Kong's iconic skyscrapers and colonial buildings once typical of Hollywood images of Hong Kong, such as those in *Love Is a Many-Splendored Thing* (1955) and *The World of Suzie Wong* (1960). No sooner does that image appear, however, than it is ironically replaced with a swish pan to an ugly quarry, where mining operations are staffed by convict labor. But rather than rest with this visual gag that Hong Kong is a prison, the sequence emphasizes the irrepressible optimism of Hong Kong people's faith in observational speculation. As the camera zooms in on two convict laborers (Hui and character actor Tsang Cho-lam), the film shows the two men betting on their meager lunch. Thus announcing the movie's positioning within gambling genre traditions, the scene also uses Hui's signature comedy to suggest a ludic and often specifically affirmative depiction of surveillance culture characteristic of Hong Kong culture in general.

Similarly, in the sequence that immediately follows the film's opening credits, *Gamblers* continues to play with gambling movie traditions by following a down-on-his-luck gambler (Michael's brother and popular pop star Sam Hui) whose fortunes suddenly turn for the better when he accidentally discovers a dishonest croupier in the process of stealing chips. Both engaging and upending gambling genre conventions, the film complicates the expected focus on gaming table surveillance to instead highlight other circumstances by which a gambler's observational acuity pays off. Typical of Hui's ludic twist on local surveillance cinema conventions, the set piece climaxes when the gambler's triumphant demand that he share in the illicit cache is interrupted by the casino's security manager, whose oversized glasses and imperturbable demeanor embody the intrusive and impersonal affect of institutional surveillance. Thus juxtaposing several forms of surveillance (including fish-eye lens shots that simulate the optical distortion of CCTV), the set piece uses the multilayered gags of traditional physical comedy to playfully illustrate Hui's vision of Hong Kong as an intensely surveilled society.[8]

WATCHING OTHERS WATCH

As the preceding examples suggest, another site of Hui's unsurpassed cinematic study of Hong Kong surveillance culture is his frequent emphasis on second- and third-order monitoring, as depicted in the many scenes in which characters monitoring other characters are themselves subject to observation. Rarely unilateral, often triangulated, and never limited to top-down, repressive forms of intrusion and control, surveillance in Hui's comedies invariably is portrayed as a granular behavior equally deployed by individuals as a means of one-upmanship or of gaining dividends and benefits for themselves. This witty reenvisioning of surveillance is a far cry from Western cinema's ominous institutional or otherwise formidably impersonal depictions of surveillance, and it often derives its comedy by exploding cultural and cinematic conventions about surveillance customs and implications. *Mr. Coconut* (1989), for example, includes an early sequence on the subway in which two men's furtive glances and nervous shifts in body position initially figure them as sexual perverts, but this ultimately is revealed as the machinations of a relentless salesman and his unwilling mark. The set piece plays on capitalism's conditioning of individuals to both surveillance monitoring and the measures by which one can turn the tables on such practices. This play then becomes the premise of the film's central plot, which tracks a family's efforts to deceive insurance investigators in order to profit from a mistakenly awarded payout. In what will become characteristic of Hui's films and many Hong Kong movies in general, surveillance in this film is economic rather than political. Moreover, although Hui's movies portray surveillance as inevitable and pervasive, his films' emphases are consistently affirmative, subversive, and focused on opportunities for individual and personal profit. For example, in Hui's *Tampopo*-inspired film, *Chicken and Duck Talk*, about a local vendor of traditional Cantonese-style roast duck challenged by the arrival of a new Western-style fried chicken fast-food chain, the small-time restauranteur played by Hui ultimately adopts the very practices of rationalized labor, monitored production, and consumer service that he had initially criticized about his competitor (Fig. 1.2). In one memorable sequence, the film shows the surveillance measures that the proprietor undertakes not to compete with a more powerful international franchise but to foil his ambitious underling, a dishwasher who hopes to steal his employer's secret recipe. Through a mock heroic send-up fusing corporate espionage and spy films, Hui uses a rip-off of the James Bond films' globally recognized musical motif to orchestrate the dodging and feinting between himself and the wayward employee.

Notably, Hui's self-casting works in conjunction with his affirmative depictions of surveillance to recall aspects of the star's own career. As previously noted, one reason for Hui's exemplariness in Hong Kong film history is his professional transition, not only from television to film but also from Shaw Brothers to Golden Harvest, where the multitalented Hui was among the first local stars to seek creative and financial control still impossible under the then increasingly archaic studio system. As Law Kar and Frank Bren have noted, this shift within Hong Kong cinema from the studios' increasingly ossified contract system to independent production did not only mirror contemporary Hollywood developments but also captured in microcosm the territory's overall shift toward agile and increasingly flexible forms of industry and manufacture.[9] No less important, the shift from centralized manufacture to diffuse and individualized film production also parallels the shift in surveillance rhetoric partly apparent when archetypal commercial studio Shaw Brothers took up traditionally left-

FIGURE 1.2. Adopting the practices of rationalized labor and industrial surveillance in *Chicken and Duck Talk* (Golden Harvest / Hui's Film Production Co., Ltd., 1988). Note that the employee (Ricky Hui) surrendering to management's timed labor practices (top) is the same person leading group calisthenics in one of the film's final shots (bottom).

leaning tenement-film traditions when it made *The House of 72 Tenants*. Hui himself occupies a key place within this cultural and industrial evolution, as the evolving surveillance motifs in the shift from early tenement films to Hui's urban and contemporary comedies suggest his proximity to trends transforming Hong Kong as a whole. Although the quasi-autobiographical media settings in films such as *The Contract*, *The Front Page*, and *Always on My Mind* position Hui's career as microcosms of local economy and society as a whole, it is the surveillance themes that run throughout Hui's oeuvre, especially the films explicitly about the subject, that best illustrate how his signature emphasis on surveillance's personal and private benefits typifies Hong Kong cinema as whole.

The Private Eyes' famous opening sequence explicitly illustrates this distinctly Hong Kong tendency toward affirmative surveillance, particularly as Hui uses his own performance as a model of surveillance's positive benefits. The sequence depicts the crowds of laborers who swell Hong Kong's streets at the start of each workday (Fig. 1.3), exhibiting a working-class empathy typical of Hui's films that is further reinforced by the catchy accompanying theme song in which Sam Hui expresses the hardships of being "we, the working people, slaves to money for life." Today the song is such a Cantopop hallmark and anthem of local culture that it is difficult to see the film's opening sequence as anything other than an assertion of Hong Kong life, but it is also worth noting how the sequence uses surveillance as a theme by which to foreground Michael Hui himself as star.[10] Contrary to British and American traditions of the charismatic and virtuoso detective—or in an exaggerated caricature of the genre's conventional "hired dick"—

FIGURE 1.3. Hui's workplace realism: morning crowds shot on location in the opening sequence to *The Private Eyes* (Golden Harvest / Hui's Film Production Co., Ltd., 1976).

FIGURE 1.4. Gumshoe detective and the star entrance: Hui's "Hong Kong everyman" asserts creative and performative agency in *The Private Eyes* (Golden Harvest / Hui's Film Production Co., Ltd., 1976).

The Private Eyes uses its titular surveillance profession to foreground the physical suffering of low-paid employment, visually depicted over the course of the opening sequence as the long shots of crowds are gradually replaced by close-ups of feet, particularly a dilapidated pair of men's loafers whose disrepair is in pathetic contrast to the well-heeled woman he tails. The obvious function of these images is to depict the labor of the gumshoe detective and thus equate the professional surveillance performed by Hui's character with the anonymous crowds among which he is introduced, but the movie also undermines this trope as the camera pans up from the shoes to reveal Hui himself (Fig. 1.4). By turning the film's titular surveillance theme from a populist paradigm of employment to a motif by which the gaze shifts from the investigator to the audience themselves, *The Private Eyes'* opening sequence further enriches Hui's affirmative surveillance tropes by using it to position the film as a star vehicle.

HUI'S VERNACULAR MODERNISM

Notably, such migration of the surveillance gaze from diegetic character to the audience themselves, as occurs in *The Private Eyes*, is not unique in world surveillance cinema, and it further illuminates the affirmative surveillance tropes throughout Hui's comedies. In an important precursor for Hui's specific focus on surveillance professions in that film as well as *Security Unlimited*, Charlie Chaplin's *Modern Times* includes an episode in which the Tramp gains temporary employment as a department store's night watchman. While on patrol the character entertains his companion by strapping on roller skates intended to facilitate his patrol but instead uses them to display his skating prowess. As shown in the reaction shots of his companion's delight, the episode thus converts the scene's nominal depiction of surveillance practice—that is, the Tramp's intended patrol—into a voyeuristic or spectacular gaze inhabited by that figure's real and diegetic spectators. Such displacement and transformation of surveillance's typical function of consolidating and reinforcing power account for the episode's otherwise incongruous inclusion within an iconic anti-surveillance film. Sharply contrasting with *Modern Times'* more commonly quoted images of proto-CCTV monitoring (Fig. 1.5), the Tramp's whimsical roller skating while on patrol is consistent with his other actions during the

FIGURE 1.5. Proto-CCTV monitoring in *Modern Times* (Charles Chaplin Productions, 1936).

FIGURE 1.6. Dividends of surveillance employment: romance in *Security Unlimited* (Golden Harvest/ Hui's Film Production Co., Ltd., 1981).

sequence—including feeding his companion from the soda fountain and encouraging her to bed down among the fur inventory—in depicting the subversive appropriation of employer resources and expectations that Michel de Certeau describes as an inevitable outcome of modern economic pressures for productivity and efficiency.[11]

Importantly, my reasons for invoking *Modern Times* alongside Hui are not unjustified, and they should not be seen as a tendency typical of much surveillance theory and comparative analysis that implies that non-Western cases can be understood only through Western models. Rather, in juxtaposing these seemingly culturally and historically disparate films, I hope to show their affinities, beginning with the mutually pragmatic emphasis on surveillance employment that contextualizes both films' generically unconventional status as surveillance comedies—an oxymoronic subgenre typified by the positive perspective by which private security is portrayed in both films. *Modern Times'* Depression-era setting, for example, legitimates the Tramp's joy when he earns the watchman position, beating scores of other unemployed people vying for the job. A similar scene occurs in *Security Unlimited* when Ricky Hui's character jumps a line of applicants in eager pursuit of a position at the private security firm. The latter movie's emphasis on the individual and personal benefits of surveillance employment is further dramatized in plot developments that depict not only promotion and wages but also romance (Fig. 1.6). As context for both films' comedy, this practical depiction of surveillance employment that *Security Unlimited* shares with *Modern Times* reiterates Hui's socioeconomic realism, particularly the importance surveillance occupies in "modern times." Like Chaplin's movies, Hui's comedy is infused with class compassion and social commentary and can be highly informed in its depiction of surveillance professions. Characters in *Security Unlimited*, for example, reference their training and service in "surveillance studies in the UK" or the "Po Sang bank robbery" (a notorious armed robbery widely remembered in Hong Kong), simultaneously demonstrating Hui's awareness of local and global surveillance history while according the comic character a mock backstory and professional legitimacy comparable to those of the surveillance professional in *The Conversation*.[12] Similarly, *Security Unlimited*'s final scene has one guard driving off with his newlywed bride in an armored security van that resembles that of Guardforce International, then Hong Kong's leading security provider (Fig. 1.7), thereby demonstrating Hui's realistic depiction of contemporary Hong Kong surveillance while also more generally illustrating the film's engagement of classical definitions of comedy as oriented toward happy endings.

More intriguingly, however, Hui's comparison with Chaplin is further motivated by the fact that the Hong Kong star studied the Hollywood silent era early in his directorial career with the express aim of exploring a means through which his work could transcend comedy's traditional linguistic and cultural limitations and further augment his exportability.[13] This occurred after *The Last Message* and before *The Pri-*

FIGURE 1.7. Social realism in surveillance comedy: on the left, a company van in *Security Unlimited* (Golden Harvest / Hui's Film Production Co., Ltd., 1981); on the right, its real-life precedent, an armored transport vehicle belonging to Guardforce, Ltd., a leading security provider in Hong Kong (photo courtesy of www.typicalben.com).

vate Eyes, when, despite his position at the top of the Hong Kong box office, Hui reportedly was disappointed by the films' earnings in Taiwan and therefore sought to further refine his already successful formula by moving away from the verbally colloquial, highly referential, and local humor for which he was known.[14] Importantly, although silent cinema's influences on Hong Kong stars and filmmakers are fairly well known, Hui's interest is intriguing because it still maintained narrative context and legibility, as opposed to the stunt-based borrowings associated with Hui's contemporary Jackie Chan (see Fig. 3.5). Indeed, it is typical of the highly cerebral Hui—who holds a university degree in sociology and who has developed detailed theses by which to construct "gag-a-minute" humor[15]—that his early interest in Hollywood silents presages what Miriam Hansen would later describe as "vernacular modernism." By looking to Hollywood silent icons such as Chaplin, Buster Keaton, and Harold Lloyd, Hui sought to fashion an extralinguistic and therefore exportable comedy comparable to the "robustness of Hollywood products abroad."[16] In fact, in a subsequent publication Hansen would also claim that Hong Kong cinema is the global film tradition whose aesthetic is most comparable to early mass media, and although the film scholar never specifically addressed Hui as a model of Hong Kong's vernacular modernism, Hui's success in attaining transcultural popularity was demonstrated by *The Private Eyes*, the star's first film after his hiatus and a movie, which under the nonsensical name of *Mr. Boo*, became a huge hit in Japan.[17]

SCENE STEALING

At its most basic, Hui's interest in Hollywood silents helps explain his international popularity, functioning like the many other intertextual references and verbal gags in his referential comedy to maximize the star's accessibility. With particular regard for the surveillance motifs that proliferate throughout his films, this means that his films' depiction of social, spatial, and data monitoring is not specific to Hong Kong, but these motifs are also aspects of urban and capitalist societies accessible to audiences in Taiwan, Japan, or any market where his films were distributed and found popularity. At times, this use of surveillance as a comic lingua franca is as simple as adaptation and imitation, such as the rigged race betting in the climax of *Games Gamblers Play*—clearly borrowed from the previous year's Oscar-winning Hollywood film *The Sting*—as well as *The Private Eyes'* multiple references to American TV detectives such as Columbo, Mannix, and Cannon. By thus channeling globally familiar images of surveillance and social control, Hui's surveillance motifs constitute a kind of vernacular modernism both in their entertainment vocabulary and the more-specific ethnographic assertion of Hong Kong society as legible to other cultures precisely because of the surveillance behaviors that city shares with modern, urban, capitalist societies throughout the globe.

More subtly and complexly, however, the affirmative tenor of Hui's surveillance comedies, particularly the suggestive affinities between his films and the intriguingly positive portrait of professional surveillance in a likely precursor film such as *Modern Times*, also foregrounds how that perspective might be based on parallels between the two stars' artistic self-presentation. Aside from its canonical place within world surveillance cinema, *Modern Times* is known for being Chaplin's first sound film, a watershed moment in the silent star's career that the icon had long resisted and to which Chaplin eventually conformed only by a characteristically subversive gag.[18] In the movie's climactic scene, the star opens his mouth for the long-awaited moment only to burst into a nonsensical aria of unintelligible gibberish that simultaneously demonstrates his adaptation to technological innovation and changing consumer tastes while preserving, through the performance's refusal of meaning, an element of personal and artistic inscrutability. Although the scene does not specifically portray surveillance with the specificity of the earlier roller-skating watchman episode, the movie's climax similarly pokes fun at the dehumanizing, anti-individualizing, and insistently forensic pressures of industrial-capitalist society. Simultaneously complying with those conditions while redirecting the audience gaze toward himself, in *Modern Times* Chaplin uses the film's surveillance themes to foreground his own artistic autonomy.

As Charles Musser describes it, in *Modern Times* Chaplin sought "not . . . to change the system so much as manipulate it," and given Hui's own remarks that "Chaplin is for me the number one," it would not be disingenuous to go so far as to suggest that their similarities are not limited to their mutually comic form of socioeconomic critique but also include the ways both artists exploit those diegetic subjects through metafilmic allusions to their own positioning within their profession.[19] In *The Contract*, for example, Hui's middle film between *The Private Eyes* and *Security Unlimited*, the star uses the film's quasi-autobiographical setting in the local entertainment industry to foreground a similarly evocative interest in artistic performance, spectacular labor, and the pleasures of the surveillance gaze. This begins in an early scene when one character (Ricky Hui) asks a magician (Sam Hui) to demonstrate sleight of hand. Interestingly, the magician—and the film itself—obliges by playing the trick twice, first at a normal pace and then more slowly and in close-up, enabling both cinematic audience and diegetic spectator to see the false thumb that enables the trick. Like all reflexive moments, the scene models how a representational product might ideally want to be consumed, with the additional fact that the sequence equates or even subordinates traditional illusion to the interest of performative skill itself. Although Michael Hui himself is absent in this sequence, as the product of a "Michael Hui film" this sequence within *The Contract* functions in a Chaplin-like manner to invite an acute spectatorial gaze that uses the film's surveillance motifs to model the kind of engrossed audience gaze that all performers desire.

Indeed, in this early sequence in *The Contract*, it is significant that the provisional "star" of the passage is not Michael but his brother Sam, a celebrity in his own right but not one holding creative or capital stake in the film to the degree of writer, director, and star. The apparent generosity of this early scene is inverted, however, by the film's climactic episode, which occurs when Michael's character accidentally disrupts Sam's magic show by hiding in one of the locking chests conventionally used by magicians to make persons and items "vanish." As does the earlier revelation of sleight of hand, this sequence gains its pleasure by destroying illusion when Michael's mistimed disappearance and reappearance, along with the magician's various props, inadvertently betrays the trap-door gimmickry underlying the magic act. Thus sending the diegetic audience into peals of laughter that the magician played by Sam had failed to earn, the scene uses a distinctly comic take on surveillance similar to Chaplin's upending in both watchman and singing sequences of *Modern Times* to instead "steal" the spotlight—in Michael Hui's case, literally steal the scene from his brother.

WATCHING THE WATCHMAN

Over the years, Sam and Michael Hui have been dogged by rumors of a rift between the two independently successful stars, but, as is always the case throughout this study, any autobiographical resonance with moments like the scene stealing in *The Contract* is less important for what it suggests about any fraternal animosity than for the way that films starring any Hui brother use surveillance themes to figure cinematic and professional aspirations, particularly in terms of the reception the films aimed to achieve. The purported rift between the two brothers is thought to have been most severe around the time of *Aces Go Places*, the blockbuster 1982 caper comedy and spy parody costarring Sam Hui that, as previously noted, has obvious similarities to *Security Unlimited*, Michael's number-one film of the previous year and the last film in which the two brothers would appear together for nearly a decade.[20] Interestingly, Sam was not the only Hui brother whom other studios and production companies hoped could cash in on Michael's popularity; in *The Pilferer's Progress* (1977) and *From Riches to Rags* (1980), both Golden Harvest comedies helmed by a pre–*A Better Tomorrow* John Woo, middle brother Ricky Hui was also charged with carrying a contemporary comedy about the foibles and escapades of Hong Kong's get-rich-quick mentality. Equally critical about this personal and professional on-screen relationship within Michael's, Sam's, and Ricky's films is the mutual importance of surveillance as a vehicle for cinematic spectacle and performative display; as Sek Kei notes, in both their individual vehicles as well as ensemble appearances the Hui brothers modeled a "less hierarchal . . . image of working peers."[21] Recall that the *Aces Go Places* series is another instance of the commercial prominence of surveillance themes within Hong Kong film history, especially in movies particularly identified with local culture and identity. That the series spoofs the James Bond films, which in the 1960s had been hugely popular in Hong Kong as throughout the world, both specifically evidences the filmmakers' efforts to emulate Hui's successful formula—including his parodies of Bond-style espionage in movies like *Chicken and Duck Talk*—and more generally shows how the questions of the gaze implicitly posed by surveillance themes provide powerful opportunities for staging cinematic ambition.

Many of Hui's films straddle these dual objectives, simultaneously presenting a nuanced glimpse of the mounting presence of surveillance in social life while using that motif to figure his own professional advancement. *The Private Eyes*, for example, follows in the rich tradition of heavily researched local television with which it was contemporary, having been prepped by Hui when the former sociology student interviewed practitioners for a sense of their working experiences and hence what scenarios he might develop into cinematic set pieces. At the same time, however, because the film is also steeped in global film traditions, particularly the Hollywood tradition of private detectives, *The Private Eyes* uses its surveillance premise to foreground its appeal to viewing pleasure and audience appreciation. As previously noted about the paradoxical introduction of Hui as both star and common laborer in *The Private Eyes*' famous opening sequence, these issues arise when the acute gaze conventionally attributed to the private "eye" becomes meaningful in Hui's films not for what it does to investigate private spaces but how it redirects the cinematic gaze back toward himself.

Perhaps not surprisingly, in *The Private Eyes*, the scene stealing that occurs in *The Contract* is explicitly identified with cinema because of that movie's generic grounding in investigation and criminal apprehension—surveillance themes more overt than in *The Contract*. In a memorable climactic episode, Hui's feckless detective finds himself held hostage in a movie theater along with many other moviegoers, whom a band of thieves plan to rob. Although Hui's usually cowardly and always cheap on-screen persona neither acts to apprehend the criminals (as might be expected of a more conventionally heroic private investigator) nor willingly surrenders his valuables, the detective still foils the robbers' plans when they haul him onto the stage with plans of cowing the remaining audience. But in a distinctly Chaplin-like twist, the detective inadvertently prevails over his captors because his querulous flinches from the gang leader's blows prove slippery and unpredictable, enabling him to escape his bonds and create enough havoc that the gang's reign of terror collapses. Like other mo-

FIGURE 1.8. Stealing the scene from Sek "Bad Guy" Kin, Hui wins by losing in *The Private Eyes* (Golden Harvest / Hui's Film Production Co., Ltd., 1976).

ments of artistic self-reference within Hui's and Chaplin's surveillance films, this comic sequence in which imperfect practices of professional surveillance enable inimitable artistic performance is clinched with reaction shots that show an audience transfixed by the scene. Thus, in *The Private Eyes*, victims robbed and held hostage are hardly paralyzed by fear, as might be expected in that situation, but rather convulse with laughter at the detective's antics. Their laughter is Hui's profit, both literally and diegetically, as it models the intended reception of Hui's film while also asserting the actor's virtuosity, as he literally steals the scene from legendary baddie Sek "Bad Man" Kin (Fig. 1.8)—the actor playing the leader of the gang of thieves, globally recognized as the nemesis in Bruce Lee's final film *Enter the Dragon* and veteran of several hundred films in which Sek starred as villain.

Of course, in visually figuring themselves as a worker and surveillance subject no different from the countless hardworking citizens vulnerable to economic contingency and severely alienated from the products of their labor, neither Chaplin nor Hui is naïve to the fact that his wealth and celebrity make him a singular, uniquely privileged individual exempted from the more oppressive conditions the films portray. But as artists whose social and economic consciousness was shaped by humble origins and whose subsequent professional success enabled unusual control over the means of their own self-representation, both comic icons manifest a deep awareness of the political and economic circumstances of industrial modernity, particularly including surveillance's power to adversely or positively impact individuals within that system. Within their particular industry of cinema, both artists acknowledge that the gaze typically perceived as intrusive and oppressive in the case of surveillance is instead a highly desired attribute and a force that their genre of comedy is uniquely effective in displaying the positive benefits that they, as stars, accrue. Chaplin's *Modern Times* and its climactic sound gag may be the more globally familiar example of comic surveillance cinema and of how even an ardent critique of surveillance nevertheless requires occasional adaptation of the mechanized technologies and Fordist-Taylorist gaze that it initially seems to resist. But like Chaplin's brief turn as a watchman in *Modern Times*, all of Hui's films, including particularly *Security Unlimited*, are even more remarkable in their unqualifiedly comic manipulation of surveillance motifs to showcase their own performative labor. Indeed, where *The Private Eyes* is particularly explicit in staging its cinematic labor through its climactic setting in the cinema, *Security Unlimited* does the same through a similar scene stealing that once again upends the gaze presumably deployed by the plot's diegetic surveillance professionals to instead direct the gaze on Hui himself.

In *Security Unlimited*, this reflexive moment in which a metafilmic scene of star performance is showcased by way of the film's surveillance plot climaxes in the film's penultimate action sequence, when the fictional Wong's Security Force personnel are employed as guards in a high-rise office building where a Japanese bank has a priceless antique Chinese jade monument on display. Jenny Lau has noted that these details of Japanese finance and Chinese antiquity convey a topicality and verisimilitude typical of Hui's films, particularly linking *Security Unlimited* to the terra-cotta soldiers discovered in China a few years earlier, as well as Japan's financial power in the early 1980s.[22] The stakes of the scene, however, go far beyond these general aspects of Hui's social realism to both specifically emphasize commercial security as an increasingly visible aspect of Hong Kong modernity and to exploit that motif to Hui's own personal and professional advantage. This occurs when a gang of knife-wielding robbers planning to steal the antiquity break into the bank, plunging the two unarmed security guards played by Michael and Sam into a situation in which they are

FIGURE 1.9. Surveillance as *dianying* (electric shadows): stopping the robbers with a play of light and sound in *Security Unlimited* (Golden Harvest / Hui's Film Production Co., Ltd., 1981).

greatly outnumbered and overpowered. Cowering behind the bank's rice paper walls and peering into the dark, the pair try to intimidate the gang by simulating the sounds of heavy weapons, troops, a canine unit, and a cavalry—but, unbeknown to them, the lights behind the pair come on, readily betraying their vulnerability to the amused robbers (Fig. 1.9).

Even without regard to the specific context and traditions of surveillance cinema, there can be no doubt that this scene is a profoundly reflexive moment reminding viewers of the labor enabling cinematic entertainment. During their auditory simulation, the two guards act out their sound effects with hand gestures and physical movements that are glimpsed on the backlit screen as shadow puppetry, simultaneously evoking a precinematic visual entertainment with a particularly rich history in Chinese culture and dramatizing the Chinese word for movies—*dianying*, meaning "electric shadows."[23] Within the specific context of surveillance cinema, moreover, the metacinematic and reflexive connotations of the scene are only more apparent. Glimpsed in a darkened room by an audience who are enraptured by the backlit screen, the effect of the two guards' son et lumière is both an obvious allusion to the conditions of cinematic production and spectatorship and a particularly explicit rendering of the performative artistry of the two stars playing the guards. Although the comic reversal of power underlying the sequence's organizing gag might recall Hitchcock's *Rear Window* as another surveillance film that similarly shows initially empowered panoptic witnesses to criminal behavior abruptly rendered vulnerable when the gaze initially associated with their position is reversed against their will, the more meaningful analogy to Hui and his most surveillant film should be Chaplin's *Modern Times*, the classic surveillance film from an artist who had a huge influence on Hui. As a subject of cinematic representation, the earlier film's cinematic image of the watchman persona heralds the manifold significance that private security offers—that is, both an aspect of urban, industrial, and capitalist modernity and a vehicle by which to portray the beneficial forms of the gaze invited by that peculiar form of industrial worker, the filmmaker and cinematic laborer.

Through this inquiry into the multicultural and transhistorical influences and popularity of Hui's films, the comedian's recurrent surveillance motifs throughout his best-known and most popular films illustrate the lateral gaze typical of Hong Kong surveillance and also demonstrate how a seemingly idiosyncratic film oeuvre is always also deeply engaged with contemporary global surveillance discourses. Hui's extraordinarily sustained and intentionally personal image of the watchman in *Security Unlimited* personifies the highly beneficial and upwardly mobile benefits of surveillance that often figure in Hong Kong's distinct variation on world surveillance cinema. It is also visible across more broadly sampled eras and subgenres in local cinema as well as in more familiar cinematic motifs. In the next chapter, I trace how the affirmative view of surveillance portrayed so effectively in Hui's films and career continued through the industry during its height in the 1980s through the early 1990s—a time that also coincided with the territory's awareness of impending reunification with China. Although the films of this era have already been extensively studied, I unearth very different themes from those typically attributed to the reunification years. And typical of Michael Hui's central place in local film and surveillance cinema more specifically, this theme is foreshadowed in the star's work. "We don't care about 1997," proclaims the catchy theme song to Hui's 1990 film, *Front Page*, which is sung by Sam Hui and plays over a montage of bustling crowds of busy workers and eager consumers whose cell phones and other temporal indicators are the only other visible differences from *The Private Eyes'* famous opening sequence. As the movie and theme song suggest, despite the decade and a half between *The Private Eyes* and *Front Page*, economic and material concerns that drive the affirmative surveillance in Hui's comedies were still paramount during reunification, providing a major context and undercurrent of contemporary film whose peculiar relationship to the cinema's pervasive surveillance themes was often misread by a critical focus on the genres of action and crime.

TWO

ON THE "CHINA WATCH"

PROSPERITY AND PARANOIA
IN REUNIFICATION-ERA CINEMA

IN CONTRAST TO MICHAEL HUI COMEDIES, the action and crime films of the 1980s through the mid-1990s are far more obvious sites for exploring Hong Kong surveillance cinema. Already known to critical and cult audiences through the work of action auteurs such as John Woo, Tsui Hark, and Ringo Lam, Hong Kong action and crime films garnered further interest among global audiences with the political and historical pressures of reunification. The 1984 Sino-British Joint Declaration announcing the territory's impending 1997 handover from colonial to Chinese rule cast additional attention on film as the territory's most visible and compelling export. Although critics rarely identified surveillance as a specific visual or narrative trope within these films, action and crime genres' conventional attributes of violence, power, apprehension, and control were obviously resonant with contemporary speculation about Communist sovereignty, and they helped promulgate a politicized Sinophobia that equated the coming change with a descent into repression and uncertainty. Indeed, because the final years before reunification also coincided with an industrial decline that had begun in the early 1990s, negative imagery in contemporary action and crime was often thought to corroborate the talent flight and fears regarding censorship then contributing to the local film industry's sudden fall in distribution deals and ticket sales. As contemporary criticism and reportage used blood-soaked and elaborately choreographed action movies such as *A Better Tomorrow* (1986), *City on Fire* (1987), *The Killer* (1989), *Wicked City* (1992), *Hard Boiled* (1992), and *The Heroic Trio* (1993) to conflate the cinema with the territory itself, such well-known and visceral films advanced a dystopian image of contemporary Hong Kong whose aesthetic and thematic attributes closely resemble Western surveillance cinema's emphasis on violence, repression, and paranoia.[1]

Yet the difference between reunification-era action and crime films and other sites of Hong Kong surveillance cinema is less profound than first appears.[2] For example, Michael Hui's comedies, as previously discussed, exemplify local cinema's persistence of surveillance themes in genres other than those typical of the Western canon, while also exhibiting the distinctly tolerant and humorous perspective that often distinguishes Hong Kong from most other world surveillance film. Similarly, during the reunification period itself, much attention was also paid to movies like Jacob Cheung's *Cageman* (1992), a sentimental social realist–type film about Hong Kong's impoverished bed-space dwellers, and the languid romances from internationally acclaimed filmmaker Wong Kar-wai, such as *Chungking Express* (1994) and *Days of Being Wild* (1990), which are atmospheric character studies about unrequited desire.[3] Although these movies belong to a different genre and artistic world than contemporary action and crime—and in the case of *Chungking Express* and *Cageman* in particular, incorporate distinctly local film traditions such as tenement movies and the *Ah Fei* (delinquent youth) genres—awareness of these alternative genres did not dampen their topical resonance. Because the movies' urban settings and themes of displacement, longing, and expiring time seemed to echo contemporary reunification concerns such as the massive increase in emigration and applications for alternative citizenship that took place during these years, films like *Cageman* and *Chungking Express* invite similar questions about the issues and contexts underlying the topical analysis widely applied to contemporary action and crime. And due to *Cageman's* obvious ties with the local tenement-movie tradition, the film raises questions regarding other ways in which surveillance themes manifest in reunification-era Hong Kong cinema.

Studies of Hong Kong film from the 1980s through the 1990s have long been hampered by this generic and methodological debate. Understandably focused on reunification and heavily weighted by the era's most visible and accessible film genres, criticism of reunification-era Hong Kong cinema is often mired in questions regarding the extent to which a genre and event ought to represent Hong Kong film and culture as a whole.[4] This critical query is often articulated as a debate over national allegory and reflectionism, which is the tendency to read narrative cinema as a relatively unmediated glimpse into the society that makes and consumes it, and has since been countered by an equally forceful critical movement advocating alternative topics and approaches.[5] Yet while Hong Kong cinema studies has benefited from the expanded critical scope, persistent scholarly interest in both reunification contexts and action and crime genres invites further inquiry into the tension between Hong Kong cinema's two distinct critical foci.[6] As films like *Cageman* and *Chungking Express* show, situating non-action reunification-era films within their alternative genres and more nuanced local contexts only reinforces their topical resonance, thereby raising questions about their similarities and differences and the continuity of these films with the dominant genre and discourse of the era.

To intervene in this critical debate, this chapter uncovers surveillance as the underlying issue in both the misunderstandings and insights surrounding critical reception of reunification-era Hong Kong film. Although anti-reflectionist critics were correct in interrogating the reductively politicized Sinophobic discourse promulgated by reunification-era action and crime genres, the subsequent turn against that genre and reunification's unquestionable importance in the era also misses the intuitive insights that were always at stake in action and crime films' conventional focus on surveillance. This subtle but specific surveillance motif within reunification-era cinema entails both a positive emphasis on surveillance's association with prosperity and economic mobility and negative connotations of political repression and violence; and it begins even earlier than precursors such as Michael Hui's comedies—during the Cold War, a time in which both Hong Kong and Hong Kong cinema emerged as key sites of global surveillance culture. To document these influences, I start by revisiting a number of well-known handover-era action and crime movies and conclude by showing how surveillance motifs common in action and crime infused other popular reunification films and genres. Like some recent film theory, this analysis is partly a defense of reflectionism and its use regarding Hong Kong cinema, but it also more simply demonstrates how surveillance motifs long privileged in local and world cinema were catalyzed by the unusual conditions of Hong Kong's transition from colonial to Chinese rule.[7] While reunification-era Hong Kong film, especially its globally visible action and crime genres, popularized Sinophobic anticommunist hysteria about repressive surveillance, the surveillance motifs always implicit within contemporary criticism's intuitive interest in action and crime were also relevant for defensive and hopeful identifications with surveillance whose formal and narrative properties positioned local cinema as tantamount to closed-circuit security monitoring. That is, the surveillance motifs evident throughout reunification-era action and crime—as in many other movies and genres of the era—are equally symptomatic of anticommunist paranoia as they are artistic and technological expressions of the prosperity and hopeful continuity of Hong Kong itself.

KING KONG IN HONG KONG

Since at least the 1984 Sino-British Joint Declaration, Hong Kong action and crime films infused the genre's conventional attributes of violence, control, and monitoring with political and historical overtones. *Coolie Killer*, for example, a stylish 1982 actioner that is often cited as a harbinger of the moody gangster dramas that by the later 1980s would become inextricable with local cinema, includes frequent scenes of photographic surveillance centered on an unknowing assassin soon to be betrayed by his enigmatic immigrant handler. Even more explicitly, *Long Arm of the Law* (1984) is widely recognized as a prescient depiction of the deleterious impact of Chinese sovereignty through its story of a gang of mainland immigrants who illegally trespass into Hong Kong, wreaking violence and destruction along the way. Pointedly implicating surveillance as both a mechanism and symbol of their threat, *Long Arm of the Law* shows the gang members rehearsing for their invasion with a military precision that highlights their backstory as former Red Guards during China's Cultural Revolution. Similarly, although *A Better Tomorrow*, like *Coolie Killer*, makes no explicit mention of China, its evocatively topical scenes of characters discoursing on Hong Kong's changes and their desire to emigrate gave resonance to an opening scene featuring CCTV and a climax hinging on secret recordings. And in 1987 alone, *City on Fire* and its spin-off, *Prison on Fire* (both starring Chow Yun-fat, the star of *A Better Tomorrow*), as well as *People's Hero*, a loose adaptation of Sidney Lumet's 1975 hostage drama *Dog Day After-noon*, all portray Hong Kong as an increasingly punitive, carceral en-vironment in which surveillance technologies and authorities endan-ger the innocent along with the guilty. Both *City on Fire* and *People's Hero*, for example, include scenes in which fax machines deliver rap-idly transmitted information identifying suspects, and the automated fences, gates, manned checkpoints, and other forms of enclosure in *Prison on Fire* and *People's Hero* prefigure *On the Run* (1988), another brutal crime drama in which both an assassin and a framed cop are helpless in trying to escape exploitation and protect their loved ones.

Indeed, by the early 1990s, as public optimism regarding reunifica-tion took a steep downturn in the aftermath of the brutal 1989 crack-down by Chinese authorities on democratic student protestors in Bei-jing's Tiananmen Square, cinematic imagery within contemporary action and crime grew only more graphic and explicit, and the corre-sponding images of surveillance grew equally more intense. Only a few months after the events in Tiananmen, for example, the 1989 *Die Hard*–like film *Crocodile Hunter* appeared, including among its brutal gang of escaped convicts a character named "Li Peng," presumably an allusion to the Communist Party leader considered responsible for the Beijing violence.[8] In the film, the gang as a whole is relentless in its ex-ploitation of local technological expertise, abducting and executing a Hong Kong computer hacker in an attempt to break into a corporate skyscraper and steal a local tycoon's priceless collection of antiquities. Similarly, *Prison on Fire II* (1991) recalls *Long Arm of the Law* by explicitly indicting mainland criminality, showing how a brutal Chinese gang upsets the provisional order of otherwise rule-abiding Hong Kong in-mates. *Wicked City*, based on a Japanese manga about parasitic, shape-shifting reptilian life-forms that prey on Hong Kong when their own resources prove insufficient, also channels *Blade Runner* in its story about investigative authorities who must locate and assassinate the genocidal parasites. Like *Prison on Fire II*, *Wicked City* makes its Sino-phobia explicit by placing the demons' lair in Hong Kong's iconic Bank

FIGURE 2.1. Big Brother in Hong Kong: *daai lou* (gang boss) identified with Orwellian totalitarianism in *Hard Boiled* (Golden Princess, 1992).

of China building, then a controversial landmark in reunification-era municipal architecture.

Also from 1992, John Woo's *Hard Boiled* revives the undercover-cop plot in *City on Fire* and the classic Hong Kong New Wave film *Man on the Brink* to underscore the undercover cop's conventional marginality by contrasting it with an Orwellian despot who, along with assassins disguised as police officers, lays siege to a hospital and co-opts the institution's CCTV technology to monitor his victims (Fig. 2.1). Although *Hard Boiled* does not specifically invoke mainland or foreign intrusion as do *Prison on Fire*, *Wicked City*, and *Long Arm of the Law*, the movie still conveys a topically resonant sense of looming fatality through its penultimate action sequence set inside a hospital morgue, depicting the impossibility of emigration and escape that this film shares with Woo's earlier movies *A Better Tomorrow* and *The Killer*. By the following year, action sequences like *Hard Boiled*'s climax in the hospital seemed to grow even more ominous, as movies like *The Heroic Trio*—an exaggerated, self-consciously comic book–style movie similar to *Wicked City*—also uses a hospital setting for an action sequence in which Hong Kong's newborn boys are abducted under the orders of an underground, Mandarin-speaking despot wearing traditional Chinese robes who hopes to raise the infants as soldiers to help him "bring back the Chinese empire." Like two 1994 police films, *Organized Crime and Triad Bureau* and *Rock n' Roll Cop*, the horrific violence unleashed by mainland criminals occasions scenes of the superior capacities of official surveillance, ranging from CCTV and Hong Kong's extensive computer command centers and established rule of law to the capacities of mainland public security (whose real and cinematic collaborations with Hong Kong police are discussed in greater length in Chapter 3).

As might be glimpsed in this brief sample of the popular action and crime films from the era, many of these films lent themselves to binary and often reductively allegorical readings about the threat of coming Chinese rule. Distinguished by dialectical, often explicitly Sinophobic plots that pit innocent, occasionally helpless Hong Kong citizens against brutish, parasitic, violent, and lawless criminal intruders, many of the best-known and most widely discussed titles in reunification-era Hong Kong film spoke to anxieties about how Communist China's different political and economic system might threaten prosperous, urban, relatively free and upwardly mobile Hong Kong. As a result, accounts of Hong Kong film that looked only at action and crime often exhibited top-down, Western-centric interpretations that focused primarily on China's perceived threat and capacity for violence, while registering little knowledge of the genres and traditions of previous decades of Hong Kong cinema. The fact that many of these films were action or crime movies both enhanced their plot symbolism and aided their global uptake, as viewers new to the cinema were no doubt most likely to stumble on action and crime and their readily accessible content as the cinema's first and most familiar mode. This tendency promulgated reductively Manichean plotlines that such films tend to favor. As Rey Chow notes in an essay published on the first anniversary after the handover, contemporary global interest in the event had become so infused by cinematic discourses of violence, threat, and oppression that its "King Kong in Hong Kong" sensationalism had taken on the lurid rhetoric and imagery of a Hollywood movie.[9]

FIGURE 2.2. Anticommunist, Sinophobic orientalism in *The Manchurian Candidate* (MGM, 1962).

ON THE "CHINA WATCH"

To be sure, the Hollywood creature film to which Chow alludes is hardly an action or crime film in the manner of most of the previously cited movies, but her metaphor highlights the degree to which a historically antecedent, fundamentally Western or Hollywoodized American film vocabulary was dominating contemporary discourse regarding Hong Kong's impending reunification. While it is possible that Chow may be thinking of *Wicked City* and its climactic image of a demon atop the Bank of China—a scene undoubtedly drawing on *King Kong*'s iconic finale to stage its nightmare of monstrous threat—the more important thrust of her claim is that during reunification, critical tendencies to use cinematic genres as de facto representations of the territory itself veered toward an anticommmunist Sinophobia that was suspiciously American. In its fearful, paranoid, and arguably hysterical depictions of the menace of authoritarian and totalitarian surveillance, this rhetoric is more akin to the demonic images of Chinese and North Korean brainwashing in iconic Hollywood movies like *The Manchurian Candidate* (Fig. 2.2) than the diversity and themes of Hong Kong cinema itself. Although not all movies of the era were as explicit

FIGURE 2.3. Provoking anticommunist paranoia with a Stalin-like villain in *The Executioners* (China Entertainment, 1993).

as *The Executioners* (1993), a loose sequel to *The Heroic Trio* whose villain clearly recalls Stalin (Fig. 2.3), many of the images in contemporary action and crime usefully corroborated anticommunist Sinophobia that had long been a thread of Hollywood and Western political culture more generally. As Shu-mei Shih notes, during reunification the "longstanding popular interest in Hong Kong action films" began to "trac[e] a very different economy from" the nuanced local history and cultural studies by which local scholars had previously sought to distinguish Hong Kong in the 1970s and early 1980s, and instead fueled a regressive ethnography in which action movies were read in ways that mirrored contemporary foreign policy.[10] Like similar critical approaches among Western critics toward mainland Chinese films, these studies participated in what Daniel Vukovich calls cinema's "long history of orientalizing Communists," where "the field [tends to] code its films as either for or against the government or Maoism"; and an orientalist, area studies–based, and effectively Cold War–inflected discourse places Hong Kong and Sinophone cinema within a long "chain of equivalence" in which any allusions to China are seen as a "vague but powerfully looming threat."[11]

Shih and Vukovich's comments are typical of anti-reflectionist scholarship in exposing the politically biased, area studies–like approach common in Western studies of Hong Kong and Sinophone film, but in advocating a more nuanced approach to film content, both scholars overlook the degree to which Hong Kong and Hong Kong cinema have always been shaped by Cold War discourse about different surveillance practices. Since World War II, the territory has been the main source of signals intelligence within the Pacific region due to infrastructure and political collaborations founded by successive waves of colonial and Japanese occupation, as well as American foreign policy interests. As Chi-kwan Mark and others show, the territory's importance as such only intensified during the Cold War, as American containment policies against Communist expansion in China and Southeast Asia willingly capitalized on the United Kingdom's relative lack of interest in the territory to assume defense and security responsibilities as a means of ensuring a beachhead within the region.[12] For Hong Kong itself, this gradual transfer of Hong Kong's foreign policy from colonial to American agendas meant that its geopolitical importance was effectively conceptualized in terms of two contrasting surveillance regimes. As the role once occupied by colonial "old China hands" was replaced by a new Cold War class of analysts and policy makers associated with the new "China watch," Hong Kong itself was caught between an authoritarian mode of surveillance associated with communism and the alternative surveillance practices of liberal, democratic anticommunism.

In film, these contrasting surveillance practices registered both locally and globally. In Hong Kong alone, as Poshek Fu has shown, the territory's film industry harbored a variety of studios and production companies whose talent and business practices spanned the spectrum of contemporary political ideology.[13] Left-leaning, occasionally mainland-funded companies, such as Great Wall, Feng Huang, Sun Luen, and Southern Film Corporation, held close ties to China that posed a stark political and aesthetic contrast with the unabashedly capitalist tendencies of leading studios like Shaw Brothers and Motion Picture and General Investment (MPGI, later Cathay), which were founded by overseas Chinese and staffed by émigré talent who had fled mainland turmoil.[14] These contrasting production sources and political sympathies reflected the ideological diversity of Hong Kong itself, then riven with refugees and economic migrants as well as leftist sympathizers, and they also paralleled or contrasted prominent Hollywood movies about Hong Kong and China such as *China Doll* (1958), *Love Is a Many-Splendored Thing* (1955), and *The World of Suzie Wong* (1960). As Christina Klein and Gina Marchetti have shown, these orientalist romances between white men and willing Chinese women were barely disguised allegories espousing contemporary American foreign policy, and although rarely acknowledged, this Hollywood history should also be considered a factor in Hong Kong's cinematic geopolitics.[15] In fact, as Charles Leary shows, in the specific case of Asia Pictures—a Chinese-language, Hong Kong–based film production company partly funded by the American CIA—the differences between Hong Kong and Hollywood and between surveillance and cinema were increasingly blurred.[16] With Asia Pictures seeking to win hearts and minds through both practical offers of employment and by the compelling images and narratives it distributed, commercial Hong Kong theaters were infiltrated by cinematic imagery and business enterprises explicitly mobilized for the purposes of promoting anticommunist feeling.

This structural variety in surveillance regimes is an integral factor in contextualizing Hong Kong cinema's diverse generic content and imagery. As previously noted, in the early 1950s *In the Face of Demolition*'s sentimental portrait of neighborhood cooperation and support dramatized the communitarian business practices of the left-leaning production company behind the film. On the opposite end of the contemporary ideological spectrum, we might look at a movie like *Air Hostess* (1959), a well-known musical romance from MPGI starring popular song-and-dance sweetheart Grace Chang as the eponymous protagonist, in which the movie's seductive portrait of Hong Kong's cosmopolitanism and place within the modern age of international jet travel includes a subplot about measures to prevent drug trafficking and apprehend those guilty of the crime.[17] Although *Air Hostess* and *In the Face of Demolition* are linguistic, generic, and stylistic opposites, both movies illustrate the persistence of surveillance as a governing motif within local cinema. As widely recognized landmarks in Hong Kong film history, the two films' roughly contemporary but antithetical political and ideological tendencies illustrate the degree to which local cinema formalized territorial history and its customs of defining itself through contrasting surveillance ideology and practice.

"MAINLANDER ENTERS . . ."

Later, of course, the different surveillance regimes portrayed in movies like *Air Hostess* and *In the Face of Demolition* would become moot as other films like *The House of 72 Tenants* and those of Michael Hui's oeuvre reflected the spread of capitalist values during the territory's rapid economic growth in the mid-1970s. My point here, however, in reviewing Hong Kong's Cold War history, particularly how the cinema mirrored contemporary geopolitics, is that a look back to the film genres and cinematic eras before the popular action and crime films of reunification reveals similar surveillance themes always present in the cinema but that had subsequently been misread as a result of the critical emphasis on handover politics. Recognizing precedents for the double surveillance themes within reunification-era action and crime necessitates reconsideration of both, with greater attention to not only the anticommunist Sinophobia underlying contemporary cinema's imagery of disorder and violence but also the ways that cinema deployed surveillance motifs as emblems of the territory's capacity for self-protection. As local author Song Mu wrote in a short story published around the same time as the Joint Declaration, a surefire commercial formula in Hong Kong film at the time was an action or crime movie in which "mainlander enters, destroys the established order, and then is himself destroyed."[18] Thus knowingly portraying the contemporary fashion for action and crime films in the reunification era, Song expresses a certainty that "the audience will love it." His story bespeaks an optimistic tenor that shifts attention away from purely paranoid and dystopian readings to those in which violence is a measure of local power and popular consumption of that screen violence as an index of local culture's continued vitality.

The popular 1980s local television series *The Good, the Bad, and the Ugly* also exemplifies the multiple and complex ways in which surveillance and its different manifestations in genre came to infuse local action and crime during the reunification. The program about a family's trials and tribulations in modern Hong Kong was known for its sensitive depictions of contemporary society and included among its recurring characters Ah Chan, a bumpkinish mainland cousin who arrives in Hong Kong with hope of a better life. As Eric Kit-wai Ma has shown, the character's plotline over the years of the program's production provides a vivid index of the mainland's changing status in the eyes of local viewers.[19] While in the early years the program portrayed the character (played by popular comedian Liu Wai-hung) with humor and sympathy, depicting his vulgar behavior and inability to fit into Hong Kong's fast and cosmopolitan society, later episodes had the character fall in with criminals and bring shame and disorder to his Hong Kong family. Such developments mirrored the perspective of many Hong Kong residents themselves, who initially empathized with their mainland cousins but, as they began to compete for jobs and other resources, grew increasingly concerned about the threat this population posed to their way of life. Not surprisingly, surveillance is an implicit theme throughout the series, initially manifested as a subtle, organic, social measure of urban assimilation but ultimately supplanted by a moral and juridical concern with criminal identification and apprehension. In this tonal and narrative shift the program presaged the generic and thematic transformation that would also characterize critical reception of contemporary film.

Intriguingly, the lead actor of *The Good, the Bad, and the Ugly* was Chow Yun-fat, then a popular television star before his breakout performance in *A Better Tomorrow* and the wave of operatic action films that movie unleashed by the mid-1980s. The link between the popular television series and the many action movies starring Chow that would subsequently occupy such critical and popular interest during reunification helps illuminate both why the latter would have been misread and how they might be reexamined. In a previous publication, I have shown how global reception of the films proliferating in response to *A Better Tomorrow*'s commercial success focused on a generic rubric that emphasized violence rather than the traditional themes of honor and chivalry for which the cycle was celebrated at home.[20] Thus emphasizing the blood rather than the heroism of the *yingxiongpian* or "hero" film cycle that *A Better Tomorrow* spawned, the global critical response to what was often called a "heroic bloodshed" film shows how

FIGURE 2.4. At ease in surveillance society: prosperous Hong Kong residents play with CCTV in *A Better Tomorrow* (Cinema City, 1986).

a political, highly topical concern about the potential for Tiananmen-style violent repression could invite the mass misunderstanding of action and crime to which the genre was subject in the politicized climate of reunification.

Yet if reflectionist approaches and the reunification-era commentary overemphasized action and crime's dystopian images of violence and repression, their initial interest in the genre also highlighted an issue long crucial to the cinema and one confirmed by closer study of genres and eras other than reunification-era action and crime—precisely the methodology advocated by the anti-reflectionist turn. The opening scene of *A Better Tomorrow*, for example, shows costars Chow Yun-fat and Ti Lung as a pair of counterfeiters mugging for security cameras (Fig. 2.4). This scene portrays Hong Kong's prosperity through the technological advancement of the secure, high-tech lab in which the pair literally print money, and it more generally asserts the characters' familiarity with that apparatus. Fax machines in *City on Fire* and *People's Hero* function in the same way, depicting the advanced technologies and information systems by which citizens of the modern territory strive to protect its wealth and order, and anticipate later scenes in *Crime Story* (1993), *Rock n' Roll Cop*, and *Organized Crime and Triad Bureau*, all of which director Kirk Wong based on real Hong Kong police cases and which include prolonged scenes of local officers using computers, telecommunications, and even traffic-control signals to create a net by which to apprehend suspects. Like a key scene in the earlier *Long Arm of the Law*, where an uncouth, sweat-suit-clad mainlander cannot escape the panoptic gaze of the territory's paramilitary police helicopter (Fig. 2.5), these reunification-era action and crime movies traffic in images of the repression and violence that arise not from totalitarian rule but from Hong Kong's more powerful resources.[21]

Similarly, *Heroic Trio* begins with a scene of one character and her husband considering the purchase of a rambling, spacious house. While this is obviously not a realistic experience for most Hong Kong residents, the scene engages the ideals of prosperity and upward mobility that the film's plot explicitly suggests is threatened by Mandarin-speaking intruders. Indeed, hospital settings in both *Heroic Trio* and *Hard Boiled*, as well as similar scenes involving an airport and electricity grid in *City on Fire* and *Wicked City*, must be recognized as being as equally important as the carceral settings of the *Prison on Fire* series. Characterized by surveillance practices but metonymizing Hong Kong

FIGURE 2.5. Hi-tech military hardware defuses pinko communism: mainland intrusion cannot evade the panoptic gaze of the Hong Kong police in *Long Arm of the Law* (Bo Ho Films / Johnny Mak Production, Paragon Films, 1984).

not as a repressive and perilously unstable environment, these scenes portray the city as a prosperous, technologically advanced, legally ordered society. Although *Hard Boiled* and *Heroic Trio* could be referencing the real, historical power well known to have been exerted by hospitals and other civic organizations in early Hong Kong history, the more general point is that an institutional symbol of municipal wealth and bureaucratic care is presented within the films as an antithesis to the capricious, parasitic, violent presence of the villains suggestively or explicitly identified with mainland invasion.[22]

CCTV HAS TWO FACES

Of all the previously mentioned reunification-era action and crime films to cast a long shadow over contemporary reception and cultural criticism, two movies in particular deserve attention for their detailed glimpses into surveillance's organizing role as an object of both identification and disidentification within local cinema. The first example, *Long Arm of the Law,* was a critical and commercial success on its original release and in subsequent scholarly discussion has shown remarkably long legs. The movie was made by experienced producer and screenwriter Johnny Mak from a script developed by high-ranking local police officer Philip Chan (whose role in the local entertainment industry is further discussed in the following chapter) during the talks that culminated in the Joint Declaration, and it appeared in local theaters only months before the official announcement that the end of British colonization would be succeeded by Chinese sovereignty.[23] Although neither the movie nor the director has the international or cult following of acclaimed auteurs such as John Woo or Tsui Hark, *Long Arm of the Law* was one of the year's top-twenty hits. Described by Esther Yau as "a kind of 'developed sector' sentiment concerning an 'underdeveloped sector,'" the movie epitomizes the highly topical but otherwise conventional crime plot that Song Mu had parodied that same year as a predictable premise in which "mainlander enters . . ."[24] Indeed, given the fact that many critical analyses of the film appeared in the 1990s, after Tiananmen and more than a half a decade since the movie's original release, it would seem that *Long Arm of the Law* gained retrospective significance as public opinion about reunification began to deteriorate in 1989.[25]

As previously noted, however, surveillance's defining role in these films provides an invaluable lens by which to reconceptualize the cinema. It accounts for the overly politicized and reductively allegorical analyses of the movies as prophecies of impending Communist sovereignty and also provides a key to the more subtle, but crucial, focus on prosperity and the economic and cultural distinctions that arise from the vastly different standards of living then at stake between Hong Kong and China. *Long Arm of the Law* is defined by this tension between mainland privation and the human and technological resources that a wealthy capitalist enclave could deploy to protect itself from such intruders. The film begins in mainland China, and, like *The Good, the Bad, and the Ugly*, initially shows great compassion in considering mainland struggles, which are depicted through sparse furnishings and primitive electricity systems, as well as neighbors gossiping about luxury appliances such as microwaves, refrigerators, and color televisions of which they have heard but can really only dream of having. However, once the mainlanders cross the border into Hong Kong, security cameras and other physical and human guards become recurring images in the film. These images are typical of the many action and crime films of the era, and a crucial plot development later in the film hinges on the Hong Kong police's use of CCTV footage from an earlier crime to advance their investigation. The climax of the film is undoubtedly the helicopter scene in which a mainlander's ridiculous pink sweat suit both continues long-standing local conventions of mocking gaudy mainland taste and literalizes his status as a "pinko" Communist, but *Long Arm of the Law* is best understood in terms of the subtler, nonmilitary modes of surveillance depicted in the security cameras and their footage that occupy such a key role in the plot. In multiple scenes of screen-within-screen imagery, such diegetic instances of CCTV footage and monitoring symbolically inscribe the movie's allegorical pretensions, positioning this reunification-era Hong Kong action and crime movie as a cautionary tale against coming Chinese intrusion. In stark contrast to previous readings, however, such surveillance motifs do not simply infuse the broadly demonic and dialectical plotlines of mainland intrusion and criminal villainy. More important, they also project a strong expression of the territory's corollary capacity to protect itself.

Hard Boiled similarly thematizes surveillance, especially CCTV security networks, as an organizing motif within its evocatively topical images and plotline. As previously noted, the undercover-cop movie includes an elaborate thirty-minute climactic action sequence involving assassins disguised as police officers, and the scene's shocking imagery of civil servants mowing down innocent civilians exerted powerful connotations in an era of post-Tiananmen paranoia. Not surprisingly, much of the film's climax depends on the genre's surveillance conventions. Typical of many other contemporary action and crime films in espousing the ideas of entrapment, emigration, and impending doom, *Hard Boiled* literalizes the anticommunist, Sinophobic fears of totalitarian control implicit in the more reductively political interpretations of such movies. It does so through a compelling coincidence whereby the movie's ominous images of CCTV monitoring further evoke Tiananmen violence because the CCTV acronym also stands for the primary Chinese state television channel and, hence, directly invites Tiananmen comparisons (Fig. 2.6).

Yet, if *Hard Boiled* resembles other contemporary action and crime films of the handover era in its topically suspicious and paranoid depiction of surveillance, it also balances that depiction with an equally important return to the traditions of liberatory, defensive surveillance long present in local cinema. This occurs when an undercover cop (Tony Leung Chiu-wai) dons a police uniform and parades a plainclothes cop before security cameras, thereby appearing to the villain as one of his assassins having successfully captured a real cop (Fig. 2.7). By cannily manipulating the CCTV technology that the villain had co-opted, the two heroes manage to free themselves from entrapment and get closer to the actual villain, ultimately bringing an end to the siege.

This scene includes multiple reunification resonances, and they consistently figure surveillance as both a mechanism of repression and violence and the means by which a prosperous city can protect itself. First, by facilitating their apprehension of the villain and arresting the casualties, the two cops' use of the security camera footage fulfills the CCTV's intended purpose, which is to deter criminality or at least facilitate apprehension. Second, this action restores the

FIGURE 2.6. CCTV as political reportage: Tiananmen footage from China Central Television.

FIGURE 2.7. Rehabilitating co-opted surveillance: preventing violence, apprehending criminality, and restoring law and order through a deceptive use of police uniforms and CCTV in *Hard Boiled* (Golden Princess, 1992).

co-opted security camera system back to its intended role of crime prevention and institutional safety, underscoring surveillance's continuing value even within a world with other, more repressive surveillance regimes. Third, in the context of post-Tiananmen reunification anxiety, the reseizing of surveillance technology from authoritarian or totalitarian uses and its reinstitution for the protection of the general populace constitutes a significant gesture of hope for local autonomy and the possibilities of domestic self-protection. As with so many of surveillance cinema's reflexive motifs, this depiction of legitimated surveillance pertains to both surveillance practices and the cinematic medium. Like *Long Arm of the Law*'s visual and thematic emphasis on surveillance technologies and especially CCTV, *Hard Boiled* thus presents *itself* as a type of surveillance film dedicated to vigilant monitoring of imminent mainland threat.

Hard Boiled further underscores this surveillance fantasy through its undercover-cop plot and restoration of the undercover officer's clothing to the official police uniform traditionally worn within his profession. Because the cop uniform he dons is taken from a felled assassin, the undercover cop's donning of the uniform is both a symbolic restoration of official police identity and a suggestive cleansing of the bloodstains associated with the fake cop-assassins in the movie's Tiananmen-like bloodbath. Though *Hard Boiled* demonstrates surveillance's reunification-era association with authoritarian power, the movie remains primarily concerned with surveillance as the prevailing emblem of local power in contemporary Hong Kong. As in so many action and crime films of the era, *Hard Boiled* uses surveillance as an indicator of the resources and ingenuity with which an already intensely surveilled society such as Hong Kong will protect itself.

FORTRESS HONG KONG?

A common term in surveillance studies of the 1990s that helps describe the defensive imagery of social and spatial monitoring within contemporary Hong Kong films like *Hard Boiled* and *Long Arm of the Law* is "fortress architecture," which describes the imposing and defensive aspects of the built environment deployed by cities and property owners to discourage loitering, prevent criminal behavior, and

otherwise restrict access.[26] "Fortress architecture" certainly describes
how Hong Kong movies of the reunification era depicted the technologies and architectural resources by which the territory conceptualized its difference from China, and such architecture was in fact an attribute of real urban landmarks and municipal infrastructure, such as
the Hong Kong and Shanghai Bank—known for its inhospitable facade
and a popular belief that it was designed to be removed and rebuilt if
reunification went awry—as well as the city's subway system, which
municipal police had helped design and whose efficient turnstiles and
clearly demarcated pedestrian passageways also had the advantage
of exposing illegal immigrants who deviated from customary traffic
flow.[27] Like the ubiquitous CCTV monitors and cameras throughout
the city that play such an important role in contemporary film, action
and crime films of the era might be understood as deploying a "fortress" aesthetic in their recurrent depiction of surveillance as a defensive, protective aspect of a prosperous, technologically advanced society. Indeed, in perhaps the cinema's ultimate reflectionist gesture,
the attributes of temporal discontinuity and tendency for blue filter or
monochromatic palettes widely associated with Hong Kong film of the
era might be understood as aesthetic simulation of the visual minimal-
ization and physical capacity for rewind, playback, and freeze frame
that characterizes CCTV surveillance footage.[28]

Yet, if the surveillance motifs of reunification-era action and crime
suggest a cinematic "fortress Hong Kong," they also complicate the repressive, inhospitable connotations with which fortress architecture
was often condemned as an unnecessarily exclusionary practice. As
A. R. Cuthbert and Janet Ng have both pointed out, urban planning
in Hong Kong is usually motivated by the goals of maximizing efficiency and commercial exposure.[29] Without being disingenuous about
the neoliberal priorities implicit in such planning, this insight nevertheless highlights the very different tenor that Hong Kong and Hong
Kong film accords urban surveillance. Fluid, diffuse, and equally as
concerned with enabling movement and consumption as with restrict-
ing access and preventing crime, the conditions of urban surveillance
mirrored in contemporary cinema often juxtapose the destruction and
repression of oppressive surveillance with more hospitable and productive forms. This diversity in surveillance regimes is evident in lo-

cal cinema not only within individual films but also across various genres, and it explains the persistence of certain images and aesthetic attributes across genres and films that might otherwise seem very different. The tenement movie *Cageman*, for example, includes a penultimate image that is virtually identical to the final scenes of *Long Arm of the Law* and *City on Fire* (Fig. 2.8), despite the vast differences between a sensitive social drama and violent action and crime. Their mutually monochromatic images of smoke-filled aftermath speak to contemporary concerns about reunification by laying blame for the devastation on the films' villains, therefore reinforcing the paranoid surveillance themes that pervade both films, while also revealing through their shared imagery the continuity of surveillance motifs through genres beyond action and crime.

Similarly, the 1996 sentimental romance *Comrades, Almost a Love Story* further exemplifies surveillance's centrality within genres and movies vastly different from the action and crime films commonly interpreted as allegories of contemporary reunification.[30] The award-winning box-office hit about two mainland émigrés who fall in love while seeking better opportunities in Hong Kong was one of the few commercial successes in the decline years of the mid-1990s, and with its sentimental image of attractive mainland immigrants (played by pop heartthrob Leon Lai and former Miss Hong Kong contestant Maggie Cheung) set to a Mandarin-language sound track, the film posed a tactically sensitive alternative to the Sinophobic end games of previous action and crime movies. If the film signals a newfound willingness by the Hong Kong film industry to accommodate or cater to coming Chinese power, a distinctly local tradition of private and capitalist surveillance motifs remains one of the film's most memorable attributes. Throughout the film, *Comrades, Almost a Love Story* features recurring scenes at an automated teller machine (ATM), which narrate the two characters' economic fortunes and hence depict their assimilation into Hong Kong's society of global capitalism and financial speculation (Fig. 2.9). As an inventive variation on the innumerable screens within screens throughout Hong Kong film, these images from *Comrades, Almost a Love Story* uphold Hong Kong surveillance as a seductive and often rewarding way of life, in stark contrast to the repressive and authoritarian mainland power motivating the film's apparent

FIGURE 2.8. Aesthetic interchangeability despite generic difference: similar scenes of urban devastation in the final image of *Long Arm of the Law* (Bo Ho Films / Johnny Mak Production, Paragon Films, 1984) and the penultimate image of *Cageman* (Filmagica Productions, 1992).

FIGURE 2.9. Hong Kong's Eastern capitalism seduces mainlander in ATM point of view shot from *Comrades, Almost a Love Story* (Golden Harvest, 1996).

Sinophilia. Indeed, if the film's Mandarin dialogue and sentimental depiction of mainlanders prefigures the current era of coproductions between Hong Kong and mainland Chinese film companies, the movie's seemingly pro-China sentimentality is subverted by imagery that positions the audience within the perspective of the ATM's security camera itself. Seeing from the perspective of a Hong Kong ATM, viewers of *Comrades, Almost a Love Story* identify with Hong Kong economic and technological surveillance and watch the mainland's conversion to Hong Kong–style capitalism.

BEYOND THE ACTION GENRE

Similar instances of Hong Kong's distinctly affirmative surveillance motifs may be found in many other generic exceptions to the topically resonant reunification-era movies. The successful 1982 comedy *Plain Jane to the Rescue*, for example, is rarely considered by Western scholarship except as an example of director John Woo's action choreography, which can be mined for suggestively topical images such as an infant born during a car chase through the territory's Cross Harbour Tunnel that Woo himself has described as an early instance of the reunification themes infusing his later films. But these reductively genre-based and allegorical studies miss how the film (the third in a series of movies based on a popular television character) finds pleasure in the economic and technological attributes of modern Hong Kong. Jokes in the film repeatedly portray local society as a technologically, bureaucratically, and financially advanced society, evident in both the rapidly expanding corporation that is the film's nominal villain, as well as the unemployment office in which the heroine occasionally works. Like Woo's other Golden Harvest comedies, *The Pilferer's Progress* (1977) and *From Riches to Rags* (1980)—which were themselves thought to have been made in imitation of Michael Hui's movies—*Plain Jane to the Rescue* shows bureaucratic and capitalist monitoring as a positive aspect of Hong Kong culture and society despite—or precisely because of—the more topical concerns regarding political change purportedly allegorized in the plot.

Similarly, the cycle of historical tragedies and romances that appeared during this era also provides an interesting glimpse into local surveillance motifs, particularly as they were positively identified with local culture rather than negatively with authoritarian China. As Ackbar Abbas and many other critics have noted, because of their cost and longer time of production, period settings and historical reenactments are rare in Hong Kong cinema after the end of the studio era, but during the handover, movies like *Red Rose White Rose* (1994), *Love in a Fallen City* (1984), *Hong Kong 1941* (1984), *Boat People* (1982), *Rouge* (1988), and *Centre Stage* (1992) were made and found audiences due to widespread yearning to explore local history and culture that reunification threatened to erase.[31] As in more conventional action and crime, surveillance is an important motif within these films. For example, Ann Hui's Vietnam-set *Boat People*, which was widely recognized as an allegory conflating Hong Kong with those trapped within Communist Vietnam, is told through the eyes of a Japanese photographer whose documentary gaze comes into increasing conflict with the Communist officials assigned to escort him through the country. Similarly, in *Love in a Fallen City* and *Hong Kong 1941*—dramas both set in World War II Hong Kong and starring a pre–*A Better Tomorrow* Chow Yun-fat as the romantic lead—local survival instincts are incarnated through the protagonist's resourceful ingenuity (including, in *Hong Kong 1941*, a variation on local undercover-cop traditions in which Chow's character enlists as a Japanese military policeman to aid his friends). And in Stanley Kwan's arty, acclaimed films, *Centre Stage* and *Rouge*, the director employs a loose documentary premise to explore two enigmatic suicides.[32] Social and spatial monitoring are implicit in both films through the general sense of historical recovery as well as diegetic representation of gossip and journalistic reportage, and because both films are metatextual, highly self-reflexive movies that incorporate filmmaking into the plot, they also suggest filmmaking—and, by extension, Hong Kong cinema more generally—as a means by which Hong Kong surveils itself.

As with *Hard Boiled* and *Long Arm of the Law*, however, of all the previously mentioned films two films in particular illustrate surveillance's centrality as an organizing motif within film genres that do not fall within the realm of action and crime. As noted in the chapter introduction, both *Cageman* and *Chungking Express* are critically acclaimed films whose topical references hinge on surveillance imagery that illustrates the subtleties of reunification-era cinema. *Cageman*, for example, combines topical allegory and local film traditions in a movie about Hong Kong's poignant "cage dwellers"—desperately poor and often illiterate men whose only housing is rented, coffin-sized lockers that may be stacked two or three deep and are crowded dozens per room (Fig. 2.10). Although the film was inspired by an actual event that the film's director, admired New Wave filmmaker Jacob Cheung, read about in a local newspaper, the movie also has topical and artistic contexts that invoke reunification-specific concerns.[33] The film's plot about impoverished residents suddenly facing eviction obviously references local tenement movies such as *In the Face of Demolition* and *The House of 72 Tenants*, while using those cinematic references to evoke a topical sense of residential disempowerment and forced transition. In fact, with specific reference to the film's cage imagery, the movie also evokes the contemporary handover crisis in its implicit similarities to contemporary rhetoric that described Hong Kong as a bird being passed from one "cage" to another (Fig. 2.11).

Like many contemporary action and crime films, then, *Cageman* layers a loosely Sinophobic anxiety about repressive surveillance with benign and even affectionate surveillance imagery whose continuity with tenement movie traditions is strongly associated with local

FIGURE 2.10. Social realism in reunification-era tenement film *Cageman* (Filmagica, 1992). A typical cage dwelling measures about two by three by six feet.

FIGURE 2.11. "From one cage to another": untitled cartoon by local artist Zunzi, July 23, 1984 (courtesy of the artist).

culture and identity. On the one hand, *Cageman* directly invites Tiananmen allusions in a protest and hunger strike organized by the residents, to which the authorities respond with jackboot tactics by sending in officers dressed in strike gear to forcibly remove the protesters.[34] On the other hand, *Cageman* also naturalizes and sentimentalizes these images by invoking tenement-movie traditions in which surveillance manifests as a proud site of local culture and society. The Tiananmen-like protest, after all, has a cinematic precedent in similar scenes from *The 82 Tenants*, a modern-day sequel to *The House of 72 Tenants* released on the 1973 film's ten-year anniversary and one of the many homages or references to the local classic within Hong Kong cinema (see Fig. C.1). *Cageman* further alludes to the original Shaw film as well as *In the Face of Demolition* through intertextual homages such as the pointed use of "Home on the Range"—a tune central to the 1973 Shaw film—and the casting of Ku Feng, one of the actors in the original Shaw film who, in *Cageman*, plays a burly laborer and fellow tenement dweller whose tireless support for his neighbors is itself an homage to Ng Chor-fan's character in *In the Face of Demolition*.

Cageman must be understood within the context of this affirmative surveillance motif, which uses the territory's poignant cage dwellers both as emblems of Hong Kong's helplessness within the impending political transition and, more hopefully, as symbols of the city's ability to find agency within highly straitened circumstances. This rehabilitative and ameliatory portrayal of local cage dwellers has some basis in that population's own sense of themselves but also is predicated on the film's revival of tenement-movie traditions, particularly their tendency to celebrate a marginalized group within local society as a metonym of Hong Kong as a whole.[35] As early as *The House of 72 Tenants*, for example, a proto-cage-dweller scene occurs when celebrated Shaw kung fu actor Yueh Hua, playing the heroic young man who breaks through floorboards to rescue a young woman (see Fig. I.9), explains to astonished witnesses that he resides at "No. 96 on this street, next to Shanghai Po, below the landlady, to the left of the communal staircase, in the Chiu Chow cigarette vendor's room, on the bunk you fixed halfway up the ceiling." Through this explicit verbal description of Hong Kong's pitiable bed-space dwellings, *The House of 72 Tenants* exemplifies tenement-genre traditions of both acknowledging privation and suffering

FIGURE 2.12. When a cage means home: reconnecting behind bars in the final scene of *Cageman* (Filmagica, 1992).

while also celebrating these conditions as positive examples of the natural surveillance pervasive to Hong Kong society.[36]

Cageman ends on a similarly rehabilitative note: The film's concluding scene takes place in a zoo where several of the movie's main characters serendipitously reencounter each other sometime after their forced relocation. Although the POV glimpses of each other through the zoo's bars (Fig. 2.12) might at first seem continuous with the negative surveillance motifs of the movie's previous imagery of enclosure and destruction, their effect is radically different. Instead of painting a dystopic and paranoid image of repressive surveillance, *Cageman*'s visually carceral but affectively sentimental final scene recalls the tenement genre's nostalgic and rehabilitative emphasis on the intimate and supportive bonds of community surveillance. Indeed, it recalls the soft-focus, slow-motion sentimentality of the movie's earlier sequences within the cage homes, whose frequent emphasis on shared possessions and mutual care continues tenement-movie conventions going back to *The House of 72 Tenants* and *In the Face of Demolition*, and whose velvety blacks and low-contrast lighting are evocative suggestions of cage homes' limited resources but also hark back to the pastel, rose-hued optimism of *The House of 72 Tenants*' Shaw palette.

DOMESTICATING SURVEILLANCE IN *CHUNGKING EXPRESS*

Although very different, Wong Kar-wai's effervescently lighthearted *Chungking Express* also exemplifies the persistence of surveillance motifs within topically resonant films that defy the action and crime genres most commonly associated with the motif. As many have noted, the atmospheric, elliptical romances Wong made in the late 1980s and through the 1990s evoke the contemporary context of reunification through their recurrent themes of longing and expiring time. *Days of Being Wild* (1990), for example, Wong's languid, nostalgic homage to the *Ah Fei* films about wayward youth popular in the 1960s, layers a playboy's search for his birth mother with a parable about a legless bird doomed to perpetual flight until his death. Similarly, *As Tears Go By* (1988), *Ashes of Time* (1994), and *Chungking Express* all include characters marked by a temporal sentence such as worsening illness or blindness or a self-imposed desire to consume food marked with a specific expiration date. Although rarely described as surveillance, the eccentric or even perverse and infantilized nature of these behaviors works in conjunction with the films' topical resonances to present a substantively different manifestation of the surveillance motifs implicated in topical readings of contemporary cinema, especially action and crime.[37] The playboy in *Days of Being Wild*, for example, seduces women by promising them that the daily repetition of their shared moment in time will be preserved in perpetuity. To further augment the eroticized cast the film gives to personal and temporal monitoring, this conceit of obsessive time marking and daily repetition then reappears in the form of an alternate romantic suitor, a beat policeman who, after regularly encountering the lovelorn woman during his daily patrol, encourages her to call him instead. Further emblematizing the eroticized surveillance in this subplot is the police call box, once an institution of Hong Kong policing that the film implies is a more reliable site of emotional response to the woman than the pay phone booth where she has futilely tried to reach her lover.[38]

As this brief outline suggests, Wong's films grant great importance to personal, spatial, and temporal monitoring, and although these movies are most commonly identified as romances, they resemble contemporary action and crime films in depicting surveillance as an attractive, even desirable aspect of Hong Kong society. This idiosyncratically seductive depiction of surveillance typical of local cinema is further apparent in *Chungking Express* and *Fallen Angels* (1995)—which both feature characters who express their affection or desire for another by secretly entering their homes or videotaping them without consent—and is especially obvious in *Chungking Express,* an upbeat, quickly paced two-part film whose cop protagonists seem to have no conventional function of investigation and apprehension but, instead, exist only as figures for romantic possibility. In the first story, for example, a detective's capacity for precise temporal observation is relevant only insofar as it records the specific moment in which he encounters women, a quality that is further endearing because he is ignorant of the criminal circumstances surrounding a mysterious woman with whom he spends a tender but unconsummated night. Similarly, in the second, longer story, the daily habits of a naïve, lovelorn beat policeman bring him to the attention of an eccentric food-counter worker whose assiduous care of his home and body are juxtaposed with the faithlessness of the cop's previous girlfriend, an airline stewardess whose mobility and easy disregard for territorial borders evoke the many Hong Kong residents who, during reunification, sought to transfer their citizenship or otherwise relocate.

As in contemporary action and crime films, *Chungking Express* uses surveillance motifs to stage its topical resonance while also manifesting its generic difference in less dystopian or negative approaches to surveillance always latent within films of the era. Conventions of contemporary action and crime films surface throughout the movie, only to be repurposed for entirely different generic and affective ends: a halfhearted shootout that closes the first vignette, for example, is nearly bloodless and figures primarily as a liberatory gesture by which the mysterious woman (actually a drug trafficker's go-between) is able to escape a repressive handler. Freeze frames and other moments of temporal discontinuity arise in *Chungking Express* not as a reminder of CCTV aesthetics but as a means by which cinematographer Christopher Doyle uses his signature undercranking and step-printing techniques to carve out romantic interludes within the banal rush of urban life (Fig. 2.13). In the context of contemporary reunification-era cinema, these moments emblematize *Chungking Express*'s generic divergence

FIGURE 2.13. Domesticating surveillance in the romanticized temporal discontinuity of *Chungking Express* (Jet Tone Productions, 1994).

from the paranoid anxieties once emphasized in action and crime and instead gesture toward an optimistic, sanguine vision where surveillance offers the means by which Hong Kong might survive. Indeed, through a subtle but powerful reworking of archetypal reunification-era crime film *Hard Boiled*, *Chungking Express* casts the same actor (Tony Leung Chiu-wai) in the blue police uniform that had played such an important role in the earlier film's action climax (compare Fig. 2.13 with Fig. 2.7), further converting that earlier movie's ambiguous reminder of Tiananmen's repressive surveillance into a neutral and even romantic emblem of local culture.

Chungking Express's ultimate instance of the domesticated surveillance that pervades reunification-era film occurs in the film's profoundly optimistic coda, in which the beat policeman retires his cop uniform and purchases the food stall where he had met his former admirer. Through this professional reinvention as a small-business owner, the former cop personifies the domesticated perspective on surveillance long characteristic of local culture and cinema. During the reunification era, this constructive and defensive notion of surveillance was inadvertently obscured by the critical and cultural prominence of action and crime films and the paranoid, overly politicized, anticommunist Sinophobia that the films seemed to portray, but it con-

tinued to surface in other genres and contemporary films that retro-
spectively help us understand those same tropes in action and crime
films. Among the period films that unusually proliferated in the early
1990s, for example, were a number of movies—such as *Lee Rock* and
its sequel *Lee Rock II* (both 1991), *Arrest the Restless* (1992), and *Powerful
Four* (1992)—which cast an oddly nostalgic look back to a time of police corruption that troubled Hong Kong during the 1960s.[39] Although
these period pieces had little correlation with the current police force—
whose greatly improved status in both film and popular culture is the
subject of the next chapter—the movies make sense as quintessentially
local glimpses of Hong Kong culture and cinema's tendency to figure
surveillance as a metonym of local identity and practical opportunity
for personal profit and upward mobility. In the next chapter, I focus on
an even more specific subset of reunification-era action and crime films
to document another, more tangible site in which Hong Kong surveillance cinema manifests its affirmative, positive tendencies. Prompted
by a cycle of movies about partnerships between Hong Kong and Chinese police that appeared in the time of industrial decline during the
final years leading up to 1997, I show how Hong Kong's uniquely affirmative surveillance culture manifests in a long-standing collaboration
between the film industry and the local police.

THREE

"ONLY" A POLICEMAN

JOINT VENTURE CINEMA AND
THE MEDIATIZATION OF THE HONG KONG POLICE

HONG KONG FILM IS SO FILLED with police images that their ubiquity obscures the cinema's unusually close relationship to the actual surveillance institution that those fictional images portray. From John Woo and Chow Yun-fat to Johnnie To and Jackie Chan, many of the industry's leading talents are strongly associated with the police plots and cop characters they have created or played on-screen. The cinema's innumerable cop images reflect its global identification with action and crime genres, but it also occludes the film industry's synergy with local law enforcement, a major factor underlying the cultural and professional success of both in the last quarter of the twentieth century. It is widely known, for example, that many of the filmmakers who would eventually become known as the Hong Kong "New Wave" gained early employment and training in government institutions, where their work included media collaboration with law enforcement agencies.[1] Prior to moving into film, for example, directors Derek Yee, Patrick Tam, and Alex Cheung all oversaw seasons of *CID*, a popular television program based on real crime stories that was developed in the 1970s in conjunction with the Royal Hong Kong Police (RHKP).[2] Similarly, Yim Ho, Ann Hui, and Alex Cheung directed individual installments of *ICAC Investigations*, a television series consisting of dramatic reenactments of cases handled by the Independent Commission Against Corruption (ICAC), a powerful government watchdog institution founded in 1974 as part of police reform.[3] Moreover, this synergy between film and local policing is not one-sided, and it continues to sustain individuals even amid the cinema's decline and reinvention. In the mid-1990s, a local officer learned so much about script development after consulting on *Organized Crime and Triad Bureau*, a 1994 procedural by noted crime filmmaker and veteran of government-funded television series Kirk Wong, that he was able to transition to screenwriting.[4] Similarly, during the post-reunification industrial retraction, Alex Cheung—whose post-TV film work included landmark New Wave crime movies *Cops and Robbers* (1979) and *Man on the Brink* (1981)—returned to the *ICAC* television series in which his career had begun.

Interestingly, however, few studies of Hong Kong cinema explore this symbiosis, largely neglecting the detail and specificity with which the police were portrayed on film. As a result, they miss the extent to which cinema worked in tandem with the force and contemporary RHKP policy. This historical collaboration was a crucial factor in the 1970s when the burgeoning media industry coincided with an institutional crisis for the Hong Kong Police (HKP), and it was channeled again in the mid-1990s when a cycle of movies about partnerships between Hong Kong and mainland police that appeared during the industrial decline explored issues of police legitimacy and continuity posed by coming reunification. This chapter shows that film and other consumer media were instrumental in the HKP's survival of the first crisis and that the mutually beneficial relationship between institution and industry established during that time helps account for the continuing prominence in film of police and police issues through subsequent years, particularly the industrial decline in the mid-1990s when commercial uncertainty regarding censorship and free expression mirrored political questions of institutional continuity. Although criticism of police behavior during the 2014 Umbrella protests shows the extent to which the HKP reputation has deteriorated in the two decades since reunification, the period between the late 1970s and early 1990s was a high point in local police imagery. At this time the cinema's prolific and often positive police images correlated with the HKP's own professional status, which by the cinema's industrial height in the 1980s had successfully erased its once-contested colonial history to become

widely regarded as one of the world's most admired and celebrated
police forces.[5]

As in the previous chapter, this discussion revisits an era and subgenre of films widely associated with Hong Kong cinema to explore
the importance of surveillance through that subgenre and the cinema
as a whole. The focus specifically on police and cop movies tracks the
real histories behind the cinema's seemingly formulaic, conventional
genres; it also shows how the industry's fictional, dramatized representations of official surveillance exemplify Hong Kong's pervasive and
unusually domesticated surveillance motifs through a police-media
collaboration that is further remarkable because it is often overlooked.
While comparable studies by John Fiske and Christopher Wilson have
documented Hollywood's overt and often highly contested role in
shaping popular wisdom about American policing, Hong Kong cinema offers an intriguing example of how official surveillance institutions can survive and prosper by embedding their fate within the
welfare of cinema itself.[6] This history of police-media collaboration in
Hong Kong is one of the most tangible instances of Hong Kong's distinctly sanguine surveillance cinema and provides an intriguing contrast with the well-known, widely documented impact on the Hong
Kong film industry by local organized crime.[7] By exploring a cinematic
subgenre that I call "joint venture" movies, I show how these reunification-era movies about partnerships between Hong Kong and mainland
police continued the cinema's long-standing affinity with official surveillance to advocate industrial and institutional continuity. Based on
an actual exchange between Hong Kong and mainland police that began in late 1992 in anticipation of the impending handover, those films'
projections of industrial and institutional vitality presaged the post-
decline Hong Kong cinema's current turn to coproduction with mainland China.[8]

THE "BIG BUSINESS" OF HKP MEDIA

Joint venture films are obviously topical in their explicit reference to
contemporary politics and in their more general staging of cop characters as proxies or surrogates for their respective societies. During
reunification the joint venture premise of Hong Kong–mainland po-

lice collaboration surfaced throughout a variety of genres, including a number outside the predictable categories of action, drama, and crime. Thus, alongside conventional cop actioners such as Jackie Chan's *Police Story III: Super Cop* (1992); Manfred Wong's critically admired road movie starring well-known mainland actor Jiang Wen, *The Trail* (1993); and action-crime procedurals such as *Rock n' Roll Cop* and *Organized Crime and Triad Bureau* (both 1994) appeared comic films, such as the *Her Fatal Ways* series (1990–94) starring female comedian Carol Cheng, and those built around Michael Hui (*Hero of the Beggars*, 1992) and Stephen Chow (*From Beijing with Love*, 1994). Also distributed were romances and other vehicles fashioned for mainland-born action star Jet Li (*The Bodyguard from Beijing*, 1994; *My Father Is a Hero*, 1995), then already a prominent figure in the Hong Kong industry for more than a decade but by the 1990s suddenly a star whose specifically Chinese associations presented valuable casting and plot opportunities to appeal to coming reunification.[9]

In fact, these movies about Hong Kong–mainland police collaborations were so widespread during this short period that, in typical Hong Kong fashion, the more successful instances spawned their own spin-offs, parodies, and imitations.[10] For example, in 1991, the first *Her Fatal Ways* film led to both *His Fatal Ways* and *Mainland Dundee*, a broad comedy about mainland cultural officers undercover in Hong Kong, whose titular allusion to the 1986 Australian crossover hit *Crocodile Dundee* paralleled the movie's Chinese title in emphasizing the same "Ah Chan"-style comedy of rustics abroad that drives *Her Fatal Ways*. By the final year before the handover, these joint venture plot conventions had become so entrenched in Hong Kong cinema that the title of *Another Chinese Cop* (1996) makes no effort to disguise its derivativeness. Similarly, in *Combo Cops* (1996)—a low-earning, briefly playing, but otherwise exemplary pastiche that appeared at the same time— mainland-born martial artist Yu Rongguang, who previously had played a mainland villain in *Rock n' Roll Cop*, reappeared as a visiting Chinese supercop who joins a Scotland Yard–trained RHKP officer in a friendly competition to train young recruits for the HKP's Special Duties Unit (SDU). Playing on previous joint venture movies and more general local cop films like *The Final Option* (a 1994 police movie hit starring biracial actor Michael Wong as the SDU head), *Combo Cops* used joint venture's take on traditional "odd couple" buddy-cop formulas to allegorize the difference between a traditional, culture-bound Chinese practice and Western-influenced emphasis on science, technology, bureaucracy, and innovation.[11]

Intriguingly, however, very little has been written about this distinct cycle within Hong Kong film history, perhaps because the subgenre is easily subsumed into more general categories of cop and crime films and the topical allegories of reunification-era cinema. Yet, as Hong Kong scholar and filmmaker Cheuk Pak Tong comments in one of the few publications to notice the phenomenon, local movies in the years immediately preceding reunification were notable for their changing depiction of China's *gonganju*, the Public Security Bureau (PSB), the provincial police that oversee government regulations and otherwise embody state power throughout the mainland.[12] As is typical of the broader category of contemporary action and crime, these movies convey concerns regarding coming reunification and are particularly intriguing for their increasingly deferential depiction of the PSB as 1997 drew closer. Like concerns about censorship and other consequences of reunification then gripping the film industry and society as a whole, this tonal shift over the course of the joint venture cycle manifests a growing, tactical unwillingness to antagonize the coming government that results in increasingly celebratory portraits of mainland authority. For example, relatively early films in the joint venture cycle, such as Michael Hui's *Hero of the Beggars* (in which Hui plays a sent-down sergeant of the People's Liberation Army [PLA] who inadvertently assists the HKP) and the entire *Her Fatal Ways* series (whose homely and bespectacled female PSB officer is reprised in *Mainland Dundee*), take an indulgent but nevertheless condescending attitude toward the mainland bumpkin character. Reminiscent of *Long Arm of the Law* and other contemporary "Ah Chan" imagery, these condescending depictions presuppose Hong Kong superiority but would soon be replaced by an increasingly idealized approach to representations of the mainland's official surveillance agency. Thus in later, more conventional action movies like *The Trail, Rock n' Roll Cop*, and Jet Li's movies *Bodyguard from Beijing* and *My Father Is a Hero*, the films' leads are all handsome, physically powerful men, photographed with the low-angle camera positioning and slow-motion cinematography typical of Hollywood action.

In its observation of Hong Kong cinema's affirmative perspective on official surveillance, Cheuk's account of joint venture movies dovetails with other accounts of Hong Kong's political pragmatism, again differing from the paranoid tropes once widely emphasized about contemporary action and crime to instead highlight the economic and practical concerns long central to local surveillance cinema. This economic-commercial aspect of joint venture movies is perhaps the subgenre's most important attribute, as is always suggested in the movies by film dialogue in which the protagonists are assigned their cross-border partnership. These scenes typically occur early into each movie and use *he zi/hap zok* or another contemporary word or phrase that translates as "joint venture," a term drawn from business to describe a collaborative enterprise between two discrete economic entities and trumpeted throughout the era by both Hong Kong and mainland governments to promote optimism regarding reunification.[13] Although the use of the phrase adds to the movies' topical verisimilitude by articulating a general thematic interest in cross-border collaboration, the term's etymological and contemporary contexts specifically emphasize vitality through economic power—an attribute crucial to Hong Kong's local and global identity; the reason behind China's desire for recovering sovereignty; and a reminder of the importance of unofficial commercial enterprises, such as cinema, in manifesting and reinforcing an influentially distinct Hong Kong identity.

In an esoteric but no less important context, joint venture movies also reflected the RHKP's own institutional ambition and its determination to survive the shift in sovereignty, recalling actual police reforms and rhetoric that once had been instrumental to HKP authority. To understand this context, one has to see the subgenre's fictional police protagonists as surrogates for real institutional representation, reflecting the force's long history of using official and unofficial media to enhance institutional legitimacy. As Norman Miners observes, the unusual prestige the force had attained by the last quarter of the twentieth century was the result of highly effective programs of indigenization and professionalization undertaken during a time of institutional

FIGURE 3.1. When "police public relations would never be the same": from the 1967 riots, leftist publication (left) and HKP response (right) (courtesy of David Hodson).

crisis.[14] Starting with the turbulent 1967 riots widely recognized as a transformative aspect of local history, the once-maligned HKP experienced a radical shift in public opinion, as the force suddenly found itself praised for its sacrifice and dedication during the siege.[15] Thus, while local and colonial histories often cite Queen Elizabeth's subsequent granting of the "Royal" honorific to the HKP in 1969 as evidence of police rehabilitation, that belated, external, and top-down emphasis on colonial recognition obscures the extent to which the force had already begun using media to promote its own status. As early as the 1940s, for example, the HKP created radio plays and short films to educate citizens about crimes and recent cases, which they broadcast through the colonial radio and TV service, Rediffusion. By the time of the riots, the HKP was countering anticolonial pamphlets disseminated by leftist activists by producing their own publications, using exactly the same size, typeface, and photo- and caption-heavy content as the anticolonial publications to present themselves as "Guardians of the People" (Fig. 3.1). These early media efforts taught the HKP both the importance of combating its colonial history and the media's value in facilitating these efforts. As Mark Gaylord and Harold Traver note, after the 1967 riots, "police public relations would never be same." "For the Hong Kong police, media relations has become big business."[16]

GOOD COPS AND BAD COPS

The chronological charting of the HKP's first phase of reform is important, moreover, as it coincides with the blossoming of Hong Kong film and media, particularly the emergence of local filmmakers that would later be identified with the Hong Kong New Wave. As most HKP histories and histories of Hong Kong in general note, the force's public favor following the 1967 riots was short-lived. It was eclipsed just several years later by the "Godber affair," a corruption scandal that in 1973 exposed extensive networks of extortion and kickback schemes that had plagued residents by permeating local policing for decades.[17] While institutional and local histories tend to emphasize this event's role in launching police reform, particularly the founding of the ICAC, the Godber scandal also prompted a specifically media-based response. In 1973, even before the ICAC's founding, the HKP launched *Police Report* and *Police Magazine*, two weekly public-service programs produced in conjunction with colonial television service RTHK.[18] In addition to educating citizens about crime prevention and seeking informants for current cases, these programs aimed to counter bad press evident throughout local television and print news, as well as in some of the highest-grossing and most culturally influential movies of local cinema at the time. In *The House of 72 Tenants*, for example, in addition to the corrupt police constable who assists the film's villainous landlady, the movie includes an elderly, lecherous police superintendent whose age and debauchery suggest the HKP's general history of police malfeasance.[19] And in more specifically contemporary allusions to Godber and the widespread culture of corruption he personified, in one scene within *The House of 72 Tenants*, emergency fire crews refuse to give aid, chanting "mou seoi, mou seoi" (no money, no water), a satiric pun common in the late 1960s and early 1970s to describe government corruption.[20]

Similarly, in a more contemporary and explicitly realistic vein, mid-

FIGURE 3.2. Local cinema joins the HKP: signing an actual RHKP recruitment pamphlet in Chang Cheh's *Police Force* (Shaw Brothers, 1973).

1970s movies like *Police Force* (1973), *Anti-Corruption* (1975) and *Jumping Ash* (1976) combine aspects of both positive and negative HKP publicity by alluding to new RHKP reforms while cashing in on widespread public attention to the institution's troubles. Unlike *The House of 72 Tenants*, all three of these films are realistic dramas explicitly set in the contemporary period, and they directly mirror aspects of HKP history recently advertised in official and critical publicity. *Police Force*, for example, which was directed by *wuxia* maestro (and John Woo mentor) Chang Cheh in a direct commission by the RHKP, follows a young man who joins the force in an attempt to track down his best friend's murderer. Fusing traditional martial arts revenge quest with the specifically urban locale and modern setting of HKP procedural, *Police Force* is symptomatic of an era in which the local police were desperate to correct widespread assumptions of its accountability and inadequacy. While the movie emphasizes the HKP's inability to close the cold case, the length of the struggle also tracks the hero's rapid rise from rookie cop to chief inspector, punctuated by many scenes of marching trainees, extensive zooms to RHKP insignia, and even closeups of contemporary HKP recruitment posters and paperwork that allude to hiring and retraining programs then just beginning to be implemented as part of police reform (Fig. 3.2).

Even more specific in both its topicality and institutional critique is *Anti-Corruption*, a drama about police extortion rings that appeared in local movie theaters at the same time local crowds were demonstrating against Godber, and *Jumping Ash*, an excitingly paced thriller drawn from international headlines about Hong Kong's then central place in international drug trafficking.[21] *Anti-Corruption* mirrors contemporary Godber-era outrage with deliberately inflammatory images of corrupt white officers luxuriating in ill-gotten gains; in one memorable scene, likely based on a real RHKP officer's claims about internal misconduct, an officer lights a cigarette with a burning British pound note.[22] Similarly, *Jumping Ash*'s handheld camera shots of staged heroin consumption, dealing, and trafficking in Hong Kong are virtually indistinguishable from a 1969 British television documentary whose highly critical depiction of rampant local crime threatened to further undermine the RHKP's already compromised legitimacy.[23] Both movies were top-grossing films of their year, demonstrating their popular resonance and the film industry's ability to capitalize on contemporary interest in RHKP status and operations. Further adding to *Jumping Ash*'s verisimilitude was the fact that the film was scripted by Philip Chan—now a prominent figure in Hong Kong film and popular entertainment but at the time already known to local audiences as an unusually visible and high-ranking ethnic Chinese officer frequently deployed by the RHKP for media purposes. Prior to enlisting in the RHKP Chan had been part of a popular local pop group, and because of his skills and his comfort in front of the cameras the RHKP often featured the photogenic young officer in media events, ranging from press conferences for the notorious "Po Sang" bank robbery in 1974 to a song about public safety for which the officer penned and recorded the lyrics, ultimately causing him to become nicknamed the "Singing Inspector" (Fig. 3.3).

Acknowledging this early parallel between Hong Kong crime cinema and the actual HKP substantially illuminates the former's history. In the more recent, reunification-driven context of suspenseful and spectacular action and crime dramas ranging from *Coolie Killer* to *Infernal Affairs*, movies like *Police Force*, *Anti-Corruption*, and *Jumping Ash* are usually remembered as prototypes of the later cinema's pounding crime narratives and visceral screen violence. But in their initial reception, those movies were likely conceived as highly visible exhibits of an ongoing civic-cultural interest in the nature of official surveillance,

FIGURE 3.3. The "Singing Inspector": former pop star and young RHKP officer Philip Chan in a televised public safety message for children (courtesy of Philip Chan).

whose success at using media to enhance its public reputation can be felt in purely commercial film images as well. Indeed, for local action auteur John Woo—who came of age during the 1967 riots, was already affiliated with Chang Cheh during the latter's work on *Police Force*, and has repeatedly cast himself as a cop in cameos in his own films—HKP history is often a latent source of his iconic action spectacles. *Bullet in the Head* (1990), Woo's *Deer Hunter*–like period film about Hong Kong during the Vietnam War, reenacts one of the most famous photographs from the 1967 riots, an image of an injured white HKP officer shortly after losing a hand while defusing a bomb. And *A Better Tomorrow*'s memorable image of the suave counterfeiter played by Chow Yun-fat lighting a cigarette with a burning US hundred-dollar bill quotes *Anti-Corruption* both to suggest the character's confidence and imminent fall and to show how heavily HKP history figures in the image palette of one of Hong Kong's most celebrated directors.

Of course, neither Hong Kong cinema histories nor studies of local policing are entirely ignorant of these intersections between early 1970s police reform and the contemporary evolution of local film, but traditional HKP histories typically emphasize material, institutional, and formal changes in policy rather than consider how the media might have assisted those changes themselves. Yet early in *The House of 72 Tenants*, for example, a handsome young officer gives chase to a purse snatcher, chiding a lazy and corrupt constable for failing to do the same. The young woman whom he aids then reflects, "I guess there are two kinds of cops—some good, some bad," thus framing and containing the critical portrayal of the corrupt constable and his dissolute, aging superior by suggesting that a new generation of locally raised police will soon restore civic order.[24]

Likewise, the inherent value of police operations and power is central to *Police Force, Jumping Ash,* and *Anti-Corruption*—all films that encode generational change into their production or plot. I've already noted how *Police Force*'s imagery of recruitment and promotion acknowledge contemporary rumblings to replace colonial officers; similarly, *Anti-Corruption* concludes with text outlining the previous year's founding of the ICAC, whose independence from the HKP was meant to replace the HKP's own failed former "anti-corruption" branch that the Godber scandals had exposed.[25] As any local viewer would have recognized, the movie and its title thus reenacted aspects of the Godber affair while showcasing the subsequent process of contemporary reform. And in *Jumping Ash*'s ultimately triumphal depiction of RHKP operations, its authorship by a well-known RHKP officer literally demonstrated the force's rehabilitation by media and its emergence as a major player in local cinema.

REPRESENTING RECRUITMENT AND REFORM

As Christopher Wilson notes about American policing, in Hong Kong, media production and self-promotion are now major sites of police labor and operations, symptomatic of the force's modernization and professionalization. While these tendencies in Hong Kong further developed with the cinema's joint venture film cycle, it is worth first exploring the general ways in which HKP media extended beyond commercial cinema and audiences for internal purposes as well. In one striking case, HKP media visibility was not confined to local borders but was also a subject abroad, as the colony's close ties with the BBC made the HKP a subject of interest for distribution in Britain and elsewhere throughout the Commonwealth. As in the case of commercial cinema, early negative publicity encouraged the HKP's involvement in providing later correctives. In the mid-1960s, for example, the RHKP gave full access to British documentarian Adrian Cowell and cameraman Chris Menges (later the Oscar-winning cinematographer for *The Mission* [1986] and *The Killing Fields* [1984]), allowing the pair to attend police operations meetings, drug raids, and stings conducted by the anti-narcotics bureau.[26] Similarly, in *Hong Kong Beat* (1978), a series of hour-long television episodes shot by the BBC in collaboration with the Police Public Relations Bureau (PPRB) for broadcast in Britain, the programs implicitly upheld and publicized HKP policies of localization and professionalization by portraying the force as a colonial institution dedicated to public service.[27] Stylistically consistent with the Griersonian tradition of British documentary present in the previously mentioned 1969 documentary, episodes show white commanding officers directing their respectful Chinese staff, speaking fluent Cantonese, and otherwise showing compassion and consideration for the dispossessed and marginalized individuals they police.

Even more illustrative of the sophistication with which territorial resources were harnessed by the HKP to improve its public image is a recruitment film made and released by the force during the 1970s re-

FIGURE 3.4. "Arresting cinema," by the PPRB: prefiguring local action cinema in a mid-1970s HKP recruitment film.

forms as part of its efforts to replace corrupt officers and equalize former colonial privilege.[28] The short, five-minute film begins with two young Chinese men spotting a recruitment poster and subsequently entering an RHKP office from which they emerge with fistfuls of money. Tactically assertive in both its address to the era's many unemployed as well as its deliberate omission of any overt references to recent corruption scandals, the recruitment film includes a voice-over explanation of the ample signing bonus and regularized standards for salary, promotion, and pension raises recently introduced as means of recruitment and corruption prevention. Further demonstrating the sophistication with which the media-savvy HKP harnessed cinematic technique to burnish its reputation, the recruitment film then shifts gears, accelerating with the sound track's contemporary music into a fast-paced, rapidly edited montage of vehicles, weaponry, and images of bare-chested, fit, young local men expertly handling such modern technologies (Fig. 3.4). While a retrospective interest primar-

ily led by Hong Kong's commercial cinema might find in this recruitment film a prescient indicator of the genres and cinematic techniques
that would later characterize Hong Kong film worldwide, a reverse on-
tology might also be true, as the many luminaries of Hong Kong crime
cinema who first got their start in police media may very well have acquired their artistic vocabulary from those official surveillance productions. In terms of the recruitment film's objective of RHKP rehabilitation by enlisting new recruits, the short film thus works on two
levels. Directly soliciting local civilians to replace the purged corrupt
and colonial officers, the recruitment film works like the contemporary
commercial film, *Police Force*, to pretend that those changes have already taken place.

Recognizing the HKP's role in its own media representations as
well as the ways that contemporary HKP reforms were mirrored in
contemporary moving-image media radically revises standard accounts of police imagery in local surveillance cinema and Hong Kong
film more generally. Most histories of Hong Kong film and popular
media typically subsume official police and surveillance television series such as *CID* and *ICAC* into other contemporary proto–New Wave
programs like *Social Worker* and *Below the Lion Rock*, which were realistic, heavily researched, and socially conscious dramatic productions
steeped in local culture and identity. But without noting those programs' specific interest in official surveillance, such an emphasis on
the programs' New Wave origins overlooks *Social Worker*'s analogous
interest in municipal administration and how it dovetails with the
criminal investigations in *CID* and *ICAC*. This emphasis thus demonstrates an overall sensibility of sociological surveillance throughout local television during this period that is a key attribute of *Below the Lion
Rock*, whose opening credits include two memorable images of police-
civilian encounter. One reason, perhaps, for this critical blindness to
the overt role of institutional surveillance within Hong Kong cinema's
creative history may be that such interventions conflict with hallowed
notions of the territory's celebrated laissez-faire capitalism. Although
all of these media-bureaucratic collaborations are representative of the
strong role of government surveillance in Hong Kong prosperity, such
works—in contrast to the sensationally unregulated industry by which

Frederic Dannen describes Hong Kong cinema's triad influences—are incongruously centralized.

The work on *ICAC Investigations* by Ann Hui, one of the best-known and most critically acclaimed New Wave luminaries to have started in government media, also is illustrative in this regard. Her artistic and critical success is indicative of both the ICAC's key role in Hong Kong film history and the remarkable power exerted by this official surveillance institution. Although two of Hui's programs for the ICAC were shelved after production and withheld from screening for more than two decades, presumably because their content was deemed inconsistent with ICAC objectives, in later years both artist and institution reference each other with respect.[29] The 1977 episode "The Man," which was one of Hui's shelved *ICAC* programs, has since been reissued for festival distribution, and at various times the ICAC website has made some of Hui's programs available for streaming, thereby showcasing both the institution's role in fostering local culture and the benefits resulting from the triumphal ICAC portrait cast by Hui's expert hands. Similarly, Hui's critically acclaimed, semiautobiographical film, *Song of the Exile* (1990), concludes with a scene of the protagonist at work at her first job within the ICAC's media department, explicitly reminding viewers that the film's diegetic and extradiegetic attributes of emergent local consciousness and incipient media professionalism can be credited to a single, specific institution of official surveillance.

TWO SINGING INSPECTORS

Perhaps even more illustrative of the powerful role of official surveillance within the commercial Hong Kong film industry is the PPRB and its subtle, but often influential, role within many fictional images of the HKP. Like the ICAC, the PPRB is a direct product of the first era of HKP reform, having originally been founded as the PPIB (Police Public Information Branch) just a year after the 1967 riots. This move by the HKP to place police media relations directly under police control expanded police operations with activities only tangentially related to traditional law enforcement and the maintenance of public order. Moreover, because of the PPRB's additional role liaising with film industry, the PPRB is just as ubiquitous in cinema as it is in Hong Kong daily life. Hong Kong residents encounter PPRB activities in multiple social, architectural, and multimedia forms, including print publications in the city's numerous police substations and kiosks, local Neighborhood Watch and Junior Police Call programs, and the long-running and widely watched biweekly public service television programs *Police Report* and *Police Magazine*.[30] Similarly, even global viewers of Hong Kong film who know the territory only through that medium may already be unconsciously familiar with the PPRB, which often surfaces in film credits as a source of consulting, production support, and municipal approval. Presumably arising as a result of the PPRB's role in granting permits for location shooting and providing access to official institutional sites, this accredited collaboration with commercial cinema is indicative of both the HKP's media involvement and the local film industry's willingness to align its commercial interests with official municipal practice.

The PPRB's role in fostering commercial and quasi-official content is also specifically apparent within the careers of Michael Hui, Jackie Chan, and Philip Chan (no relation), who are linked to each other and the HKP through the PPRB's influence on their careers or individual works. In his Jack Webb–like transition to entertainment from official policing, Philip Chan is the paradigmatic instance of the HKP's unofficial representation in commercial media, as the former officer's film appearances invariably capitalize on his police biography. He is typically cast as a ranking officer in a variety of police and cop genres, including dramas such as the 1991 corruption tragedy *The Tigers* and comedies and generic parodies such as *Pantyhose Hero* (1990) and the Stephen Chow undercover-cop satire *Fight Back to School III* (1993). While all of these films presumably use Philip Chan's police bona fides as forms of verisimilitude or metatextual allusion, they also demonstrate the extent to which the once-controversial HKP had been so effectively rehabilitated in popular imagery and public culture to become naturalized as a site of consumer pleasure. By the time John Woo's 1992 undercover actioner *Hard Boiled* was released, Philip Chan's supporting role as the jaded police captain overseeing leads Chow Yun-fat and Tony Leung functions both as a play on the actor's official police biography and as a metatextual device to inaugurate a new generation of local police movie stars.

FIGURE 3.5. Police heroism, action stardom, and the aesthetics of arrest: Jackie Chan channels Buster Keaton in the opening sequence of *Police Story* (Golden Harvest, 1985).

Jackie Chan's *Police Story* (1985) also illustrates the multiple forms of police-cinema interaction in Hong Kong. Perhaps one of Hong Kong cinema's most globally recognized films, *Police Story* occupies a key place in Chan's oeuvre as the star's first directorial feature and a movie by which the star aimed to regain the bankability that had been interrupted by a brief and initially unsuccessful foray into Hollywood. Intriguingly, the HKP's institutional and cultural history is hinted at in the film's iconic opening action sequence, in which Jackie Chan's character apprehends a wanted crime boss by bravely standing before a speeding bus (Fig. 3.5). Primarily meant to display Chan's inimitable stunt work, the freeze-framed image is also a literal instance of the frequent conflation of cinematic and criminal arrest that underlies so much surveillance cinema. While global fans of the movie often cite that moment as characteristic of the cinema's penchant for temporal discontinuity, more informed local viewers could have read in the scene allusions to a specific HKP history.[31] To "stop the bus, get on the bus, or get run over by the bus" was once an oft-quoted phrase from the corruption years, invariably cited to explain the logic under which cops and other citizens tolerated those practices.[32]

Even more pointed in *Police Story*'s informed depiction of official police operations is a comic subplot regarding the protagonist's professional celebrity, as his bravery brings the officer to the attention of HKP administration, particularly the PPRB. The media relations de-

partment immediately drafts the officer as a poster boy for HKP professionalism, requisitioning him from traditional police practices of
crime prevention and investigation (Fig. 3.6). These blithe but highly
informed images of PPRB practice are typical of the detailed understanding of contemporary HKP operations that often infuses local police and crime films and continues through *Police Story*'s well-known
spin-offs, sequels, and imitations. For example, *Police Story 2* (1988) continues the original film's Philip Chan–like career arc by recycling the
original film's PPRB imagery in posters and TV spots incorporated
into the film's sets. In the popular *Lucky Stars* series of ensemble action comedies (1983 and afterward) made in emulation of both the *Police Story* and *Aces Go Places* series, Philip Chan and Jackie Chan both
make occasional cameo appearances.[33] Perhaps most overtly, Michael
Hui's 1986 comedy *Inspector Chocolate* resembles *Police Story* in making
the PPRB and HKP public relations a subplot while specifically evoking contemporary HKP reforms through repeated scenes in which the
protagonist's superior officer stands before an organizational chart
and reminds the hero about current administrative mandates to promote more officers (Fig. 3.7). Adapting traditional cop-buddy formulas to pair Hui's characteristically impulsive and crabby officer with a
naïve rookie (pop star Anita Mui), who also happens to be a contestant
for the Miss Hong Kong Pageant, *Inspector Chocolate* follows Chan's *Police Story* in portraying a police administration increasingly concerned
with public reputation and media accessibility.[34]

FIGURE 3.6. Surveillance and celebrity: the PPRB in action in *Police Story*
(Golden Harvest, 1985).

FIGURE 3.7. Publicizing police reform: promotional mandates in *Inspector Chocolate* (Golden Harvest / Hui's Film Production Co., Ltd, 1986). HKP organizational charts were widely circulated during the reform years.

Not surprisingly, the plot of Jackie Chan's *Police Story* ultimately returns to action, but even this return to Chan's signature genre and the bravery and corporeal risk for which Chan is famed are only facets of a multimedia publicity campaign in which Chan's visage benefits both him and the HKP. In further recollection of Philip Chan's biography, *Police Story* showcases Jackie Chan as a singer who recorded the theme song that plays over the film's credit sequences, even incorporating into Chan's famous end credits footage of the star singing. Thus explicitly presenting the action icon in the model of Philip Chan's "Singing Inspector," the movie further realizes its diegetic interest in HKP and PPRB activity with an extradiegetic association with *Police Report* and *Police Magazine*, the decades-long and still-ongoing weekly HKP public service broadcasts to which Chan has loaned his movie theme song since *Police Story*'s original release. By thus lending the HKP the invaluable promotional asset of his stardom while acquiring through these broadcasts a regular, high-profile reminder of one of his most iconic roles, Jackie Chan exemplifies the symbiotic relationship between local police and the Hong Kong film industry.[35]

NATURALIZING POLICE POWER BY 1997

While Jackie Chan's civic boosterism is not unknown, his specific police collaborations and their parallels with the cinematic careers of

Philip Chan and Michael Hui demonstrate how well established the police-film collaboration was by the late reunification period.[36] By the time of the joint venture cycle, this police-media symbiosis was so entrenched that the cinema continued to depict institutional concerns even without the direct connections that existed earlier in their mutual history. Like commercial films about the HKP in the 1970s, joint venture films are highly informed and detailed regarding reunification's coming impact on the force. The movies abound with specific conventions, including bilingual dialogue, scenes announcing joint venture partnership, early and concluding scenes at the Hong Kong–China border, an almost fetishistic focus on police uniforms, and carefully chosen extradiegetic attributes such as mainland-born or otherwise racially or linguistically marked stars. In addition to dramatizing the official and jurisdictional issues at stake in cross-border policing, these representational attributes mirrored actual issues confronting the HKP in regard to reunification. For example, immediately following the announcement of the 1984 Sino-British Joint Declaration, both institutional and civic concern focused on issues of police authority, raising questions about whether China would assume police authority, what powers of investigation and arrest the HKP would hold—including who and what might be considered a "political" investigation—and who would provide the military protection and border security previously provided by the British colonial military.[37] Most of these issues were decided well before 1997 through negotiated agreements that ultimately determined to leave the HKP largely unchanged, with the exception of decolonizing revisions such as dropping the force's "Royal" honorific and replacing the crown on the colonial crest with the new bauhinia insignia of the Special Administrative Region (SAR).[38]

The *Her Fatal Ways* comedies illustrate joint venture cinema's reflection of the widespread and highly visible concerns underlying the future of local policing.[39] Like so much reunification-era cinema, the series revolves around a broadly allegorical premise that maps Greater China's geopolitical tensions. In the first film, a running joke throughout the movie contrasts an HKP officer's repeated assertions of personal and professional neutrality to the political dogmatism of both the visiting mainland cadre and the HKP officer's father, a fervent former officer of the Kuomintang (KMT) Nationalist Party expelled to Taiwan by the Communists. Subsequent installments in the series grew even more specific on the issues facing reunification policing. The second film contains a moment in which an HKP Special Branch captain played by biracial actor Anthony Wong requests of the visiting mainland officer that "after 1997, my men and I will not be punished for our prior service" and that the Chinese government understand that they "serve only Hong Kong." Alluding to one of the most significant transformations planned for the post-1997 HKP—that is, disbandment of Special Branch, the political unit historically deployed by the colonial government to investigate Communist activities—the film, despite being a comedy, articulates a serious and topically relevant vision of police neutrality as a necessary condition for police legitimacy.[40]

Similarly, in *The Bodyguard from Beijing*, contemporary concerns about mainland authority and the subsequent nature of future police power are dramatized through an attack on official uniforms, an issue recurrent throughout the joint venture subgenre. Clearly based on the blockbuster 1992 Hollywood romance *The Bodyguard*, the Hong Kong movie stars mainland-born Jet Li as a decorated PLA officer who must protect a Hong Kong taipan's pampered fiancée after she witnesses a murder. Evoking widely publicized contemporary debates about whether Chinese military or police would displace the HKP and what uniform the post-reunification police might sport, *Bodyguard from Beijing* shows the woman chafing under the mainlander's surveillance, ordering him to wear plainclothes and indignantly telling him, "This is Hong Kong—the Chinese military has no place here!" Typical of plot points throughout many other joint venture films—such as the tension between the rigid comportment and formal dress of the mainland officer and the leather-jacketed, ponytailed Hong Kong officer in *Rock n' Roll Cop*; or "makeover" scenes in all *Her Fatal Ways* comedies in which a brusque and ungainly female PSB officer is remade through Hong Kong consumerism into a timorous and beautiful love interest (Fig. 3.8)—*Bodyguard from Beijing*'s tension over official Chinese surveillance's uniformed presence both recalls specific contemporary debates regarding the future HKP uniform and highlights post-Tiananmen political concerns regarding the HKP's potential displacement by the mainland's very different surveillance forces.[41]

As might be guessed by joint venture films' emergence after Ti-

FIGURE 3.8. Domesticating the mainland presence: from militant Chinese security officer (left) to timid beauty (right) in *Her Fatal Ways* (Bo Ho Films, 1990). Note the Republic of China (Taiwan) flags in the image on the left, contesting the authority of the Chinese state asserted by the cadre's uniform.

ananmen, at stake in the movies' topically politicized adaptation of the well-trodden cop-buddy film conventions is an increasingly imperative desire to both assimilate and distinguish between local policing and foreign military occupation, an issue greatly exacerbated by Tiananmen. Since the 1967 riots, the HKP's iconic *luk yee* (green coat), an olive-green uniform directly descended from a nineteenth-century British military field uniform, had been an icon of local identity and cultural history, fondly depicted in local cinema, especially the soft-focus nostalgia of the period movies that appeared in the early 1990s. At the same time, however, the recent context of Tiananmen and the uncertainty that tragedy posed for Hong Kong's future under Chinese rule cast attention on the HKP uniform's unfortunate resemblance to that of the Chinese PLA. The subsequent imperative to differentiate between HKP and PLA uniforms, which directly affected the RHKP, adds additional interest to the blue police uniforms depicted so prominently in *Chungking Express* and *Hard Boiled* (see Figs. 2.7 and 2.13). Although *Chungking Express* was made and released after the RHKP's switch in early 1994 to a new blue uniform based on the force's winter uniform, *Hard Boiled*'s early use of police blues works with the film's monochromatic blue filter and moody jazz orchestration to heighten the film's noir elements and suggest a specifically urban, apolitical force more akin to British and American police than paramilitary former colonial institutions. Thus maintaining some institutional continuity while dispelling strong associations with either sovereign, these movies' show-casing of the new HKP uniform work—like the official uniform change itself—to assert the institution's difference from Tiananmen-style authority and effectively prioritize the force itself as a keystone of local governance and continuity.

Similarly, both *Rock n' Roll Cop* and the sequels to the prescient Joint Declaration–era hit *Long Arm of the Law* are particularly explicit in their indictment of PLA-identified attributes. For example, although *Long Arm of the Law*'s two sequels, released in 1987 and early 1989, pre-date Tiananmen and the joint venture cycle, they merge the first film's plot of mainland intruders with Hong Kong traditions of undercover surveillance to craft a joint venture precursor in which former PLA officers go undercover in Hong Kong with HKP knowledge. Although all three *Long Arm of the Law* movies display a notably compassionate view of mainland privation consistent with their pre-Tiananmen production, they also include uncannily prescient scenes regarding unconstrained official surveillance power. *Long Arm of the Law II*, for example, includes a scene in which the mainland leader berates an HKP handler for "just following orders" and exclaims, "If I were ordered to shoot a child, I would not follow [the order]." Even more cynical in its identification of brutality with the mainland military, *Long Arm of the Law III* casts Elvis Tsui, the same actor who plays the mainland leader in the previous film, as a relentless PLA officer with the surname "Mao." He proudly carries next to his red-jacketed military ID a photo of himself with Deng Xiaoping and wreaks havoc in Hong Kong by flouting HKP orders that he surrender his gun and not wear his PLA uniform or otherwise practice strong-arm tactics.

By the time of late joint venture films, however, the subgenre's turn toward a politically strategic esteem for mainland policing had to overcome these post-Tiananmen anxieties regarding mainland capacity for violence. *Rock n' Roll Cop*, for example, gives its mainland officer a detailed backstory in which an inflexible former PLA soldier (Wu Hsing-guo, a classically trained Taiwan-born performer useful for his formal deportment and properly accented Mandarin) prioritized military service over his girlfriend, abandoning her to nearly die during a back-alley abortion. Thus using its 1994 setting and the mainland officer's commission of military brutality against innocents to roughly align his actions with Tiananmen, *Rock n' Roll Cop* presents its mainland protagonist as a figure who, according to buddy-film conventions, must both reform and be reformed by his companion—a "Hong Kong Dirty Harry" whose rogue departures from HKP protocol personify the territory's scrappy resourcefulness. The climax of their partnership occurs at the border as a mainland criminal about to be remanded to Hong Kong taunts mainland officers—who suffered considerable losses in their efforts to apprehend him—that he "will go free in Hong Kong" because the territory "has rule of law." Outraged, the once scrupulous former PLA officer joins his men in swarming the border gates and abducting the criminal with the HKP officer's assistance, as aerial shots spotlight the similarities of society and space on both sides of the border. This scene of unauthorized but lethally empowered mainlanders storming the Hong Kong border inverts the ominous scenes of invading mainland criminals in *Long Arm of the Law* while also demonstrating remarkable similarities to the reversal of demonic and heroic surveillance in *Hard Boiled*. Thus presenting this triumphal and cathartic scene as a symbolic recuperation of mainland capacities for violence, *Rock n' Roll Cop* also subordinates that quasi-military power to HKP guidance, as the movie concludes with the HKP officer facing the camera to intone, "After 1997 these borders will no longer exist, and we won't be pointing guns at each other." Claiming that only then "can [they] go back to being police officers," *Rock n' Roll Cop*'s concluding statement exemplifies the joint venture subgenre's deep identification with real institutional issues and the degree to which local cinema continued to stake its continuity on its long-standing identification with the HKP.

AFTER THE HANDOVER CEREMONIES

As *Rock n' Roll Cop*'s closing scene suggests, a nominally quiescent notion of joint venture's commitment to transcend politics is nevertheless still freighted by political implications, clearly positioning the police as a means of maintaining stability as Hong Kong transitioned into Chinese sovereignty. These fictional allusions to a real institutional predicament reflect the HKP's importance in reunification, and, in retrospect, they also presage through the plots of cross-border partnership

FIGURE 3.9. Joint venture cinema and the romance with China in the final image of *Bodyguard from Beijing* (Golden Harvest, 1994).

Hong Kong cinema's post-reunification turn toward coproduction with mainland China. As noted throughout this book, Hong Kong surveillance is often economically motivated rather than political, and in the particular case of local policing's extensive media history, it should not be surprising that detailed and highly specific movies depicting contemporary policing should use that premise to also consider the future of local cinema itself. In fact, *Rock n' Roll Cop* opens with a dense symbol of Hong Kong cinema's various surveillance tropes and influences through a scene in which the HKP officer is working undercover as a vendor of pirated Hollywood movies. And similarly portraying Hong Kong cinema's use of Hollywood commercialism to naturalize the mainland presence, *Bodyguard from Beijing* follows its American inspiration in eroticizing surveillance techniques and behavior, ultimately concluding with an astonishingly hagiographic portrait of Jet Li in full PLA uniform, whose position before a waving Chinese flag vividly suggests the degree to which joint venture cinema was advocating cross-border partnership as the key to future territorial vitality (Fig. 3.9).

Indeed, well before the first joint venture film, Hong Kong genre movies were using plots regarding police jurisdiction and institutional culture to allegorize local cinematic aspiration. *Banana Cop* (1984), for example, is an early odd-couple cop movie about the differences between a UK-raised ethnic Chinese officer in Scotland Yard and the Hong Kong convict that he is assigned to escort as part of an investigation into a Chinatown criminal. Shot on location in London and released at the conclusion of talks regarding the Joint Declaration, the film differs from the contemporary *Long Arm of the Law* in focusing more on the legacies of Hong Kong's departing colonial sovereign than coming Chinese rule.[42] As in later joint venture films, however, the movie uses the odd-couple premise to stage a gradual but begrudging partnership that positions Hong Kong, especially Hong Kong film, as a source of vitality that supersedes its nominal political and cultural superior. Throughout the film, the Hong Kong convict played by diminutive local pop icon Teddy Robin constantly outwits the stiff British detective played by George Lam (a supporting actor known for his height and bushy, neo-Victorian mustache), thereby subverting the trench-coated would-be Sherlock Holmes as well as the traditionally Western genre of procedural and detective investigation that character represents (Fig. 3.10).

Similarly, even in the greatly reduced Hong Kong cinema of the post-handover years, joint venture conventions and other Hong Kong

FIGURE 3.10. Outsmarting Western surveillance cinema: on location in England, diminutive Hong Kong icon Teddy Robin outruns the titular hero in *Banana Cop* (Cinema City, 1984).

cop-movie traditions continue to provide a major source of cinematic renewal. The same focus on British legacies that drives *Banana Cop*, for example, recurs in *The Longest Summer* (1998), an oblique, depressing drama directed by Fruit Chan about decommissioned former local recruits to the British military who turn to crime as a result of unemployment due to the colonial withdrawal and the time's general economic malaise.[43] Although obviously not a joint venture film, *The Longest Summer* is consistent with that precedent, as well as the more general history of Hong Kong cinema's rich archive of movies about official surveillance institutions, in that it uses that subject as a vehicle to confront challenges facing cinema itself. As in Fruit Chan's other works, the film casts amateur and untrained actors—including several decommissioned local servicemen available because of unemployment[44]—and is characterized by an avant-garde, self-consciously nonspectacular or uncinematic aesthetic that incorporates documentary footage shot by the director during the reunification ceremonies and then edited for cynical, pointedly deflationary purposes. (For example, one of the scenes built from the documentary footage critiques public anxiety about the incoming PLA soldiers through an ostentatiously melodramatic and slow-motion action sequence in which HKP officers overreact to a perceived bomb, only to preventively detonate a watermelon.)

Like *The Longest Summer*, a number of noteworthy figures and films of the post-reunification era of cinematic retraction engage images and themes reminiscent of joint venture while deploying those conventions in deconstructed and revisionist perspectives that align those institutional representations with questions regarding the fate of Hong Kong cinema itself. For example, the two independent films *The Final Night of the Royal Hong Kong Police* (1999 and 2002), which were directed by former *ICAC* television series director Lau Shing-hon and funded by a government arts grant specifically created to help revive local cinema during the economic decline, also incorporate footage from the handover ceremonies as part of their deconstructed, realist aesthetic modeled on the principles of the filmmaking movement Dogme 95.[45] As their title indicates, the two films exemplify local cinema's long tradition of portraying specific aspects of HKP history by recalling joint venture's recent attention to the specific circumstances and issues of institutional identity at the time of reunification. Both films use the much-publicized moment when the HKP replaced the colonial crest with the new emblem of the Chinese SAR to anchor narratives equally engaged with aesthetic questions about cinematic continuity and heritage. The first film, subtitled *One Body, Two Flags*, dismantles the conventionally spectacular and special effects–driven genre of ghost stories through handheld POV shots and voice-over narration to present a fallen officer's memories of his three decades of local policing before his death while on duty on the day of the handover. Similarly, in the second film, subtitled *The 5th* in reference to police use of Beethoven's Fifth Symphony to drown out local activists during events leading up to the handover, growing tension between a young HKP recruit and his lover, an ardent pro-democracy activist, signals a shift in public feeling about the post-reunification police, whose critique of the once-privileged HKP office extends to their cinematic representations as well.[46]

More expansively and prominently, longtime director Johnnie To's rise to critical acclaim during the years of the post-reunification cinematic retraction has been closely related to police and crime movies—genres that he takes up with some of the self-conscious allegorizing of reunification-era cinema but that he also dismantles into a disaffected, cynical world that confounds the previous era's tropes of heroism and territorial continuity. As many have noted, To's films from this era explore group dynamics and the impact of fate and contingency on individual agency; although his protagonists are not always cops, their stories and settings do always emphasize surveillance customs and behaviors.[47] The reunification-year film *Lifeline* (1997), for example, is a *Backdraft*-style study of municipal firefighting services that recalls police procedurals in highlighting the firefighters' training and orchestrated action. (Not insignificantly, both police and fire emergency services belong to what the Hong Kong civil service conventionally calls the "disciplinary forces.") The director explores similar, more explicitly police-sited issues in his widely referenced film *PTU* (2003) and its many spin-offs, whose depiction of the HKP's paramilitary riot control units often shows more interest in institutional culture and the vagaries of bureaucratic regulation than conventional cop movies' straightforward depictions of moral righteousness and law enforcement.[48] *Breaking News*, To's 2004 movie about the competing media campaigns between the PPRB and a group of criminals who have taken a family hostage, is a particularly explicit instance of the auteur's signature interest in HKP practices and surveillance behaviors more generally. Engaging local cinematic conventions of both portraying police mediatization and using police movies to display artistic aspiration, *Breaking News* opens with a seven-minute tracking shot and juxtaposes the screens within screens presented by the PPRB command center with the fast-moving and highly individualized transmissions of social media.

"WHO CARES ABOUT JACKIE CHAN?"

Further augmenting To's idiosyncratic, characteristically deromanticized engagement of Hong Kong cinema's police and joint venture tropes is the director's realization of that diegetic interest with an extradiegetic commitment to the local film industry itself. As I discuss in greater detail in Chapter 4, To's post-reunification ascendance to international critical acclaim is intriguing not only because he attained commercial success at a time of industrial retraction but also because he did so without surrendering to the trend toward coproduction that joint venture cinema presaged. His films from this era pointedly make use of local casts and crews, in contrast to industry trends toward mainland partnerships, and occasionally come into conflict with mainland censors. The latter is widely associated with To's acclaimed triad films, *Election* (2005) and *Election 2* (2006), whose study of a crime syndicate's internecine competition for leadership was widely interpreted as a critique of Hong Kong's lack of democratic processes and was subsequently banned in China. However, the director's unwillingness to fall in line with the tactical accommodationism of the previous era's joint venture movies is also apparent in his 2009 *PTU* spin-off, *Tactical Unit—Comrades in Arms*, which despite a subplot about an illegal immigrant did not take the obvious and more cost-effective route of casting a mainland actor for that role but instead incurred additional expense by hiring a Mandarin dialogue coach for a local star.[49] And with his whimsical, nostalgic 2008 pickpocket film, *Sparrow*, To subverted the strong hand of Chinese censorship that had previously banned

Election by exploiting a mainland policy to distribute *Sparrow* in China as a provincial film.[50]

Through their mutual depictions of official surveillance as a vehicle for post-reunification Hong Kong film, Fruit Chan and Johnnie To maintain the police-media symbiosis long characterizing local cinema, even though their movies originate within a very different industrial environment and with a look and feel that are very different from the benign and heroic police movies and tropes present at the cinema's height. *The Longest Summer*, in fact, includes a moment when the character played by Sam Lee, the young amateur actor who had debuted to much acclaim in Fruit Chan's *Made in Hong Kong*, rhetorically asks, "Who cares about Jackie Chan?," thereby using his announcement of a new generation of actors to acknowledge a shift toward more cynical, less iconically cinematic police images. In To's oeuvre, such an ambivalent, pointedly deromanticized police role is often incarnated by Simon Yam, one of the director's favorite leads and a longtime action and crime star whose unusual ability to toggle back and forth between "good" and "bad" characters is further intriguing given the fact that Yam is the younger brother of a former deputy commissioner of police. However, to best appreciate how closely related local cinema and official surveillance once were at their height, we ought to reconsider *The Longest Summer*'s ironic query about Jackie Chan's cultural value by examining one of the star's classic movies for its characteristically detailed depiction of local policing, especially its centrality for territorial vitality and entertainment's role in promoting police legitimacy.

In *Project A* (1983) and *Project A, Part 2* (1987), set at the start of the twentieth century, Jackie Chan plays a captain in the Water Police—historically the first official police force in the territory and now the largest civil marine patrol in the world.[51] Set amid the competing activities of colonial rule, Chinese Nationalist intrigue in early Republican China, and purely self-interested parties like pirates and corrupt government officials, both *Project A* films present the Water Police as an exemplar of local culture and identity. Both films are filled with close-ups of the Water Police crest and scenes of goose-stepping cadets parading in front of colonial police headquarters, clearly exalting the force's discipline and training as an ideal of early Hong Kong. As costume productions, the two *Project A* films constitute an interesting version of Chan's typical identification with cop characters and vividly demonstrate through their loose historicism and unusually high production values the star's commitment to using his celebrity to advance the HKP institution itself. In fact, one of *Project A, Part 2*'s most beloved sequences is a set piece—often compared to the famous "crowded stateroom" sequence in the Marx Brothers' 1935 comedy *A Night at the Opera*—which climaxes when Chan and two other characters burst into a rhythmic chant, declaring, "Who keeps Hong Kong safe for the Chinese people? The Hong Kong Police, that's for sure!"

Whether or not one is familiar with HKP history or that of the Water Police more specifically, the *Project A* films are remarkable both for the unequivocally positive image they give local policing and the implicit value that topic provides for individual film stars and consumer entertainment more generally. Ignoring the actual history of HKP corruption and contested legitimacy, the films use their period setting to trumpet an idealized portrait of local police practice that echoes contemporary HKP rhetoric. For those familiar with HKP specifics, such unqualified admiration for the Water Police is justified by its history, as the Water Police undertook localization and professionalization initiatives much earlier than the land force. In fact, *Project A, Part 2* concludes with a telling scene during which Chan's character—who throughout the movie has been heavily recruited by colonial officials, corrupt local officers, self-interested pirates, and Chinese Nationalist revolutionaries—rebuffs all overtures and instead invokes his police profession as grounds for his refusal, reminding them that "only by being a police officer can [he] keep Hong Kong safe for the Hong Kong people." Such a claim of professional neutrality must have been resonant during the reunification process, and it resembles the star's formal support for HKP activity evident in his loaning of the *Police Story* theme song to HKP media productions. Simultaneously rewriting HKP history while using the police genres to reinscribe himself as an archetype of local culture and cinema, Chan, with *Project A, Part 2*, anticipates joint venture movies in his declaration of policing as a model of local vitality and political neutrality. Contrary to later, post-reunification crime movie cynicism such as Fruit Chan's "who cares about Jackie Chan?," *Project A, Part 2* exemplifies the symbiosis between police and local cinema that sustained both professions at their mutual height in the 1980s.

As demonstrated in the next chapter, however, the overt, explicit, and unreservedly positive depiction of HKP history and operations that once characterized Hong Kong cinema during the 1980s changed as the growing willingness to comply with Chinese sovereignty signaled in joint venture movies was further impacted by China's entrenchment and the growing discrepancy between the mainland's explosive growth and Hong Kong's economic malaise. In cinema, this mainland ascendancy, heralded by joint venture and portrayed with such paranoia in other contemporary action and crime films, was particularly evident in the subgenre of undercover-cop movies long central to local film. Covert operations and undercover motifs remain one of the most striking signs of surveillance's continuing importance within Hong Kong film, manifest even in accommodationist joint venture movies such as *Police Story 3: Supercop, My Father Is a Hero, Long Arm of the Law III*, and the Stephen Chow Bond parody, *From Beijing with Love* (1994). But later Hong Kong undercover movies appearing in the post-reunification coproduction era complicate the once-ubiquitous and overtly positive HKP imagery with tragic plots and ambiguous protagonists implicitly querying the possibilities for local survival and individual agency. Yet even if these recent undercover movies offer an unusually depressing and cynical perception of local agency more akin to Fruit Chan's and Johnnie To's deconstructed post-reunification images of official surveillance, they still reiterate Hong Kong cinema's rich surveillance traditions. As I show in Chapter 4, despite the very different landscape of Hong Kong film evident in the two decades since reunification, by continuing the undercover tradition of classic Hong Kong films such as *Man on the Brink* and *City on Fire*, local cinema continues to be a prime indicator of global trends in surveillance culture.

FOUR

"REPRESENTING THE CHINESE GOVERNMENT"

HONG KONG UNDERCOVER IN AN AGE OF SELF-CENSORSHIP

SURVEILLANCE REMAINS A CRUCIAL ASPECT of contemporary Hong Kong cinema, even despite the cinema's decline and China's subsequent emergence as a global film market. In fact, through the tangible form of censorship and self-censorship, surveillance has arguably never been greater in the history of Hong Kong cinema, as the hypercommercial and once relatively uncensored industry has reshaped itself around a series of Chinese government policies that since 2003 have enabled foreign filmmakers to bypass state quotas on import films by incorporating a required component of mainland talent, locations, and financing.[1] As a result, film industries in Hong Kong and throughout the world now register a distinct tendency to cater to a state characterized by its strong surveillance powers. The dramatic uptick since reunification in coproductions between Hong Kong and mainland Chinese film companies is an obvious manifestation of this phenomenon, as is the general pandering among industries and filmmakers eager to enter the lucrative Chinese market.[2] Much attention has already been paid to Hollywood pictures like *Iron Man 3* (2013) and the *Red Dawn* remake (2012), which were reedited for Chinese distribution, but a similar conflict occurred much earlier and much closer to home when the Hong Kong film *Infernal Affairs* was recut for China with a drastically different ending.[3] Abruptly truncating the original film's tragedy by depicting the gang mole's swift punishment and the protagonist's survival, the mainland version of *Infernal Affairs* has none of the original film's ambiguity and cynicism. While Martin Scorsese's Oscar-winning Hollywood adaptation, *The Departed*, maintains much of the Hong Kong original's moody sensibility, the recut mainland version exhibits the distributors' consideration of mainland demands that films not "endanger social ethics" or otherwise "instigate crime."[4]

Interestingly, however, neither film nor surveillance studies explores this connection between surveillance content and context that shapes movies such as the mainland version of *Infernal Affairs*. While censorship, self-censorship, and other forms of artistic collusion or catering to centralized power are established topics of film history, they are strangely absent in most studies of surveillance cinema, whose typical focus on film image, style, and narrative tends to favor diegetic content over extradiegetic context such as production and reception.[5] In the case of Hong Kong surveillance cinema in particular, this silence is especially egregious given China's influence over the current industry and Hong Kong's historical role as a former regional cinematic leader. Although much can be said about the symbolic irony of Hollywood's waning hegemony evident in the rewriting or editing of big-budget action spectacles to appease Chinese power, Hong Kong's three *Infernal Affairs* films provide a more subtle but no less important instance of cinema's adaptations to the constraints and pressures imposed on film by tangible surveillance policies. For example, in addition to the altered ending in the mainland version of *Infernal Affairs*, the second film in the series is a prequel whose handover setting provides an evocative backdrop for the series' covert operations plot. In the final film—a coproduction between several mainland companies and the Hong Kong producers behind the original—the trilogy's latent linking of diegetic surveillance with extradiegetic buckling to rising Chinese power manifests in a joint venture plot in which esteemed mainland actor Chen Dao-ming co-stars in a crucial role as an enigmatic mainland security officer.

One reason perhaps that the *Infernal Affairs* films have not launched discussion of the connection between diegetic and extradiegetic surveillance is the undercover genre's inherent subtlety and accessibility. Much of the attention paid to coproductions and related trends in Hong Kong and Sinophone film has focused on *wuxia* and *dapian* (big

story) films—spectacular, big-budget films often set in remote and exotic locations in which an A-list Sinophone director brings together
stars and creative talent from both sides of the Hong Kong–China border.[6] In the case of *wuxia*, movies like *Hero* (Zhang Yimou, 2002), *The
Promise* (Chen Kaige, 2005), *The Warlords* (Peter Chan, 2007), *An Em-
press and the Warriors* (Tony Ching Siu-tung, 2008), *Red Cliff* (John Woo,
2008–9), *The Grandmaster* (Wong Kar-wai, 2013), and *The Assassin* (Hou
Hsiao-hsien, 2014) revive a genre once banned on the mainland and
subsequently central to the Hong Kong film industry. By thus reclaiming mainland interest in a globally recognized element of Chinese cultural history, the new *wuxia* films announce, as David Desser suggests,
"the new reality of China as an emergent power on the world scene."[7]
Mobilizing an unmistakably triumphal nationalism through both diegetic and extradiegetic expressions of mainland Chinese power, these
neo-*wuxia* or *wuxia* revival films have at times been accused of Fascist or Communist aesthetics, and they exemplify cinema's primacy
in contemporary Chinese soft power.[8] As Anthony Fung notes about
contemporary Chinese entertainment in general, twenty-first-century
Chinese media specialize in "narcotizing" spectacles whose sumptu-
ousness and massified imagery featuring armies of extras captivate
audiences in ways that distract them from potential suspicions regarding the authoritarian power structures on which such spectacles both
obscure and depend.[9]

In the midst of such aggressive visual and narrative imagery, it is
not surprising that Hong Kong's comparatively less spectacular small-
budget urban crime dramas and psychological thrillers are sometimes consigned to peripheral status and treated as discrete phenom-
ena on the margins of this other, more aggressive type of film. With
the influx of high-profile *wuxia* releases garnering local and global attention for their strident assertion of a culturally distinct alternative
to Hollywood, Hong Kong cinema and its diverse, often Hollywood-
influenced traditions of highly exportable genres can be overlooked.
Thus, while *Infernal Affairs*' critical and commercial success sparked a
number of copycat movies, such as *Eye in Sky* (2007) and the *Overheard*
trilogy (2009, 2011, 2014), whose similar surveillance and covert operations plots reentrenched undercover policing as a vital subgenre of
Hong Kong's post-decline survival, the proliferation of *Infernal Affairs*

imitations might also be interpreted as a symptom of Hong Kong cinema's exhaustion and deteriorating creativity since reunification. Both eclipsed by its Oscar-winning American adaption and vulnerable to a stultifying mainland recut, *Infernal Affairs* may be a global icon and one of the most successful of retraction-era Hong Kong movies, but with its Hollywood co-opting and mainland reediting *Infernal Affairs* is also a poignant reminder of the real constraints shaping even the most successful recent Hong Kong surveillance films.

However, ignoring recent Hong Kong surveillance films or otherwise occluding the ways that movies like *Infernal Affairs* or the *Overheard* trilogy engage current Chinese political and economic ascendancy greatly underestimates the agency of one of Hong Kong surveillance cinema's most enduring forms. As this chapter shows, undercover motifs continue to be a prime attribute of a number of notable recent Hong Kong and Sinophone films such as *Drug War*, Johnnie To's 2012 coproduction about a collaboration between a mainland narcotics officer and the Hong Kong drug manufacturer who assists him during an undercover operation, as well as a subgenre of joint venture–style *wuxia* mashups I call "period undercover." Like the overt identification of surveillance with China that I previously showed at work in the Sinophobic paranoia infusing reunification-era action and crime, surveillance and undercover motifs in post-decline Hong Kong cinema continue to be deeply allusive to contemporary Chinese power. As motifs long deployed by local cinema to portray Hong Kong's unique political and cultural agency, their continued appearance in film from this era puts the cinema—particularly its beloved undercover-cop and covert-operations plots—in an ideal position from which to contest the pressures exerted by China, the reigning political and cinematic superpower to which Hong Kong otherwise appears subordinate. Although Hong Kong cinema must share its signature surveillance motifs with period undercover, a new and as-yet-unremarked subgenre of *wuxia*-style *dapian* that has emerged during the coproduction era, those motifs offer an alternative, recuperative reading in which, despite its global hegemony, Chinese film still emulates Hong Kong, and Hong Kong cinema's surveillance motifs remain a resonant site of cultural and cinematic vitality. As this chapter will show, Hong Kong undercover movies model for Hollywood and other world cinemas a paradigm of survival in a new age of Chinese political, economic, and cinematic power.

UNDERSTANDING "OLD CHINESE MOVIES"

Most assessments of Hong Kong cinema in the face of China's rise are implicitly tragic narratives emphasizing decline and retraction, despite the cinema's continued production and visibility. Laikwan Pang, Mirana Szeto, and Yun-chung Chen, for example, describe the contemporary Hong Kong film industry as having been reduced to two modes: one in which the cinema engages in a lucrative collusion with the content and policy demands of mainland China; or one in which it resigns itself to modest returns when it continues to make movies designed for local Hong Kong audiences.[10] This dialectical choice confronting contemporary Hong Kong film manifests in generic, linguistic, and aesthetic differences, such as the upgraded production and scalar enhancements that Yiu-wai Chu and Stephanie DeBoer find in the spectacular and often expensively star-studded, computer graphic (CG)–enhanced coproductions, particularly in comparison to more modest Hong Kong–based comedies and social dramas such as *Aberdeen* (2014), *Floating City* (2012), *Vulgaria* (2012), *A Simple Life* (2011), *Echoes of the Rainbow* (2010), *The Way We Are* (2008), *Mr. Cinema* (2007), *My Life as McDull* (2001), and the *Golden Chicken* series (2002, 2003, 2014).[11] While the Mandarin-language trend in Sinophone cinema features huge casts in epic plots set in epochal moments of Chinese national history, the Cantonese-language body of work recalls local traditions of social realism by pursuing more intimate stories about individuals and families set within a banal urban environment that is unmistakably recognizable as Hong Kong.

This bilateral description of Hong Kong cinema's options as a response to mainland Chinese power, however, neither acknowledges Hollywood's importance for local cinema nor connects it to the tradition of surveillance motifs within local and global cinema that have always connected Hong Kong with Hollywood. As argued throughout this book, Hong Kong film's recurrent surveillance motifs are never simply only ethnographic reflections of local culture but also self-conscious artistic and aspirational expressions by which the cinema asserts its place within world culture and global modernity. Under the current conditions of mainland Chinese cinematic ascendancy, this means that Hong Kong's long-standing engagement with Hollywood and other world film traditions provides an important alternative that complicates any reductively binary account of Hong Kong cinema's options for survival, as *Infernal Affairs* exemplifies. As Tony Rayns wryly notes of *Infernal Affairs*, the film seems to have been made "by people who have clocked up many hours with David Fincher and Michael Mann movies," and according to Law Wing-sang, it was precisely this aspect of the movie's anonymously homogeneous offices and urban imagery that obscured *Infernal Affairs'* continuity with Hong Kong's rich tradition of undercover films.[12] Yet far from suggesting that *Infernal Affairs* succeeds by visually and aesthetically distancing itself from local identity and urban culture, Law claims that what appears at first a superficially or nominally Hollywoodized aesthetic is instead the cinema's ingenuity at packaging highly local stories in ways that remain commercially viable. As a self-consciously modern global city that prides itself on its place within international networks of finance and consumer capital, Hong Kong is portrayed in *Infernal Affairs* like the sterile images of millennial Berlin and London that David Martin-Jones describes in European crossover hits like *Sliding Doors* and *Run Lola Run* (both 1998), both of which similarly relied on an element of Hollywood commercialism to revitalize their respective cinemas.[13] As Martin-Jones notes of those movies, such homogenizing images of a culturally distinct urban space should not be seen as a wholesale surrender to one style of filmmaking but as subtle attempts to preserve local culture and cinema, a covert masking of local film style through a loose Hollywood gloss that in *Infernal Affairs* is particularly resonant through the movie's covert operations plot and the rich tradition of undercover motifs to which that film belongs.

Indeed, Hollywood film is crucial to one of *Infernal Affairs'* most memorable surveillance sequences, inviting questions of local agency during a suggestive commentary on traditional Chinese cinema. This scene occurs when the gang mole within the police confers with his boss during a clandestine meeting in a movie theater while they are unknowingly being observed by the undercover officer within the

FIGURE 4.1. "I can't understand these old Chinese movies": gangster exits cinema in *Infernal Affairs* (Media Asia, 2002).

gang. Just before the mole exits the theater, the boss casts a disinterested gaze at the movie screen and its image of a woman in traditional dress leading a horse in a rural environment, prompting the boss to remark that he "can't understand these old Chinese movies" (Fig. 4.1). Within the diegetic confines of the plot, such a comment illuminates that character's psyche, whose indifference to history and heritage stands in contrast to the undercover agents and the strong role they necessarily accord to personal memory—themes that are subsequently explored in greater detail in the prequel. However, given this scene's reflexive allusions to film taste, *Infernal Affairs'* movie theater sequence also has important extradiegetic allusions that become evident in the next scene, which shows the undercover officer tracking the mole as they both exit the cinema, passing posters advertising the latest Hollywood fare (Fig. 4.2). Implicitly juxtaposed with the "old Chinese movie" in the previous scene, these Hollywood spectacles pose a different option of cinematic aesthetics that *Infernal Affairs* broaches only to also dismiss them. As both gang mole and undercover officer pass the Hollywood posters quickly and without interest, the Hong Kong movie's equal indifference to this alternative cinematic tradition suggests its deliberate positioning as a different, distinct film style equally aware of Chinese and Hollywood possibilities but shaping itself in opposition to both.

FIGURE 4.2. Hollywood spectacle vs. Hong Kong undercover: covert ops at the multiplex in *Infernal Affairs* (Media Asia, 2002).

As an example of surveillance cinema's distinct imagery and themes, this passage from *Infernal Affairs* is particularly effective because its references to action conventionally associated with Hong Kong and Hollywood cinema foregrounds its remaking of that action. Unlike the kinesthetic and spectacular action traditionally associated with Hong Kong and Hollywood, this surveillance scene recalls gambling and tenement movies by subordinating violence and physical conflict to visual observation and interpersonal monitoring. This attribute is made particularly obvious in the way that the scene—unlike the contemporary Hollywood movies advertised in the posters, *Men in Black II* and *K-19: The Widowmaker* (both 2002)—substitutes suspense for speed; and its most spine-tingling moment of danger arises not with physical assault but betrayal of a character through a cell phone's ringing. Set in an empty walkway outside an anonymous affluent urban shopping center devoid of local color, this sequence is typical of *Infernal Affairs'* apparent channeling of Hollywood—but because no more attention is paid to the Hollywood imports than the old Chinese movies, *Infernal Affairs* presents itself as neither. Yiu-wai Chu observes a similar tendency in coproduction-era crime movies and urban thrillers such as *Cold War* (2012) and the street-racing drama *Motorway* (2012), whose loose emulation of the hugely lucrative *Fast and Furious* series (2001 and beyond) similarly deploys Hollywood style and technique as a "third way beyond the 'big budget Mainlandized inauthentic' versus 'small-budget local authentic' dichotomy [that] would prove to be very important for the revival of Hong Kong cinema." Likewise, *Infernal Affairs*, with its quintessentially local plot of covert operations, literally goes undercover itself as a Hollywood-ready version of exportable surveillance fare. In the resonant surveillance motifs by which Chu describes the downsized post-reunification Hong Kong cinema, *Infernal Affairs* was one of the earliest instances of local cinema's "cold war[,] declared not only on the hostage-takers in the film but also on the co-production model that has been 'hijacking' the industry over the past decade."[14]

"REPRESENTING THE CHINESE GOVERNMENT"

Interestingly, in *The Departed*, the pursuit sequence that starts in the movie theater also references Sinophone cinema and the contemporary context of Chinese ascendancy, albeit in ways that betray the Hollywood adaptation's cultural clumsiness. Although Martin Scorsese's Hollywood positioning and international prestige surely make for a very different relationship to Sinophone culture and cinema than that of Hong Kong filmmakers, his film exhibits a cultural and industrial paranoia about mainland power that emulates *Infernal Affairs'* subtle surveillance motifs while also betraying an American heavy-handedness. *The Departed*, for example, has a complicated relationship to its Hong Kong original, as the film's South Boston and other similarities to the biography of notorious mobster and FBI informant Whitey Bulger attempt to naturalize the Asian movie into an American story even as Scorsese unabashedly reproduces shots and scenes from *Infernal Affairs*.[15] This American recasting of a foreign property is typical of Hollywood hubris and the privileges of a global film superpower, but rather than completely elide and displace the Sinophone original, *The Departed* still incorporates several references to China, surveillance, and cinema that suggest both its creative origins and contemporary geopolitics. The former arises early in *The Departed* through a plot point about "buyers representing the Chinese government" who want to purchase illicit American surveillance technology. In the Hong Kong original, these characters were Thai drug dealers, a highly regional reference that the Hollywood film recasts in a distinctly American uneasiness with Chinese power reminiscent of the demonizing of Russians and Muslims in other eras of Hollywood history.[16] Like the Chinese villains in roughly contemporary films such as *Spy Game* (2001) and *Tomb Raider 2* (2003), *The Departed*'s Chinese buyers personify contemporary American fears about rising Chinese political and economic power.[17] Indeed, although *The Departed* precedes the actual revelations about Chinese corporate spying that sparked American public and political furor in 2013, by specifically naming surveillance technology as the objective of the Chinese buyers, *The Departed* exemplifies both ongoing anticommunist Sinophobia about Chinese totalitarianism and American tendencies to cite those proclivities in justification of their own countersurveillance operations.[18]

Of course, one likely reason that *The Departed* alludes to Chinese surveillance is Scorsese's intertextual homage to acknowledge the Hong Kong original, but even that context further highlights the film's engagement with contemporary American and Hollywood anxieties about Chinese ascendancy. The only ethnic Asian actor to have a speaking role in the film is a go-between played by American-born Robert "Toshi" Kar Yuen Chan, who delivers his lines in badly accented Cantonese. This representational inaccuracy of having a buyer "representing the Chinese government" speaking Cantonese rather than official Putonghua may be an attempt on the part of the filmmakers to acknowledge *The Departed*'s Hong Kong source text, but by using an American-born actor known for a Japanese name, *The Departed* both exemplifies Western ignorance about the varieties of Asian ethnicity and invites ongoing critique of Hollywood's unwillingness to cast Asian, non-Western, or other "foreign" and minority actors.[19] And further demeaning and diminishing its Sinophone source material, *The Departed* includes a debasing reference that transposes *Infernal Affairs'* original cinema scene from the homogeneous American-style multiplex in the Hong Kong original to a Chinatown porn theater. Thus ignoring the original film's depiction of Hong Kong as a cosmopolitan, affluent city modeled on American experiences and replacing it with tired conventions of seedy, inscrutable, and perverse oriental culture, the Hollywood remake's strenuous efforts to both co-opt and debase the Hong Kong original inadvertently betray its own awareness of Hollywood decline.

PERIOD UNDERCOVER

Another instance of contemporary surveillance movies "representing the Chinese government" is the recent cycle of *wuxia*-style period undercover movies, which counterintuitively merge the historical settings and spectacular aesthetics strongly associated with coproductions with the subversive plots and imagery of Hong Kong's long tradition of covert-operations motifs. For example, *Bodyguards and Assassins* (2009) depicts a grassroots effort to protect Chinese revolutionary leader Sun Yat-sen from imperial mercenaries as he passed through Hong Kong during his exile from China. *Legend of the Fist: The Return of Chen Zhen* (2010) inexplicably revives Bruce Lee's legendary hero (who was shot to death in the final freeze frame of *Fist of Fury* [1972]) as a Shanghai nightclub manager who moonlights in the anti-Japanese resistance. Also set in the era of Japanese occupation are *The Silent War* (2012), an overtly surveillance-focused film from the *Infernal Affairs* creative team that recasts that film's star (Tony Leung Chiu-wai) as a blind piano tuner who is recruited by Chinese intelligence for his acute hearing, and *The Chef, the Actor, the Scoundrel* (2013), an action-comedy about three undercover agents whose feigned haplessness disguises their efforts to co-opt a Japanese biological weapon. Thus grafting Hong Kong's undercover motifs to a historical setting and extravagant, often CG-enhanced production, period undercover films requisition Hong Kong undercover plots for the service of a neo-*wuxia*-style nationalism. Indeed, while these films' urban and more recent historical settings might seem inconsistent with the historical and geographical remoteness typical of traditional *wuxia*, period undercover movies also include movies like *14 Blades* (2010), *Let the Bullets Fly* (2010), *Wu Xia* (2011), and *The Four* trilogy (2012–14), which are consistent with traditional *wuxia* in their remote settings and more distant past but also feature covert heroes and plots. For example, *14 Blades*, *Wu Xia*, and *The Four* trilogy all center on mercenaries or highly skilled representatives of imperial authority who uphold current governance while living anonymously, and even the Tarantino-like comic western *Let the Bullets Fly* still concludes in a denouement whose numerous impersonations, revelations, and double crosses have a former bandit reforming and augmenting the very governing office he previously had planned to exploit.

As this brief sketch of period undercover films illustrates, undercover motifs remain a potent genre within Hong Kong surveillance cinema, to the point that they are actively imitated in Chinese-style *dapian*, the very market with which Hong Kong cinema now competes. But if period undercover's emergence is indicative of China's Hollywood-style hegemony in its ability to adopt attributes and creative properties initially identified with a smaller market, this very attempt by Mandarin-language period undercover films to co-opt Hong Kong undercover motifs for its own nationalistic agendas only affirms Hong Kong cinema's continued artistic and cultural influence. To be sure, undercover and covert-operations plots are not unknown in mainland film. During the 1950s and 1960s, for example, Chinese state film companies made a number of movies about espionage and counterespionage that used those topics to legitimate and celebrate Communist surveillance.[20] Yet these films were typically set in the contemporary period and had no connection with the *wuxia* genre then still banned under Communist power. Thus, despite the mainland precedent of midcentury espionage and counterespionage films, period undercover's more recent and likely influence is *Lust, Caution*, the 2007 film by Hollywood-trained, Taiwan-born director Ang Lee, about a group of Hong Kong drama students who attempt to entrap a collaborator in Japanese-occupied Shanghai. The film garnered considerable attention among Sinophone and global audiences, partly because of its status as Lee's first Chinese-language film after the unexpected worldwide success of his 2001 *wuxia* homage, *Crouching Tiger, Hidden Dragon*, as well as explicit sex scenes that earned lead actress Tang Wei a media ban in China. And just as *Crouching Tiger, Hidden Dragon*'s status as the highest-grossing foreign-language film in American history helped encourage further *wuxia* productions, *Lust, Caution* provided a high-profile precedent for the many Mandarin-language period films about covert operations that developed alongside the *wuxia* revival.

Interestingly, though, despite *Lust, Caution*'s loose generic and stylistic parallels with period undercovers and the Chinese nationalism that genre signals, the movie's plot explicitly asserts Hong Kong as a site of political and artistic renewal. Like the original short story by

Eileen Chang on which the film is based, the movie heightens Hong Kong's political symbolism by specifically identifying the drama students with Hong Kong rather than the real students from Beijing's Yenching University on whom Chang's story is known to be based. Unlike the confusingly generalized Sinophone and Asian references in Hollywood responses to Chinese power such as in *The Departed* and the *Red Dawn* remake, this recasting to Hong Kong upholds a distinct Hong Kong–identified cultural and cinematic symbolism that drastically differs from the period undercover films that *Lust, Caution* seems to have made possible. Because the undercover agents in both film and original story fail at their activities and are summarily executed, the narrative bears an ambivalent and tragic tone at odds with the Chinese triumphalism crucial to *wuxia*, *dapian*, and period undercovers. Indeed, for Leo Lee, who has shown that Chang's story may have been initiated at the suggestion of an American foreign policy officer, both story and film are consistent with the author's own biography as a cosmopolitan Shanghai exile ambivalent about Chinese nationalism and sympathetic to Western cultural influences.[21] Like *The Departed*'s oddly Cantonese-speaking buyers representing the Chinese government, *Lust, Caution*'s subtle but pointed portrayal of covert operations as an activity identified with Hong Kong performance simultaneously acknowledges the territory's mediating role in the film's creation while also exhibiting an almost American, Cold War–era paranoia about the terrors of China's rise to power.

In other words, *Lust, Caution* is a Hong Kong undercover movie masquerading as a movie about Chinese nationalism, and despite its historical position between early mainland espionage films and the similarly mainland-focused cycle of period undercover, *Lust, Caution* reaffirms Hong Kong surveillance cinema's continuing local and global influence. Through its explicit narrative invocation of Hong Kong as an artistic initiator of covert surveillance, the Hollywood-helmed Sinophone surveillance film is a striking reminder of the original context and resonance of the Hong Kong undercover tradition before its coopting by period undercover films. It also serves as a reminder of the tradition's function as a subversive alternative to the contemporary context of mainland surveillance that shapes the coproduction context in which *Lust, Caution* was made and released. Although the movie, like *Crouching Tiger, Hidden Dragon,* is closer in style and subject to period undercovers, *Lust, Caution*'s tragic departure from that subgenre's triumphant Chinese nationalism positions the film more in the vein of *Infernal Affairs* and the rich tradition of surveillance and undercover movies long central to Hong Kong that was reinforced by *Infernal Affairs*' many successors. These coproduction-era surveillance movies— which include *Eye in the Sky* (2007), the *Overheard* trilogy (2009–14), and *Drug War* (2013)—also do not fit easily into the reductively binary account of Hong Kong cinema's options of engaging in the lucrative appeasement of mainland China's policy demands or settling for modest returns in order to continue to make movies for local Hong Kong audiences. Instead, these post-reunification surveillance and undercover movies suggest that it is precisely the cosmopolitanism and portability of their surveillance motifs that despite Chinese ascendancy continues to make Hong Kong cinema the vanguard of cinematic and cultural influence.

UNDERCOVER AND *OVERHEARD*

Just as *Infernal Affairs*' Hollywood attributes obscured the film's place in the local tradition of undercover movies, some of the most prominent movies of the subsequent undercover cycle that appeared in the wake of its success are also distinguished for their synthesis of vernacular content with a Hollywood-style universality. For example, *Eye in the Sky,* an ensemble *policier* from the *Infernal Affairs*' screenwriter, depicts the competing surveillance regimes deployed by a team of experienced thieves as well as the HKP officers specializing in surveillance and covert operations working to apprehend them. (The English title is a colloquial term commonly used in Hong Kong to describe CCTV.) Although the movie's location shots and explicit institutional representation clearly signify Hong Kong, the film has less in common with the sociopolitical specificity of joint venture movies and other handover era surveillance and cop films than with *Infernal Affairs*' cosmopolitan universalism. Indeed, in a process of global uptake very similar to that of *Infernal Affairs*' Hollywood adaptation, *Eye in the Sky* was later remade by South Korean filmmakers into their 2013 local blockbuster *Cold Eyes,* which was one of the most successful local movies that year.

Like *The Departed, Cold Eyes* demonstrates the portability of Hong Kong surveillance by reproducing many of the original film's memorable shots and sequences. In the specific case of *Cold Eyes'* regionally lateral adaption from Hong Kong to South Korea, the movie's adaptation likely reflects South Korea's affinities with Hong Kong as a neighboring East Asian society also shaped by its capitalist differentiation from a totalitarian society. At the same time, however, because *Cold Eyes* appeared at time of ebb and flow in the region's *hallyu*, or "Korean wave" cinema, the movie also exemplified a more general commercial opportunism in using surveillance cinema formulas as a means of surviving and prospering during a time of industrial transition. Like *Infernal Affairs*, the Korean remake attains accessibility by affecting an urbane ethos vaguely identified with Hollywood. As Michael Shapiro observes of the Hong Kong original, *Eye in the Sky* begins with a scene of interpersonal surveillance within the subway reminiscent of a similar passage in Samuel Fuller's 1953 noir, *Pickup on South Street*. This intertextual emulation, Shapiro notes, "reflects two aspects of Hong Kong, one singular and one shared with all modern cities."[22]

Similarly, in the *Overheard* trilogy, the specifically local context of Hong Kong's real estate history and the role that mainland finance plays in the local economy are set within broader themes of aspiration and upward mobility whose universalism resembles that of the first *Infernal Affairs*. The *Overheard* films were made by the same creative team behind *Infernal Affairs*, and recurring images throughout all three films are the headphones used by characters for audio surveillance, clearly recalling *Infernal Affairs'* prominent scenes of headphone usage and other forms of eavesdropping. Although the second and third films in the *Overheard* series parallel the *Infernal Affairs* trilogy in becoming increasingly local and topical—as made evident by their incorporation of Mandarin-speaking characters and focus on political and economic episodes specific to Hong Kong history—the first movie is notably international and cosmopolitan. This film includes among its lead characters two specifically Asian American figures (the villain played by biracial Michael Wong and an émigré cop played by US-raised Daniel Wu) who evoke Hong Kong's place within a global rather than regional network. More pertinently, the movie manifests a notably universal quality, because the plot, which depicts the consequences

FIGURE 4.3. Financial speculation, voyeuristic spectatorship, and the dividends of surveillance: jubilation on the trading floor in *Overheard* (Pop Movies, 2009).

of three HKP officers investigating insider trading who decide to use information obtained through a surveillance operation for their personal gain, emphasizes the officers' actions as sympathetic and understandable, and hence as something with which everyone can identify.

Overheard conveys this local as global conceit through a variety of tropes and premises, such as a terminally ill cop who resorts to insider trading in hopes of leaving a windfall for his family, and also in one of the film's most memorable surveillance sequences. This passage—the equivalent of the famous cell phone pursuit chase sequence past multiplex movie posters in *Infernal Affairs*—occurs on a day-trading floor, a quintessentially Asian or even specifically Hong Kong customer-service enterprise in which users rent time on powerful financial computers to manage their personal trades and stock speculations.[23] Having overcome their moral, ethical, and professional prohibitions against engaging in the very criminal activity they had been charged with investigating, the three plainclothes officers watch the trading screens with rapt attention as the stock on which they have placed their life savings ascends, to their jubilation as well as the admiration of a growing circle of fellow traders who gather around them (Fig. 4.3). Significantly, much of the scene's setting, language, and even cinematic conventions is directly continuous with local traditions of surveillance film, such as the spectators that traditionally ring casino tables in gambling movies (Fig. 4.4), including even an elderly female gambling addict who dryly comments on the developments. Yet, despite these highly local attributes, the overall effect of *Overheard*'s contemporary, urban setting and the expertly managed dramatic motivation leading up to the characters' financial speculations are also highly empathic, as the proliferating screens within screens—especially the digital stock quotes that are superimposed onto the action—present an extralinguistic and therefore globally accessible image of information monitoring, particularly relevant during the global economic downturn at the time of the film's release.

As noted previously, Rey Chow and Aihwa Ong claim that it is this very familiarity of Hong Kong's postcolonial, capitalist modernity that makes the territory a prototype of global modern subjectivity in general.[24] But if Chow and Ong's observation usefully corroborates the underlying premise of the current generation of Hong Kong undercover films, by emphasizing the indexical relationship between local circumstances and modern subjectivity, such a claim diminishes how effectively local cinema uses artistic and generic attributes specific to film and Hong Kong film traditions in particular to communicate that experience to both local and global audiences. In the past, Hong Kong cinema conveyed its critical engagement with surveillance through its sophisticated engagement of themes and motifs already well known from world, especially Western, cinema and often in a very different

FIGURE 4.4. More conventions of the gambling film: interested spectators ring a casino table in *Games Gamblers Play* (Golden Harvest/ Hui's Film Production Co., Ltd., 1974).

variation on the intrusive and omnipotent surveillance gaze typically experienced in the best-known and most influential Western exemplars of the world surveillance cinema canon. In the new, current post-decline age of coproduction resulting from Chinese hegemony—in which surveillance is not only a diegetic theme within Hong Kong cinema but also a practical issue that Hong Kong films must confront in their efforts to attain local, regional, and global commercial success— this gaze has metamorphosed yet again. It is now a seemingly dystopic and tragic view of surveillance antithetical to earlier traditions of Hong Kong surveillance cinema but that uses its apparent universalist accessibility as a powerfully subversive and sympathetic vision at odds with the more overt forms of power visible in other contemporary Sinophone film. This ingenious inversion of Hong Kong's once-unique variations of surveillance cinema into a surveillance cinema redolent of Hollywood accessibility is the underlying attribute that unifies recent Hong Kong surveillance and undercover movies like *Overheard* with *Eye in the Sky* and *Infernal Affairs*. Distinguishing themselves from the period undercover films that constitute their commercial and ideological competition, these films find an alternative to contemporary mainland Chinese hegemony by presenting Hong Kong disempowerment as a paradigm for global modernity in general.

TIANJIN VICE

Of course, unlike *Infernal Affairs* and *Eye in the Sky*, at the time of this book's writing, the *Overheard* films have yet to be remade for foreign markets, but their aspirations for global relevance are evident in the fact that they have been acquired for English-language remake by the same Hollywood executives who presided over *Infernal Affairs'* reinvention as *The Departed*.[25] Like *Infernal Affairs*, *Overheard* exemplifies a coproduction-era evolution of the Hong Kong undercover tradition in which attributes that previously distinguished the subgenre have themselves gone undercover, enabling the subgenre to function as a vehicle through which Hong Kong surveillance cinema can enjoy continued relevance despite industrial accountability to mainland power. Like any good mole, recent Hong Kong undercover movies like *Infernal Affairs*, *Eye in the Sky*, and *Overheard* constitute a subversive agency,

pointedly rejecting period undercover films' adoption of covert surveillance plots into the tactical accommodationism and overt nationalism of joint venture, coproduction, and the *wuxia* revival. Instead,
these films carve a cinematic site in which the minority perspectives
of Hong Kong surveillance paradoxically are prescient for the world at
large.

It is precisely this covert, undercover quality to recent Hong Kong
undercover movies that also infuses *Drug War*, the 2012 crime drama
from Johnnie To that was the subject of much publicity as the director's
first globally recognized coproduction. (Actually preceded in To's coproduction oeuvre by the 2011 romantic comedy *Don't Go Breaking My
Heart*, *Drug War*'s much-publicized but factually incorrect reputation
as To's first coproduction further underscores the political symbolism
of the surveillance themes implicit within its police plot.)[26] Financed by
a partnership between To's Milkyway production company and mainland company Shanghai Hairun, *Drug War* takes place in the mainland cities of Tianjin and Jintai and stars mainland actor Sun Honglei
as a narcotics detective determined to take down a large drug ring involving criminal interests on both sides of the Hong Kong–China border. Unlike joint venture movies, however, *Drug War*'s crime drama ne-
glects any narrative depiction of official partnerships between Hong
Kong and Chinese surveillance, altogether omitting HKP agency from
the film. In fact, the only Cantonese speakers portrayed in *Drug War*
are criminals—the Hong Kong–born drug manufacturer (played by
Hong Kong heartthrob Louis Koo), who bases his operation on the
mainland, and the investors behind a major drug buyer. Through diegetic plot and content alone, *Drug War* presents a striking image of
Chinese power, as the movie's criminalizing of Hong Kong figures and
corresponding heroic depictions of mainland drug busts reverse the
Sinophobia that once characterized Hong Kong film around the time
of the handover. In fact, in further demonstration of the film's uncom-
promising depiction of the inflexibility and violence of the Chinese
state, *Drug War* goes so far as to conclude with a prolonged depiction
of the Hong Kong drug manufacturer's sentencing and execution, thus
roundly asserting the relentlessness of mainland law enforcement
while provoking uneasy reminders of the Chinese government's capacity for swift and inexorable violence.

As an undercover cop movie by one of Hong Kong's leading direc-tors, however, *Drug War* is rooted in a subversive tradition of antiestab-lishment feeling that invites alternative ways of conceptualizing the film's depictions of official surveillance and mainland Chinese power. Covert operations are at the core of the film's thematic and dramatic in-terest, made evident by both the movie's opening scene—which intro-duces the officer and his assistants working undercover during a sting to arrest couriers at a freeway toll booth—and the investigative plot in which the narcotics officer gets to the core of the drug ring by imper-sonating an eccentric northern shipping magnate who will transport the manufactured drugs throughout Asia. As is always the case in sur-veillance cinema, surveillance motifs enable reflexive gestures toward the accomplishments of film itself, particularly in Sun's revelatory per-formance as an officer whose relentless determination to apprehend his suspects includes a formidable gift for acting. In the scenes where the taciturn cop instantly transforms into a gregarious profiteer with a thick northern accent, the undercover movie highlights the officer's flexibility and ambiguity, attributes more consistent with the Hong Kong tradition of undercover cop movies than those of model workers typically espoused in Communist propaganda. Like the surveillance agents of *Infernal Affairs* and *Overheard*, *Drug War*'s covert officer per-sonifies a modern subjectivity whose ambivalence and ambiguity have little in common with period undercover films and the Fascist aesthet-ics of neo-*wuxia*. Indeed, because the officer's undercover role has him pretending to be a northerner in order to get a job done, the film alle-gorically depicts its own role of pragmatically simulating one surveil-lance regime while advancing its own, different surveillance agenda.

A telling scene from the film that illustrates *Drug War*'s mix of sur-face Sino-nationalism with submerged Hong Kong–style undercover motifs occurs at the Jintai harbor, in which the investigating officer and Mandarin- and Cantonese-speaking criminals confer in a wary entente between two different manifestations of surveillance agency. The scene is Sun's tour de force performance-within-a-performance as the shipping magnate, and it begins with the arrival of an enigmatic buyer and his Cantonese-speaking associate whom we are told are merely proxies for the group of Hong Kong–based criminal investors whom the police suspect will be monitoring the negotiations covertly.

FIGURE 4.5. Chinese nationalism under surveillance in mainland undercover-cop movie *Drug War* (Milkyway Image / Shanghai Hairun, 2012). Note the fleet of waving Chinese flags, highlighting the film's co-production status (compare with Figure 3.9).

During the scene, both police and criminals monitor each other with visual and auditory surveillance technology such as cameras, binoculars, hidden microphones, and earpieces, similar to the contrasting surveillance practices between cops and criminals recently depicted in *Overheard*, while also recalling through the linguistic contrast the mainland–Hong Kong conflict of early handover-era movies like *Long Arm of the Law*. Unlike both of these antecedents, however—and in stark contrast to nearly all of Johnnie To's surveillance films before this movie—*Drug War* does not privilege Cantonese characters and indeed seems to exalt mainland surveillance. Significantly, the climax of the scene is a stunningly large-scale and literally flag-waving CG-enhanced nationalist image in which the cop impersonating the shipping magnate orders a fleet of vessels to set sail in a show of power that will persuade the buyers of his criminal authenticity and clout (Fig. 4.5).

In both its plot and visual pageantry, *Drug War*'s key scene at the Jintai harbor thus might recall reunification-era mainland movies like *The Opium War*, a lavish 1997 historical epic by celebrated Communist filmmaker Xie Jin that uses the nineteenth-century history of official resistance to British drug trafficking to celebrate Chinese paternalism and governance. As evident in the two films' similar titles, despite their very different historical settings and genres, both movies portray a Chinese state official determined to stop the influx of narcotics debasing the country through its deleterious effects on individuals and its embarrassing symbolism as infractions against state authority. Equally important are the two films' respective temporal symbolism; *The Opium War* was made and released at a time of high Chinese triumphalism during Hong Kong's reversion to China, and *Drug War* recalls and continues that sentiment through its coproduction-era allegory of director To's once staunch commitment to Hong Kong cinema finally surrendering to mainland Chinese power. Although neither *Drug War* nor *The Opium War* is a period undercover movie, both films are symptomatic of the coproduction era in literally and narratively illustrating China's transformative impact on the production and imagery of Sinophone film.

At the same time, however, *Drug War*'s undercover plot and the ambivalence with which the genre is typically portrayed in Hong Kong film suggest other influences or interlocutors, such as the moody, disaffected narcotics detectives of landmark 1980s American television series *Miami Vice*. Johnnie To is often compared with Michael Mann, *Miami Vice*'s creator—for example, To's 1999 crime movies *The Mission* and *Running out of Time* have many similarities with Mann's 1995 *Heat*, including elaborately orchestrated urban shoot-outs and, in *Running out of Time*'s cat-and-mouse thriller, recurring overhead shots of detective and master criminal as they outwit each other. Similarly, although *Miami Vice* is probably best remembered globally for the stylish costumes, cars, and locations with which the series became a cultural and consumer phenomenon, by also depicting narcotics investigations, To's *Drug War* recalls covert operations' importance in *Miami Vice*, which often showcased the narcotics officers' charismatic ambivalence by depicting the officers adopting criminal aliases to conduct their investigation and assimilating with the criminal populations they were supposed to apprehend.

To be sure, *Drug War* has none of *Miami Vice*'s visual glamour, and indeed the ugly or nondescript spaces of Jintai's industrial harbor and the urban freeways and backroads of rapidly developing Tianjin again illustrate post-decline Hong Kong surveillance cinema's capacity to disguise its specificity in favor of appearing universal. Like *Infernal Affairs*, To's undercover cop movie resembles a "Michael Mann or David Fincher" movie in the general sense of an urban surveillance thriller based on an ambiguous hero familiar throughout global film and popular culture. Not insignificantly, *Drug War*, like *Sparrow*, premiered in Europe nearly a half year before its Hong Kong and Chinese release, further demonstrating To's strategic positioning as an auteur adept at using international film festivals and other global critical pathways to bypass regional pressures on Hong Kong filmmakers.[27] And at the time of this book's completion, remake rights for *Drug War* had already been sold for South Korean adaptation, further undermining any socialist accommodationism perceived in the film's status as a coproduction.[28] Instead, through its *Infernal Affairs*–like accessibility, *Drug War* presents an image of mainland Chinese policing that To himself at times proudly notes has no mimetic relationship with the actual Chinese state.[29]

Surveillance therefore remains a crucial aspect of Hong Kong film, despite the cinema's current diminished and subordinate status in the face of Chinese ascendancy. Precisely because of China's historical reputation for authoritarian surveillance and the particular ways that this manifests in cinema, contemporary Hong Kong film has adapted to its new position by ceding its former industrial supremacy and, instead, collaborating in ways that might at first seem to announce its resignation to its newly subordinate status. *Drug War* exemplifies this characteristically pragmatic but resourceful perspective on surveillance power so typical of Hong Kong and Hong Kong cinema through its ambivalent and chameleonic undercover hero who, within surveillance cinema's reflexive conceits, is clearly a surrogate for To and for Hong Kong film in general. Indeed, as one of the most critically acclaimed and politically freighted films from a Hong Kong director since *Infernal Affairs*, *Drug War*, and especially its continuation of Hong Kong's rich tradition of undercover cop movies, exemplifies the cinema's ability to survive and distinguish itself within Sinophone cinema's redrawn geopolitical landscape. By cooperating with and capitalizing on contemporary trends toward coproduction, but adapting and subverting its nominal Chinese nationalism by maintaining a distinctly "Hong Kong" sensibility within its undercover motifs, *Drug War* strikes a blow against the cinematic expressions of Chinese soft power evident in period undercovers and the *wuxia* revival. Although

Drug War and the cycle of post-millennial undercover movies precipitated by *Infernal Affairs* are often seen as exceptions to the binary analyses of Hong Kong cinema's post-decline options, the subgenre provides a vital means by which the cinema might preserve its global influence.

To restate the issue in terms originally posed by *Infernal Affairs*, the choice is not between "old" and new "Chinese movies" but rather within a triadic relationship between Hong Kong, China, and Hollywood, particularly the surveillance motifs with which all of the cinemas engage. By reinvesting in the undercover motifs and plots of covert operations long central to local cinema, post-decline Hong Kong film finds the potential to remain influential. Whether through intentionally universalized Hong Kong undercover movies like the first *Infernal Affairs* or *Overheard* films, or through the complicated case of Johnnie To's *Drug War*, Hong Kong undercover movies model global influence by cinematically going undercover themselves. Indeed, as in the case of *Drug War*, iconic Hong Kong surveillance films provide a model by which Hollywood and other world film industries may continue to be original even while appearing to conform to Chinese pressures for political palatability.

IN THIS BOOK, I have shown how the social, spatial, and data monitoring practices known as surveillance shape Hong Kong film, informing both its celebrated visual energy and announcing the cinema's intervention in world film and global culture. The cinema's pervasive and often idiosyncratic surveillance motifs are a crucial factor of Hong Kong's spectacular aesthetics and important both for what they suggest about the unique cultural and historical circumstances of Hong Kong and how its colonial and postcolonial history situate the city and cinema at a unique position from which to challenge Chinese soft power. This is both a top-down argument for "provincializing" the existing Western surveillance canon and a bottom-up attempt to present a regional film culture typically subject to area studies as a theoretical intervention in surveillance studies. In an age of Chinese ascendancy and declining American influence, and as the world increasingly resembles Hong Kong in becoming a densely crowded site of expanding wealth disparity and neoliberal governance, it is Hong Kong, especially Hong Kong film, that is the vanguard of global surveillance culture.

Despite the inevitable fading from public consciousness that occurred once reunification was complete and as it was eclipsed by the subsequent rise of China, Hong Kong continues to be a flashpoint in global discourse about surveillance and security. Since the 2003 SARS epidemic, for example, every subsequent outbreak of bird flu seems to revive global interest in the territory's efforts toward contagion control and disease prevention. Similarly, during the 2008–10 series of acid attacks that frightened shoppers and residents within the popular Mong Kok shopping district, Hong Kong again garnered global attention both because of contemporary anxieties about terrorism and domestic security and because the municipality's subsequent response to the events—including intensifying CCTV monitoring and an early, successful use of consumer metadata to locate and identify an unknown suspect[1]—showcased the technologies and policies that place Hong Kong at the forefront of global surveillance practice. In further illustration of the unusually tolerant, sophisticated, and often pragmatically affirmative surveillance culture that distinguishes Hong Kong and Hong Kong film from the rest of the world, one of the most curious developments of the acid attacks was the local reaction to news that the government had compiled and accessed the passenger mobility and purchase data recorded on "Octopus" cards, the territory's mass-transit stored-value smart cards, to facilitate apprehension of the suspected perpetrator. In sharp contrast to the fierce and ongoing opposition in many Western countries to mandatory ID cards and government monitoring of private phone calls, local reaction to the Hong Kong government's use of the data was somewhat jaded and inventive and raised questions of profit sharing alongside issues of privacy.[2]

Ubiquitous examples of Hong Kong's powerful but highly domesticated surveillance experiences, Octopus cards are one of the world's first and most extensive examples of stored-value transport cards. They gave rise to London's Oyster card and join a number of other surveillance technologies and practices—such as fingerprint collection and analysis, which first originated in India[3]—that were first innovated in colonial or nonhegemonic sites before influencing putative world leaders along with the rest of the world. Although this book focuses on Hong Kong, similar arguments might be made about other places worldwide. As David Lyon, Randy Lippert, and Aaron Doyle demonstrate, for example, the rapid global expansion in CCTV use has been relatively undocumented, partly due to different laws and cultural practices that enable their unchecked growth as well as the Global North's ongoing bias that overlooks case studies outside its own borders.[4] Yet this oversight does more than simply pose an empirical or statistical challenge to tired assertions of the United Kingdom as the most surveilled country in the world. Rather, as this book shows, postcolonial and non-Western spaces are often the most intriguing sites of surveillance theory and practice. By expanding and complicating the existing surveillance canon with customs and cultures from outside the Global North, these examples diversify the discourse. Moreover, their various surveillance practices pose fascinating challenges to standard models of what might be called the UKUSA paradigm of Western hegemony in surveillance theory.

Although few cinemas can equal Hong Kong film in both its extraterritorial influence and prolific, long-standing surveillance motifs, Hong Kong is not alone in cinematically engaging world surveillance cinema trends. For example, Bombay film in the 2000s featured a variety of urban techno-thrillers and crime-based actioners whose paranoid ethos and tightly plotted gaze were adopted for local stories regarding Hindu-Muslim tension. Spanish horror films like *[Rec]* (2007) and *Tesis* (1996) make extensive use of in-camera editing and other video imagery drawn from landmark American independent film *The Blair Witch Project* to fashion a new kind of "digital horror."[5] As does Hong Kong film, these other non-Hollywood surveillance movies manifest a cultural and cinematic engagement with the aesthetic and epistemological issues of post-9/11 high-tech security while transforming their content and imagery for the peculiarities of their home industry and individual artistic and cultural conditions. Like *Cold Eyes*—the South Korean adaptation of Hong Kong's *Eye in the Sky*, which continued a wave of modern techno-thrillers popular in the country since the 1990s[6]—these non-Hollywood surveillance movies use their reflexive and representational surveillance imagery both to demonstrate their home culture's participation in global surveillance practices and to assert the achievements of the cinemas themselves. Indeed, because some films—like *[Rec]*, which was remade in America into 2008's *Quarantine*—would themselves become adopted by Hollywood, these other examples of global surveillance cinema recall *Infernal Affairs* in demonstrating the transnational resonance of non-Hollywood surveillance cinema.

However, Hong Kong film remains unique in world surveillance cinema because of its curious take on the dystopian and paranoid dimensions by which surveillance is typically portrayed. While foreign adaptations of Hong Kong–made films such as *Cold Eyes* and *The Departed* provide the most obvious instances of the cinema's resonance with global surveillance culture, Hong Kong cinema's most intriguing dimension lies within its unique genres and frequently affirmative treatment of surveillance customs and behaviors. Studies of Hong Kong film's transnational influences invariably note that the CGI-realized 360-degree-view action sequences in the Hollywood sci-fi blockbuster *The Matrix* were modeled on Hong Kong martial arts films.[7] While that connection highlights the irony of deep-pocketed Hollywood finding inspiration in the visual and technical strategies of a much less wealthy industry, it also speaks to the influence of Hong Kong surveillance cinema in that its omniscient visual aesthetic—which is derived from a distinctly Hong Kong film genre and idiom—sets a global standard for Hollywood spectacle. Similarly, at the time of this book's completion, Johnnie To's typically genre-defying boardroom musical *Office* (2015) was scrambling local and global influences in such a way that its Sinophone, loosely Hong Kong–based approach to surveillance and oversight would enchant critics and audiences worldwide. Adapting to screen a stage musical that was itself based on an early twentieth-century Noel Coward play, *The Office* is set in a Chinese company during the 2008 Asian financial crisis and vividly realized through 3D capture of a purposefully minimalist theatrical set. The film thus depicts an alienating, anonymous, modernist corporate environment of transparent walls presided over by a monstrous clock that recalls both Coward's Hollywood contemporary, *Modern Times*, and Hong Kong tenement- and cop-movie traditions of eavesdropping, professional monitoring, and social and institutional surveillance.

Another instance of Hong Kong cinema's unique insights for global surveillance culture became apparent in the difference between two globally prominent episodes in which Hong Kong figured as the centerpiece of real-life surveillance and security issues. The first event occurred in 2013, when National Security Agency whistleblower Edward Snowden flew to Hong Kong to expose the US government's domestic spying program. Because he chose Hong Kong as his initial base of operations for leaking the documents and responding to the media during the immediate outcry over the disclosure, the city's current and historical status in global surveillance and security history became the object of mass attention. Snowden explained that he had chosen the territory for its "long history of freedom of the press," while others questioned the significance of having taken refuge "in China, an enemy of the U.S."[8] While Snowden's allusions to Hong Kong's complex role in global surveillance were highly informed—including his reference to a "CIA stronghold just down the street" that, unknown to most, was a legacy of the territory's Cold War strategic importance—the histrionic rhetoric of his claims also played right into contemporary Sinophobia, as he speculated that he could be "abducted and smuggled across the border." Regardless of whether one sees Snowden as a reviled traitor or heroic defender of civil society, his presence in Hong Kong ensured the territory's place at the forefront of global surveillance and security discourse.[9] At the same time, though, by echoing paranoid terms typical of Hong Kong's Cold War history and its current subjectivity to China, Snowden conjured a compelling image of Hong Kong surveillance that had little to do with Hong Kong itself.

In contrast, in the second episode just a year later, the 2014 Umbrella protests by Hong Kong residents against the Chinese government once again put the territory in the global spotlight, with the additional interest that this episode showed how surveillance and security issues affecting primarily Hong Kong residents mapped onto issues relevant to populations beyond its own borders. The initial reason for the protest was that China rescinded previously stated agreements to increase democratic elections, to which local residents responded through organized, peaceful demonstrations that reflected both the city's long history of civic protest and municipal regulations that require all public gatherings to obtain prior authorization and follow strict guidelines for behavior. In a gesture symptomatic of Hong Kong's dense media environment and its ability to capitalize on its place within global networks, both government and protesters were astute in their use of media and technology to enable internal communications while promoting their cause abroad. Protesters made use of new social networking applications to overcome government blocks on wireless and cellular technology; government retaliated by mimicking that application to eavesdrop on protesters; and when police began to crack down on crowds by using pepper spray, protesters raised their arms in silent surrender, deliberately recalling the "Black Lives Matter" protests regarding police brutality in America earlier that year.[10] Notably, in this contrasting episode of Hong Kong's leading role in global surveillance practice, the object of attention was the collective effort of local citizens rather than those of an individual white expatriate personifying American intelligence supremacy and its heroic subversion. This more diffuse, but still highly coordinated, surveillance culture that arises from Hong Kong's tendencies for internal cooperation has cinematic and cultural precedents in everything from tenement films to the civilian support for police during the 1967 riots that helped change the HKP reputation. Indeed, although local support for the 2014 protests was never universal and grew more divided as the demonstrations continued into a second and third month, the movement's ability to present a highly local issue as continuous with civic concerns among different global populations demonstrated the qualities by which Hong Kong and its idiosyncratic surveillance culture and cinema are relevant for the contemporary world.

One compelling precedent for Hong Kong's acuity at grassroots countersurveillance is *The Other Hong Kong Report*, an annual publication assembled and authored by local scholars and activists to review and assess current life in ways expressly conceived in opposition to official reports long produced by the former colonial and present Chinese governments. Yet as argued throughout this book, cinema's imagery and accessibility often make narrative film an equally or arguably even more effective site of surveillance criticism, and both Hong Kong cinema's rich domestic traditions and its astute engagement with world film have made it an unusually perceptive predictor of world surveillance trends. Thus it should not be a surprise that even the themes of the 2014 Umbrella protests also had a precedent in local film. By all accounts, *72 Tenants of Prosperity* is an utterly conventional instance of local cinema typical of the time of its release, and its relevance for Hong Kong surveillance cinema derives in part from its ordinariness.[11] As its title suggests, the 2010 comedy is yet another installment in the long-established local tradition of remakes and homages to the local classic *The House of 72 Tenants*. As such, in the post-decline context of Hong Kong-China coproductions, *72 Tenants of Prosperity* at first seems to oc-

cupy a position in contemporary Hong Kong film on the side of modest, small-budget movies meaningful only to local audiences rather
than accessibly spectacular or universal themes that might appeal to
broader Chinese audiences and Hollywood-style global distribution.

Reinforcing this categorization of *72 Tenants of Prosperity* as a movie
limited to local audiences is the film's predominantly Cantonese dialogue and highly specific plot and setting, which loosely center on
the romantic and professional rivalry between two men whose mobile
phone retail stores oppose each other on Sai Yeung Choi street, a popular shopping venue in densely crowded Mong Kok. Equally referential of both local surveillance cinema and contemporary Hong Kong
surveillance culture, the movie includes a subplot regarding the recent
acid attacks (which in reality all occurred on Sai Yeung Choi) as well
as backstory and plot developments meaningful only to audiences familiar with Hong Kong film history, especially *The House of 72 Tenants'*
legacy. The movie's main characters are said to be middle-aged versions of young people from the original film, and *72 Tenants of Prosperity* begins by restaging a well-known opening sequence in Shaw's
The House of 72 Tenants before cutting in freeze frame to modern-day
Mong Kok. Linked to a plot about the crisis posed to residents by rising rents and threats of eviction, these cinematic references in *72 Tenants of Prosperity* both recall Hong Kong's long tradition of civic demonstration and prefigure the 2014 Umbrella protests. Through scenes
of organized civic protest that draw on landmark local tenement movies ranging from *In the Face of Demolition* to *Cageman* (Fig. C.1), *72 Tenants of Prosperity* shows how quintessentially Hong Kong–based surveillance imagery illuminates and even foreshadows local surveillance
culture.

Challenging this seemingly local account of *72 Tenants of Prosperity*, however, is the fact that the film was partially financed by Sil-
Metropole, a Hong Kong production company with extensive ties to
the mainland, and the way the movie narratively acknowledges its
participation in contemporary trends toward coproduction and ame-
nability to Chinese state policy and censorship. Hints of the movie's
compliance with Chinese soft power are evident in a subplot about a
mysterious Mandarin-speaking businessman, whose initial appearance in the film employs all the cinematic conventions of Chinese vil-

FIGURE C.1. Film tradition and public history: civic protest in tenement-movie homage, *The 82 Tenants* (Shaw Brothers, 1982).

lainy before he is revealed as an angel investor who uses his financial power to paternalistically prevent rent increases, unify the two rival men by employing their sons, and otherwise save the neighborhood. Although this denouement might seem to push the film in the accommodationist direction of contemporary coproduction and the mainland heroism of the earlier joint venture subgenre, the fact remains that *72 Tenants of Prosperity* imagines Mandarin-speaking clout transformed by Hong Kong–style capitalism. With this demonstrably pragmatic appeal to mainland resources and power enfolded into an unquestionably Hong Kong–specific tradition of surveillance cinema, *72 Tenants of Prosperity* works like some post-reunification Hong Kong undercover films—or even the early reunification-era romance *Comrades, Almost a Love Story*—to cinematically portray local surveillance culture absorbing or transforming the more powerful regime.

As an utterly conventional Hong Kong film of its era, then, *72 Tenants of Prosperity* exemplifies the unique, distinct quality of Hong Kong surveillance, whose pragmatic, domesticated, and even affirmative tendencies position it as a model of how to survive and prosper under surveillance conditions increasingly affecting the world at large. This insight and prescience so characteristic of Hong Kong film as a whole are particularly appreciable in the movie's subversive domestication of

Chinese authority by Hong Kong surveillance cinema. It is also apparent in the movie's shuttling between local and global references and jokes that present Hong Kong's inclusive, granular, individual, and privatized surveillance as meaningful to all populations. Thus, in one scene, an elderly woman gathering discarded bottles and cardboard to recycle (a poignant reminder of Hong Kong's wealth disparity and a fixture of Hong Kong's streets) garners pity and sympathy, only to have her proudly point to a binocular-wielding assistant spotter positioned on a rooftop as her own "eye in the sky." Similarly, an early sequence in the film that starts with the cast singing an updated cover of Sam Hui's classic theme song to *The Private Eyes* underscores the movie's local resonance, before segueing into a large-scale musical dance number choreographed like *West Side Story* and set to the tune of Michael Jackson's "Beat It."

In summary, by suggesting that a local movie like *72 Tenants of Prosperity* provides some precedent for the 2014 Umbrella protests, I am not suggesting that the movie directly prefigured its developments but rather that anyone watching the film—or almost any sample of Hong Kong surveillance cinema of the past half century—should not have been surprised by either the content or form of the 2014 protests or by Snowden's decision to flee first to Hong Kong. As previously noted, the street protests of 2014 have precedents that go back in local history for decades, and the organic, grassroots monitoring by civilian populations of government or establishment power that those protests represent have been further enshrined in local culture through the many fictional scenes of civic protest and other motifs of lateral surveillance within some of Hong Kong cinema's most emblematic films. Similarly, throughout the roughly eighteen-month period between Snowden's interviews from a Kowloon district hotel in the summer of 2013 and the street protests that blockaded traffic in several parts of Hong Kong in autumn of the following year, local and global coverage invariably expressed surprise that this tiny city previously known best as a capitalist paradise could so suddenly display fierce political protest or occupy such strategic geopolitical significance. This disingenuousness is understandable for outsiders, but it ignores the city's history and the territory's long-standing value in global politics. Indeed, even if local residents forgot or never knew about either of these facts—a profoundly blasé or indifferent response to surveillance that Hong Kong surveillance culture in some ways actively encourages—these circumstances have been memorialized for decades throughout some of local culture's best-known films.

In regard to surveillance, where Hong Kong goes, so goes the rest of the world. These insights are apparent in Hong Kong daily life; but in the manner of the well-known Western canon of surveillance cinema, Hong Kong film also offers through its distinct narrative ethics and visual aesthetics a powerful source of surveillance imagery and commentary. These insights available through cinema and Hong Kong film in particular stand in stark contrast to other well-known non-Hollywood surveillance films, such as *The Lives of Others*, a 2006 German film about the East German Stasi that invariably came up in conversations during the writing of this book. But as engrossing and moving as *The Lives of Others* is, its retrospective look at a uniformly condemned surveillance history under an authoritarian European regime nearly half a century in the past is of limited use for the present. A tragedy primarily focused on surveillance's repressive and violent consequences, *The Lives of Others* is typical of most canonical surveillance cinema both in its critical depiction of secret police and its liberal Western desire to distance itself from surveillance practice. Unlike Hong Kong film, *The Lives of Others* elides society's complicity within the ongoing surveillance systems that continue to shape our world.

Hong Kong's 72 *Tenants of Prosperity*, by contrast, is a roughly contemporary film that offers a vastly different lens by which to explore surveillance modernity. While I recognize that *The Lives of Others* presents a valuable contribution to an ever-expanding archive of world surveillance film, such a canon will be most useful once it encompasses the full range of global surveillance imagery. This book presents Hong Kong as one of the most vibrant and diverse contributions to world surveillance cinema, but that cinema is not alone in challenging Hollywood hegemony and the parallel Western biases that for too long have confined surveillance studies. From East and West, past to present, and through a generic variety that places comedy, romance, tenement, and gambling movies alongside sci-fi, crime movies, political dramas, and techno-thrillers, world surveillance cinema has much to teach us. This means exploring not only Hong Kong, Hong Kong cinema, and what it means to be "Hong Kong on a bad day." It means also looking toward cinema from places like Seoul, Mumbai, Recife, and Barcelona for their version of "rear window ethics" and aesthetics. As Hong Kong cinema shows, world film has many more venues from which we can learn about different surveillance cultures to find out what it tells us about our ourselves.

CHINESE GLOSSARY

SELECT NAMES AND TERMS

Ah Chan	阿燦
Asia Pictures	亞洲影業有限公司
ban jian fang (*baan gaan fong*)	板間房
Chan, Philip (Chan Yan-kin)	陳欣健
Chang Cheh	張徹
Chang, Grace	葛蘭
du pian (*dou pin*, or gambling film)	賭片
Feng Huang	鳳凰
gonganju (Public Security Bureau)	公安局
Great Wall	長城
Hero Story	英雄故事
Hui, Michael	許冠文
Hui, Sam	許冠傑
joint venture	合資
Lee Tit	李鐵
Leung, Tony (Leung Chiu-wai)	梁朝偉
Liu Wai-hung	廖偉雄
mou seoi, mou seoi (*mei qian, mei shui*)	無水無水（沒錢沒水）
Ng Chor-fan	吳楚帆
Police Magazine	警訊
Song Mu	松木

Southern Film Corporation	南方影業公司
Sun Luen	新聯
Woo, John	吳宇森
Zhonglian (Union Film Enterprises)	中聯（中聯電影企業有限公司）
Zunzi (Wong Kei-kwan)	尊子（黃紀鈞）

FILM AND PROGRAM TITLES

14 Blades	錦衣衛
72 Tenants of Prosperity	72家租客
82 Tenants, The	82家房客
Aberdeen	香港仔
Aces Go Places	最佳拍檔
Air Hostess	空中小姐
Always on my Mind	搶錢夫妻
Another Chinese Cop	中國O記之血腥情人
Anti-Corruption	廉政風暴
Arrest the Restless	藍江傳之反飛組風雲
As Tears Go By	旺角卡門 （熱血男兒）
Ashes of Time	東邪西毒
Assassins, The	銅雀台
Backyard Adventures	後窗
Banana Cop	英倫琵琶 (香蕉探長)
Below the Lion Rock (TV series)	獅子山下
Better Tomorrow, A	英雄本色
Boat People	投奔怒海
Bodyguard from Beijing, The	中南海保鑣
Bodyguards and Assassins	十月圍城
Breaking News	大事件
Bullet in the Head	喋血街頭
Cageman	籠民
Casino, The	吉祥賭坊
Centre Stage	阮玲玉
Challenge of the Gamesters	千王鬥千霸
Chef, the Actor, the Scoundrel, The	廚子戲子痞子
Chicken and Duck Talk	雞同鴨講
Chungking Express	重慶森林
City on Fire	龍虎風雲

Cold War	寒戰
Combo Cops	國產雪蛤威龍
Comrades, Almost a Love Story	甜蜜蜜
Contract, The	賣身契
Coolie Killer	殺出西營盤
Cops and Robbers	點指兵兵
Crime Story	重案組
Crouching Tiger, Hidden Dragon	臥虎藏龍
Days of Being Wild	阿飛正傳
Dividing Wall, The	一板之隔
Don't Go Breaking My Heart	單身男女
Drug War	毒戰
Echoes of the Rainbow	歲月神偷
Election	黑社會
Election 2	黑社會以和為貴
Empress and the Warriors, An	江山美人
Enter the Dragon	龍爭虎鬥
Executioners, The	現代豪俠傳
Eye in the Sky	跟蹤
Fallen Angel	墮落天使
Fight Back to School III	逃學威龍3之龍過雞年
Final Night of the Royal Hong Kong Police, The	皇家香港警察的最後一夜
Final Option, The	飛虎雄心
Fist of Fury	精武門
Floating City	浮城
Four, The	四大名捕
From Beijing with Love	國產凌凌漆
From Riches to Rags	錢作怪
From the Queen to the Chief Executive	等候董建華發落
From Vegas to Macau	賭城風雲
Front Page, The	新半斤八兩
Games Gamblers Play	鬼馬雙星
God of Gamblers	賭神
Golden Chicken	金雞
Good, the Bad, [and] the Ugly, The (TV series)	網中人

Grandmaster, The	一代宗師
Hard Boiled	辣手神探
Her Fatal Ways I–IV	表姐，妳好嘢！
Hero	英雄
Hero of the Beggars	丐世英雄
Heroic Trio	東方三俠
His Fatal Ways	老表，你好嘢！
Hong Kong 1941	等待黎明
House of 72 Tenants, The	七十二家房客
ICAC (TV series)	香港廉政公署電視劇集
Imp, The	凶榜
In the Face of Demolition	危樓春曉
Infernal Affairs	無間道
Infernal Affairs 3	無間道III: 終極無間
Inspector Chocolate	神探朱古力
Jumping Ash	跳灰
Killer, The	喋血雙雄
Last Message, The	天才與白痴
Lee Rock	五億探長雷洛傳：雷老虎
Lee Rock II	五億探長雷洛傳II之父子情仇
Legend of the Fist: The Return of Chen Zhen	精武風雲–陳真
Let the Bullets Fly	讓子彈飛
Lifeline	十萬火急
Long Arm of the Law	省港旗兵
Long Arm of the Law II	省港旗兵續集
Long Arm of the Law III	省港旗兵第三集
Longest Summer, The	去年煙花特別多
Love and the City	都市情緣
Love in a Fallen City	傾城之戀
Love Parade	花團錦簇
Lucky Seven	七擒七縱七色狼
Lust, Caution	色, 戒
Made in Hong Kong	香港製造
Magic Touch, The	神算
Mahjong Heroes	打雀英雄傳
Mainland Dundee	表哥我來也！

Man on the Brink	邊緣人
Moment of Romance, A	天若有情
Motorway	車手
Mr. Cinema	老港正傳
Mr. Coconut	合家歡
My Father Is a Hero	給爸爸的信 (父子武狀元；赤子威龍)
My Life as McDull	麥兜故事
My Lucky Stars	福星高照
Needing You	孤男寡女
Office	華麗上班族
On the Run	亡命鴛鴦
Opium War, The	鴉片戰爭
Organized Crime and Triad Bureau	重案實錄O記
Out of the Dark	回魂夜
Overheard	竊聽風雲
Pantyhose Hero	脂粉雙雄
People's Hero	人民英雄
Pilferer's Progress	發錢寒
Plain Jane to the Rescue	八彩林亞珍
Poker King	撲克王
Police Force	警察
Police Magazine	警訊
Police Story II	警察故事續集
Police Story III: Supercop	警察故事III：超級警察
Powerful Four	四大探長
Prison on Fire	監獄風雲
Prison on Fire II	監獄風雲II逃犯
Private Eyes, The	半斤八兩
Project A	A計劃
Project A, Part 2	A計劃續集
Promise, The	無極
Rear Entrance	後門
Red Cliff	赤壁
Red Rose White Rose	紅玫瑰與白玫瑰
Rock n' Roll Cop	省港一號通緝犯
Rouge	胭脂扣
Running out of Time	暗戰

Security Unlimited	摩登保鑣
Silent War, The	聽風者
Simple Life, A	桃姐
Social Worker (TV series)	北斗星
Song of the Exile	客途秋恨
Sparrow	文雀
Sup Sap Bup Dup	十三不搭
Tactical Unit—Comrades in Arms	機動部隊-同袍
Teppanyaki	鐵板燒
Tigers, The	五虎將之決裂
Trail, The	大路 (狹路英豪)
Vulgaria	低俗喜劇
Way We Are, The	天水圍的日與夜
Wicked City	妖獸都市
Wu Xia	武俠

PREFACE

1. D. A. Miller, *The Novel and the Police* (Berkeley: University of California Press, 1989).

2. J. S. Nye Jr., *Soft Power: The Means to Success in World Politics* (New York: PublicAffairs, 2004); and J. S. Nye Jr. and W. Jisi, "Hard Decisions on Soft Power: Opportunities and Difficulties for Chinese Soft Power," *Harvard International Review* (Summer 2009): 18–22. For just a few examples of the extensive contemporary studies of Chinese soft power, see Joshua Kurlantzick, *Charm Offensive: How China's Soft Power Is Transforming the World* (New Haven, CT: Yale University Press, 2007); Sheng Ding, *The Dragon's Hidden Wings: How China Rises with Its Soft Power* (Lanham, MD: Lexington Books, 2008); Michael Barr, *Who's Afraid of China? The Challenge of Chinese Soft Power* (London: Zed Books, 2011); and Yiu-wai Chu, "The Rise of China and Its Soft Power," in *Lost in Transition: Hong Kong Culture in the Age of China* (Albany: State University of New York Press, 2013), 19–41.

INTRODUCTION

1. See, e.g., Tom Gunning, "What I Saw from the Rear Window of the Hotel des Folies-Dramatiques, or the Story Point of View Films Told," in *Ce que je vois de mon ciné: La représentation du regard dans le cinéma des premiers temps*, ed. Andre Gaudreault (Paris: Merudiens Klincksieck, 1988), 33–43, "Tracing the Individual Body: Photography, Detectives and Early Cinema," in *Cinema and the Invention of Modern Life*, ed. Leo Charney and Vanessa R. Schwartz (Berkeley: University of California Press, 1996), 15–45, and *The Films of Fritz Lang: Allegories of Vision and Modernity* (London: BFI, 2000).

2. Catherine Zimmer, *Surveillance Cinema* (New York: NYU Press, 2015), and "Surveillance Cinema: Narrative between Technology and Politics," *Surveillance & Society* 8, no. 4 (2011): 427–40; Sébastien Lefait, *Surveillance on Screen: Monitoring Contemporary Films and Television Programs* (Lanham, MD: Scarecrow Press, 2012); and Garrett Stewart, *Closed Circuits: Screening Narrative Surveillance* (Chicago: University of Chicago Press, 2015), and "Surveillance Cinema," *Film Quarterly* 66, no. 2 (2012): 5–15. For other uses of the "surveillance cinema" rubric, see Mia Galuppo and Chris Godley, "Surveillance Cinema: 14 Movies Featuring Big Brother," *Hollywood Reporter*, June 21, 2013, http://www.hollywoodreporter.com/gallery/surveillance-cinema-14-movies -featuring-566300/1-v-for-vendetta.

3. Norman K. Denzin, *The Cinematic Society: The Voyeur's Gaze* (London: SAGE Publications, 1995); John S. Turner, "Collapsing the Interior/Exterior Distinction: Surveillance, Spectacle, and Suspense in Popular Cinema," *Wide Angle* 20, no. 4 (1998): 93–123; Thomas Y. Levin, "Rhetoric of the Temporal Index: Surveillant Narration and the Cinema of 'Real Time,'" in *Ctrl [Space]: Rhetorics of Surveillance from Bentham to Big Brother*, ed. Thomas Y. Levin, Ursula Frohne, and Peter Weibel, 578–93 (Cambridge, MA: MIT Press, 2002). Also see Wheeler Winston Dixon, *It Looks at You: The Returned Gaze of Cinema* (Albany: State University of New York Press, 1995), which is not as explicitly focused on surveillance as Turner and Levin but is exactly contemporary to Denzin and parallels that book's study of cinematic reflexivity.

4. For example, Norman Denzin's chapter on Asian detective figures such as the fictional Charlie Chan, Mr. Moto, and Mr. Wong still focuses only on Hollywood cinema.

5. Michael T. Kaufman, "What Does the Pentagon See in 'Battle of Algiers'?," *New York Times*, September 7, 2003, section 4, 3.

6. Law Wing-sang, "Hong Kong Undercover: An Approach to 'Collaborative Colonialism,'" *Inter-Asia Cultural Studies* 9, no. 4 (2008): 522–42, and "The Violence of Time and Memory Undercover: Hong Kong's *Infernal Affairs*," *Inter-Asia Cultural Studies* 7, no. 3 (2006): 383–402. For a wry commentary on Hollywood's easy adaptation of *Infernal Affairs*, see Tom Scocca, "Martin Scorsese, Now a Great Hong Kong Director," *New York Observer*, October 9, 2006.

7. *Rear Window* opened in New York on August 1, 1954. *Backyard Adventures* opened in Hong Kong sixteen months later, on December 7, 1955, less than half a year after *Rear Window* played in Hong Kong.

8. David Lyon, *Surveillance Studies: An Overview* (Cambridge: Polity, 2007), 140. For other critical and theoretical references to such films among surveillance studies, see Christopher Gad and Lone Koefed Hansen, "A Closed Circuit Technological Vision: On *Minority Report*, Event Detection and Enabling Technologies," *Surveillance & Society* 11, no. 1/2 (2013): 148–62; Michael J. Shapiro, "Every Move You Make: Bodies, Surveillance, and Media," *Social Text* 83, no. 2 (2005): 21–34; Richard Maxwell, "Surveillance: Work, Myth, and Policy,"

Social Text 83, no. 2 (Summer 2005): 1–19; and Dietmar Kammerer, "Video Surveillance in Hollywood Movies, *Surveillance & Society* 2, no. 2/3 (2004): 464–73.

9. For information on UKUSA, see Nicky Hager, *Secret Power: New Zealand's Role in the International Spy Network* (Nelson, New Zealand: Craig Potton, 1996); and James Bamford, *The Shadow Factory: The NSA from 9/11 to the Eavesdropping on America* (New York: Anchor, 2009).

10. Few scholarly studies have yet been published about *Neighboring Sounds*, but for an excellent essay on the film's "intimate relationship between security and paranoia," see A. O. Scott, "The Leisure Class Bears Its Burden," *New York Times*, August 23, 2012, C1.

11. See, for example, Gina Marchetti and Tan See Kam, eds., *Hong Kong Film, Hollywood and the New Global Cinema: No Film Is an Island* (New York: Routledge, 2007); and Chuck Kleinhans, "Becoming Hollywood? Hong Kong Cinema in the New Century," in *Chinese Connections: Critical Perspectives on Film, Identity, and Diaspora*, ed. Tan See-Kam, Peter X. Feng, and Gina Marchetti (Philadelphia: Temple University Press, 2009), 109–21.

12. Hong Kong gambling films remain little studied, but for additional discussion, see Brenda Chan, "Gamblers and Trickers: The Forgotten Gambling Films of the 1970s," *Journal of Chinese Cinemas* 4, no. 2 (2010): 89–104, and "Identity and Politics in Hong Kong Gambling Films of the 1990s: *God of Gamblers III* and *God of Gambler's Return*," *New Cinemas: Journal of Contemporary Film* 9, no. 1 (2011): 35–48.

13. *God of Gamblers* presents probably one of the most famous instances of Hong Kong gambling triumph identified with advanced optical skills. The eponymous hero prevails in the film's climactic match because of "special contact lenses, recently imported from Germany." For an earlier example of gambling explicitly identified with Hong Kong entertainment, see *Challenge of the Gamesters* (1981), written by Wong Jing and directed by his father, the celebrated Wong Ting-lam. Although *Challenge of the Gamesters* is set in Republican China (and long before any sizable film industry in Hong Kong), it shows the defeat of a Japanese gambler through an elaborate scheme in which Chinese Nationalists borrow Hong Kong film crews to construct a set that will enable them to deceive the villain.

14. Although Hong Kong's gambling film tradition was initially influenced by a contemporary trend in early 1970s Japan, Hong Kong cinema's subsequent fecundity and longevity of the genre arguably surpass those of the Japanese original cycle, which was limited to a comparatively brief, decade-long span. For one scholarly reference to *Snake Eyes*, see Levin, "Rhetoric of the Temporal Index," 588–91.

15. Although widely recognized by local film scholars and critics, the tenement film is still largely unknown among Western scholars. For English-language references to the phenomenon, see Leung Ping-kwan, "Urban Cinema and the Cultural Identity of Hong Kong," in *The Cinema of Hong Kong:*

History, Arts, Identity, ed. Poshek Fu and David Desser (Cambridge: Cambridge University Press, 2000), 227–51; and Li Cheuk-to, "Postscript," in *A Study of Hong Kong Cinema in the Seventies,* The Eighth Hong Kong International Film Festival Catalogue (1984; repr., Hong Kong: Hong Kong Urban Council, 2002), 127–31.

16. Jane Jacobs, *The Death and Life of American Cities* (New York: Random House, 1961). On natural surveillance in policing and criminology, see Jake Desyllas, Philip Connoly, and Frank Hebbert, "Modelling Natural Surveillance," *Environment and Planning B: Planning and Design* 30 (2003): 643–55.

17. Although the phrasing of the English subtitles recalls *The Three Musketeers'* famous motto, the Chinese phrase used in the movie (*ren ren wei wo, wo wei ren ren*) more accurately translates as "I live for everyone, and everyone lives for me."

18. *In the Face of Demolition* was released in late November 1953; the Shek Kip Mei fire occurred only weeks later on Christmas Day that same year. For the fire's precipitating role in local history, see Manuel Castells, Lee Goh, and R.Yin-Wang Kwok, *The Shekkipmei Syndrome: Economic Development and Public Housing in Hong Kong and Singapore* (London: Pion, 1990); and Alan Smart, *The Shek Kip Mei Myth: Squatters, Fires and Colonial Rulers in Hong Kong, 1950–1963* (Hong Kong: Hong Kong University Press, 2006).

19. Grace Ng, ed., *One for All: The Union Film Spirit* (Hong Kong: Hong Kong Film Archive, 2011). Also see Hector Rodriguez, "Organizational Hegemony in the Hong Kong Cinema," *Post Script* 19, no. 1 (Fall 1999): 107–19.

20. Actually a film adaptation of a stage play that had been successfully performed in Hong Kong only months earlier, the Shaw movie is not the first cinematic treatment, but it is the first to specifically portray Hong Kong. (The first film treatment was adapted in 1963 from a Shanghai stage and radio play.) As for tenement films in general, scholarly studies of *The House of 72 Tenants* are still relatively few, particularly outside the Chinese language. See Li Cheuk-to, "Postscript."

21. *The House of 72 Tenants* was distributed in Cantonese, despite appearing at a time in the early 1970s when Mandarin films all but dominated the local film market. Although a number of the film's characters were said to be recent emigrants from Shanghai, Chiu Chow, and elsewhere (who presumably would have spoken their provincial dialect), by depicting them speaking Cantonese, the movie reinforced both the film's theme that Hong Kong could be a unifying identity and the movie's ties to local television network TVB, whose Cantonese broadcasts were partly responsible for the decline in the production of and attendance at Cantonese films.

22. In *The House of 72 Tenants* instances of actual freeze frame are supplemented by another device, probably drawn from the recent local stage production that partly inspired the Shaw production. The actors temporarily pause

the first time they appear on-screen, presumably allowing for the applause that might occur in a theatrical production; it also allows movie viewers time to read subtitles that give the actor's and character's name. Although not technically freeze frame, this convention adds to the overall sense of recurrent pauses within the film.

23. Gilles Deleuze, "Postscript on the Societies of Control," *October* 59 (Winter 1992): 3–7.

24. For the "new" surveillance, see Gary T. Marx, *Undercover: Police Surveillance in America* (Berkeley: University of California Press, 1988), 206–33; for lateral surveillance, see Mark Andrejevic, *iSpy: Surveillance and Power in the Interactive Era* (Lawrence: University Press of Kansas, 2007); for sousveillance, see Thomas Mathiesen, "The Viewer Society: Michel Foucault's 'Panopticon' Revisited," *Theoretical Criminology* 1, no. 2 (1997): 215–34; for the "surveillant assemblage," see Kevin D. Haggerty and Richard V. Ericson, "The Surveillant Assemblage," *British Journal of Sociology* 51, no. 4 (2000): 605–22; for the sensor society, see Mark Andrejevic and Mark Burdon, "Defining the Sensor Society," *Television & New Media* 167, no. 1 (2015): 19–36; for the soft cage, see Christian Parenti, *The Soft Cage: Surveillance in America from Slavery to the War on Terror* (New York: Basic Books, 2004). Also see James Rule, *Privacy in Peril* (Oxford: Oxford University Press, 2007).

25. See, e.g., Derek Malcolm, "The Blade Cuts Sharper," *The Guardian*, November 26, 1992. For the film's production history, see Paul Sammon, *Future Noir: The Making of* Blade Runner (New York: HarperPrism, 1996).

26. Wayne Arnold, "Military Hardware Is Adapted to Fight SARS," *New York Times*, May 12, 2003. American airports, for example, did not begin mandating temperature checks until the 2014 Ebola outbreak in Africa and only on a limited and provisional basis. Sabrina Tavernise, "Newly Vigilant, U.S. Will Screen Fliers for Ebola," *New York Times*, October 9, 2014, 1.

27. Harold Traver, "Orientations toward Privacy in Hong Kong," *Perceptual and Motor Skills* 59, no. 2 (1984): 635–44, 637; E. N. Anderson Jr., "Some Chinese Methods of Dealing with Crowding," *Urban Anthropology* 1, no. 2 (1972): 141–50, 148; see also Nuala Rooney, *At Home with Density* (Hong Kong: Hong Kong University Press, 2003). An exception to this general dearth of studies specifically exploring Hong Kong surveillance is A. R. Cuthbert, "The Right to the City: Surveillance, Private Interest and the Public Domain in Hong Kong," *Cities* 12, no. 5 (1995): 293–310, and "Ambiguous Space, Ambiguous Rights—Corporate Power and Social Control in Hong Kong," *Cities* 14, no. 5 (1997): 295–311.

28. Lau Siu-Kai, *Utilitarian Familiarism: An Inquiry into the Basis of Political Stability* (Hong Kong: Chinese University of Hong Kong Social Research Centre, 1977); and Lau Siu-kai and Kuan Hsin-chi, *The Ethos of the Hong Kong Chinese* (Hong Kong: Chinese University Press, 1988); Ma Ngok, *Political Development in Hong Kong: State, Political Stability, and Civil Society* (Hong Kong:

Hong Kong University Press, 2007); Leo Goodstadt, *Uneasy Partners: The Conflict between Public Interest and Private Profit in Hong Kong* (Hong Kong: Hong Kong University Press, 2005); Elizabeth Sinn, *Power and Charity: A Chinese Merchant Elite in Colonial Hong Kong* (Hong Kong: Hong Kong University Press, 2003); Steve Tsang, *A Modern History of Hong Kong* (London: I. B. Tauris, 2004). Also see Rance P. L. Lee, "Bureaucratic Corruption and Political Instability in Nineteenth-Century China," in *Corruption and Its Control in Hong Kong: Situations up to the Late Seventies*, ed. Rance P. L. Lee (Hong Kong: Chinese University Press, 1981), 105–32.

29. Ambrose King (as Jin Yaoji), "Zhongguo Ren Dui Siyinquan De Lijie," *Ming Pao Monthly* (February 1994): 56–62. Also see his earlier English-language publication, "Administrative Absorption of Politics in Hong Kong: Emphasis on the Grass Roots Level," *Asian Survey* 15 (1975): 422–39, which influenced Lau Siu-kai and others.

30. See, e.g., Rey Chow, "From Biopower to Ethnic Difference," in *The Protestant Ethnic and the Spirit of Capitalism* (New York: Columbia University Press, 2002), 1–17, and *Writing Diaspora: Tactics of Intervention in Contemporary Cultural Studies* (Bloomington: Indiana University Press, 1993); Aihwa Ong, "Flexible Citizenship among Chinese Cosmopolitans," in *Cosmopolitics: Thinking and Feeling beyond the Nation*, ed. Pheng Cheah and Bruce Robbins (Minneapolis: University of Minnesota Press, 1998), 134–62, and *Neoliberalism as Exception: Mutations in Citizenship and Sovereignty* (Durham, NC: Duke University Press, 2006).

31. Ding-Tzann Lii, "A Colonized Empire: Reflections on the Expansion of Hong Kong Films in Asian Countries," in *Trajectories: Inter-Asia Cultural Studies*, ed. Kuan-Hsing Chen (New York: Routledge,1998), 122–41.

32. For more recent and generically specific discussion of Hong Kong cinema's ability to use action to capitalize on its minority perspective, see Meaghan Morris, "Transnational Imagination in Action Cinema: Hong Kong and the Making of a Global Popular Culture," *Inter-Asia Cultural Studies* 5, no. 2 (2004): 181–99.

33. Yiman Wang, *Remaking Chinese Cinema: Through the Prism of Shanghai, Hong Kong, and Hollywood* (Honolulu: University of Hawai'i Press, 2013); Paul S. N. Lee, "The Absorption and Indigenization of Foreign Media Cultures: A Study on a Cultural Meeting Point of the East and West: Hong Kong," *Asian Journal of Communication* 1, no. 2 (1991): 52–72.

34. One particularly interesting, relevant example of surveillance as an artistic as well as narrative trope is *Who Do You Think You're Fooling?*, a 1994 short film by independent filmmaker Mike White that juxtaposes dialogue and imagery from *Reservoir Dogs* and *City on Fire* to demonstrate the extent to which the Hollywood film borrows from and reproduces aspects of the Hong Kong film.

35. Ackbar Abbas, *Hong Kong: Culture and the Politics of Disappearance* (Minneapolis: University of Minnesota Press, 1997); Yiu-wai Chu, *Lost in Transition: Hong Kong Culture in the Age of China* (Albany: State University of New York Press, 2013).

36. The film still lacks much scholarly examination; for one study, see Jenny Lau, "A Cultural Interpretation of the Popular Cinema of China and Hong Kong," in *Perspectives on Chinese Cinema*, ed. Chris Berry (London: British Film Institute, 1991), 166–74.

37. *Aces Go Places* opened in Hong Kong in early January 1982; *Blade Runner*'s US opening took place in late June of the same year, and the film opened in Hong Kong in late December 1982.

38. The use of miniature robots to metonymize Hong Kong culture is a recurring convention in local film throughout the early 1980s, suggesting both the territory's small but technologized economy and the fact that such items were an increasingly common manufacture in Hong Kong industry's tendency for swift reproduction of affordable gadgetry. For another sustained use of the trope, see *The 82 Tenants* (1982), an homage to the 1972 classic *The House of 72 Tenants*, in which tenement residents use a remote-controlled miniature helicopter to pester their landlord.

39. Lai's celebrity endorsement deal with Hutchinson Telecom was the first and perhaps most memorable partnership in a long and still-active tradition of collaborations between Hong Kong's entertainment industry and one of the world's most competitive mobile phone markets. Lai's television ads remain the subject of fond remembrance, as can be seen in the activity and comments surrounding the YouTube uploads of his old TV spots; the ads were also featured in a public exhibition in 2007. Frederick Yeung, "Industry Remembers Those Classic Adverts," *South China Morning Post*, May 30, 2007.

40. Glenn Greenwald, *No Place to Hide: Edward Snowden, the NSA, and the U.S. Surveillance State* (New York: Metropolitan Books, 2014), 94.

41. Paul Virilio, *War and Cinema: The Logistics of Perception* (London: Verso, 1989).

42. Richard Slotkin, *Gunfighter Nation: The Myth of the Frontier in Twentieth-Century America* (New York: Atheneum, 1992); Dana Polan, *Power and Paranoia: History, Narrative, and the American Cinema, 1940–1950* (New York: Columbia University Press, 1986); Siegfried Kracauer, *From Caligari to Hitler: A Psychological History of the German Film* (Princeton, NJ: Princeton University Press, 2004).

43. Quentin Lee's incisive and increasingly influential treatments of surveillance are studied in Katrien Jacobs, *People's Pornography: Sex and Surveillance on the Chinese Internet* (Bristol, UK: Intellect, 2012). Also see the art and essays of scholar-artist Chow Yiu Fai, discussed in the autobiographical essay "The Inevitable III: Screens on Screens, an Artistic Attempt," *Situations* 7, no. 2 (2014): 89–106. For a broader survey of contemporary Hong Kong video artists

that also inadvertently demonstrates a recurring interest in issues of social, spatial, and data monitoring, see Hector Rodriguez, "The Fragmented Commonplace: Alternative Arts and Cosmopolitanism in Hong Kong," in *Multiple Modernities: Cinemas and Popular Media in Transcultural Asia*, ed. Jenny Kowk Wah Lau (Philadelphia: Temple University Press, 2002), 128–48.

44. See, for example, David Bordwell, *Planet Hong Kong: Popular Cinema and the Art of Entertainment* (Cambridge, MA: Harvard University Press, 2000), on the "arresting incidents," "delirious and outlandish scenes that so appeal to Western fans" (122, 121). See also his influential essay on Hong Kong action aesthetics, which shows how the cinema's staccato, "pause-beat-pause" rhythm "arrests us" with its exaggerated stylizations. David Bordwell, "Aesthetics in Action: Kungfu, Gunplay, and Cinematic Expressivity," in *At Full Speed: Hong Kong Cinema in a Borderless World*, ed. Esther C. M. Yau (Minneapolis: University of Minnesota Press, 2001), 73–93, 86. Similarly Michael J. Shapiro cites "such moments of arrest in an otherwise hyperkinetic" cinema as typical of Hong Kong's modernity. "Intercity Cinema Hong Kong at the Berlinale," *Journal for Cultural Research* 12, no. 1 (2008): 98–119, 116. In her claim that temporal discontinuity is "simply part of the common grammar of Hong Kong cinema," Joelle Collier may not specifically use the term but suggests cinematographic arrest as a defining attribute of Hong Kong film. Joelle Collier, "A Repetition Compulsion: Discontinuity Editing, Classical Chinese Aesthetics, and Hong Kong's Culture of Disappearance," *Asian Cinema* 10, no. 2 (1999): 67–79. Interestingly, a similar use of the term with reference to Hong Kong visual culture also occurs in Rey Chow's discussion of local cartoonist Larry Feign. See Chow, *The Protestant Ethnic and the Spirit of Capitalism*, 81.

45. Abbas, *Hong Kong*, 47.

CHAPTER ONE

1. For the common linking of Hui and *The House of 72 Tenants* as watersheds in Hong Kong film history, see Stephen Teo, *Hong Kong Cinema: The Extra Dimensions* (London: British Film Institute, 1997), 50–60, and "The 1970s: Movement and Transition," in *The Cinema of Hong Kong: History, Arts, Identity*, ed. Poshek Fu and David Desser (Cambridge: Cambridge University Press, 2000), 90–110; Kwai-Cheung Lo and Evan Man Kit-Wah, *Age of Hybridity: Cultural Identity, Gender, Everyday Life Practice and Hong Kong Cinema of the 1970s* (Hong Kong: Oxford University Press, 2005) (in Chinese).

2. Norman K. Denzin, *The Cinematic Society: The Voyeur's Gaze* (London: SAGE Publications, 1995).

3. See, e.g., Franco Moretti, "Planet Hollywood," *New Left Review* 9 (2001): 90–101.

4. Alison Wakefield, *Selling Security: The Private Policing of Public Space* (Portland, OR: Willan Publishing, 2003); Clifford Shearing and Philip Sten-

ning, "Modern Private Security: Its Growth and Implications," *Crime and Justice* 3 (1981): 193–245.

5. Leo Ou-Fan Lee, *Shanghai Modern: The Flowering of a New Urban Culture in China, 1930–1945* (Cambridge, MA: Harvard University Press, 1999). Characteristic of Hui's referentially dense verbal comedy, the star's use of *bou biu* to reference professional watchmen ignores the more common usage in colloquial Hong Kong Cantonese of *gun lei jyun* or even *sik cu*, another loan word adapted into Cantonese from English "security." Pointedly anachronistic, Hui's *bou biu* joke also occurs in passing in *The Magic Touch* in a scene where his character uses the term to introduce his companion to an elderly relative who lives in the rural—and hence "timeless"—New Territories.

6. For example, Stephen Teo, Law Kar, and Jenny Lau all separately invoke "Hong Kong's Everyman," the "Hong Kong Everyman," and Hui's "comedy of the everyday man." See Law Kar, "Michael Hui: A Decade of Sword Grinding," in *A Study of Hong Kong Cinema in the Seventies*, The Eighth Hong Kong International Film Festival Catalogue (Hong Kong: Hong Kong Urban Council, 1984), 62–68, 65; Teo, *Hong Kong Cinema*, 141; and Jenny Lau, "Besides Fists and Blood: Hong Kong Comedy and Its Master of the Eighties." *Cinema Journal* 37, no. 2 (1998): 18–34, 26.

7. Perhaps not surprisingly, the *sik cu* or *gun lei jyun* watchmen common in Hong Kong commercial and residential buildings have been the subject of several other memorable Hong Kong movies, such as *Rosemary's Baby*–style horror film, *The Imp* (1981), and Stephen Chow's *Out of the Dark* (1995), a parody of Luc Besson's *Léon: The Professional*.

8. On the alternative, and often conflicting, scenarios that physical comedy comprises in the silent era, see Noel Carroll, "Notes on the Sight Gag," in *Comedy/Cinema/Theory*, ed. Andrew S. Horton (Berkeley: University of California Press, 1991), 25–42.

9. Law Kar and Frank Bren, *Hong Kong Cinema: A Cross-cultural View* (Lanham, MD: Scarecrow Press, 2004). Also see Matthew Turner, "'6os/9os: Dissolving the People," in *Hong Kong Sixties: Designing Identity*, ed. Matthew Turner and Irene Ngan (Hong Kong: Hong Kong Arts Centre, 1995), 13–36; and Michael Curtin, *Playing to the World's Biggest Audience: The Globalization of Chinese Film and TV* (Berkeley: University of California Press, 2007). On Golden Harvest in particular, see *Golden Harvest: Leading Change in Changing Times* (Hong Kong: Hong Kong Film Archive, 2013); Teo, "The 1970s"; Mike Walsh, "Hong Kong Goes International: The Case of Golden Harvest," in *Hong Kong Film, Hollywood and the New Global Cinema: No Film Is an Island*, ed. Gina Marchetti and Tan See Kam (New York: Routledge, 2007), 167–76; and Steve Fore, "Golden Harvest Films and the Hong Kong Movie Industry in the Realm of Globalization," *Velvet Light Trap* 34 (1994): 40–58.

10. For Sam Hui's popularity and the cultural importance of *The Private*

Eyes' theme song, see Leung Wing-fai, "Multi-media Stardom, Performance and Theme Songs in Hong Kong Cinema," *Canadian Journal of Film Studies* 20, no. 1 (2011): 41–60.

11. Michel de Certeau, *The Practice of Everyday Life* (Berkeley: University of California Press, 1984).

12. In *The Conversation*, for example, the protagonist's professional background and expertise are established through allusions to his work on the "Chrysler fins scandal" and the "'68 elections." The Po Sang Bank robbery was a daring daytime robbery of a local branch of the bank, then a significant Hong Kong financial institution, by armed and masked intruders. The 1974 assault was the object of considerable public attention for being the biggest and most weaponized robbery in local history.

13. See, e.g., "Il fait rire toute l'Asie," *Cahiers du Cinema*, September 1984, 37.

14. On the linguistic and cultural limitations of Hui's early comedy, see Law Kar, "Michael Hui"; and Ng Ho, "A Portrait of the Comedian as a Schizophreniac," in *A Study of Hong Kong Cinema in the Seventies*, The Eighth Hong Kong International Film Festival Catalogue (Hong Kong: Hong Kong Urban Council, 1984), 69–72.

15. On Hui's theories about the maximum time that can pass between gags, see, e.g., "Il fait rire toute l'Asie."

16. Miriam Bratu Hansen, "Fallen Women, Rising Stars, New Horizons: Shanghai Silent Film as Vernacular Modernism," *Film Quarterly* 54, no. 1 (2000): 10–22, 12.

17. Miriam Bratu Hansen, "Benjamin and Cinema: Not a One-Way Street," *Critical Inquiry* 25, no. 2 (Winter 1999): 306–43. For the Japanese marketing of Michael Hui, see Kinnia Yau Shuk-ting, "From Shaw Brothers to Golden Harvest: Raymond Chow and Japan," in *Golden Harvest: Leading Change in Changing Times* (Hong Kong: Hong Kong Film Archive, 2013), 43–49; and Cheuk-fan Leung, "The Lure of the Exotic: Hong Kong Cinema in Japan," in *Border Crossings in Hong Kong Cinema*, ed. Law Kar (Hong Kong: Leisure and Cultural Services Department, 2000), 156–59.

18. There are many studies of *Modern Times*, but for one analysis similarly engaged with the movie's reflexivity, see Garrett Stewart, "Modern Hard Times: Chaplin and the Cinema of Self-Reflection," *Critical Inquiry* 3, no. 2 (1976): 295–314.

19. Charles Musser, "Work, Ideology and Chaplin's Tramp," *Radical History Review* 41 (1988): 36–66, 62; Karen Fang, "'Absurdity of Life': An Interview with Michael Hui," in *Not Just a Laughing Matter: Interdisciplinary Approaches to Political Humor in China*, ed. Sharon Wesoky and King-fai Tam (New York: Springer, forthcoming).

20. Although Sam has a cameo in *Chicken and Duck Talk*, Sam did not return as costar in a Michael Hui film until *Front Page* (1990), when Sam's lucrative *Aces Go Places* (1982–89) series had run its course.

21. Sek Kei, "The Vicissitudes of Golden Studios: From Factory-Oriented Production to Star System and Satellite Operation," in *Golden Harvest: Leading Change in Changing Times* (Hong Kong: Hong Kong Film Archive, 2013), 26–33, 31.

22. Lau, "Besides Fists and Blood," 29.

23. The dramatic representation in Hong Kong film of shadow puppetry's ontological relationship to cinema is not unique to Hui's movies; it also surfaces among his contemporaries. Also in 1981, just a few months after *Security Unlimited* was released, the critically acclaimed movie by New Wave filmmaker Allen Fong, *Father and Son*, also included a scene in which the protagonist—a film-loving child loosely based on Fong himself—first exhibits his interests by toying with shadow puppetry.

CHAPTER TWO

1. Examples of critical emphasis on reunification-era action and crime films are now too numerous to require review, but the emphasis began with local film festivals and continued into scholarly and journalist reportage. See, for example, the 14th Hong Kong International Film Festival, whose theme and catalog were titled *The China Factor in Hong Kong Cinema* (Hong Kong: Urban Council, 1990); the 24th Hong Kong International Film Festival, whose main themes and catalog included "Border Crossings in Hong Kong Cinema" (Hong Kong: Urban Council, 2000); Li Cheuk-to, "The Return of the Father: Hong Kong New Wave and Its Chinese Context in the 1980s," Esther Yau, "Border Crossing: Mainland China's Presence in Hong Kong Cinema," and Leo Ou-Fan Lee, "Two Films from Hong Kong: Parody and Allegory," all in *New Chinese Cinemas: Forms, Identities, Politics*, ed. Nick Browne, Paul G. Pickowicz, Vivian Sobchak, and Esther Yau (Cambridge: Cambridge University Press, 1994), 160–79, 180–201, 202–16, respectively; Julian Stringer, "'Your Tender Smiles Give Me Strength': Paradigms of Masculinity in John Woo's *A Better Tomorrow* and *The Killer*," *Screen* 38, no. 1 (1997): 40; Jillian Sandell, "Reinventing Masculinity: The Spectacle of Male Intimacy in the Films of John Woo," *Film Quarterly* 49, no. 4 (1996): 23; Tony Williams, "Space, Place, and Spectacle: The Crisis Cinema of John Woo," *Cinema Journal* 36, no. 2 (1997): 67–84; Edward Wong, "Hong Kong's Final Cut?," *Los Angeles Times*, June 15, 1997; and especially Lisa Odham Stokes and Michael Hoover, *City on Fire: Hong Kong Cinema* (London: Verso, 1999), a book-length survey of a variety of Hong Kong films that takes its title from Ringo Lam's action and crime movie.

2. Although "action" and "crime" genres are not exactly interchangeable, this chapter follows common audience tendencies to aggregate the two terms into a broad category of spectacular, action-based plots motivated by clear moral or physical conflict. Similarly, this chapter uses "handover" and "reunification" interchangeably to reference the period from 1984 to 1997, when Hong Kong was awaiting its impending transition from colonial to Chinese rule.

3. For reunification-era studies of *Cageman* and Wong Kar-wai, see Ackbar Abbas, *Hong Kong: Culture and the Politics of Disappearance* (Minneapolis: University of Minnesota Press, 1997); Curtis K. Tsui, "Subjective Culture and History: The Ethnographic Cinema of Wong Kar-wai," *Asian Cinema* 7, no. 2 (Winter 1995): 93–124; Stokes and Hoover, *City on Fire*, 171–75.

4. Prominent critiques of previous approaches to Hong Kong film include Rey Chow and David Bordwell, who in *Planet Hong Kong: Popular Cinema and the Art of Entertainment* (Cambridge, MA: Harvard University Press, 2000) urge viewers to be "skeptical of relying too much on the reflection metaphor" (36). Chow's many publications on the topic include "Nostalgia of the New Wave: Structure in Wong Kar-Wai's *Happy Together*," *Camera Obscura* 14, no. 3 (1999): 30–49, and "Introduction: On Chineseness as Theoretical Problem," *boundary 2* 25 (1988): 1–24. Reflectionist approaches to Hong Kong film go back to Ian Jarvie, *Window on Hong Kong: A Sociological Study of the Hong Kong Film Industry and Its Audience* (Hong Kong: Centre of Asian Studies, Hong Kong University, 1977), and are reviewed in Hector Rodriguez, "The Emergence of the Hong Kong New Wave," in *At Full Speed: Hong Kong Cinema in a Borderless World*, ed. Esther Yau (Minneapolis: University of Minnesota Press, 2001): 53–69.

5. For a sample of Hong Kong cinema studies since reunification that pursue an auteur or industrial approach or focus on genres and eras beyond reunification action and crime, see Stephen Teo, *Director in Action: Johnnie To and the Hong Kong Action Film* (Hong Kong: Hong Kong University Press, 2007); Stephen Teo and Vivian Lee, "Placing Value in the Missing and the Lost," *Journal of Chinese Cinemas* 4, no. 2 (2010): 83–87; Laikwan Pang, *Cultural Control and Globalization in Asia: Copyright, Piracy, and Cinema* (New York: Routledge, 2006), and *Creativity and Its Discontents: China's Creative Industries and Intellectual Property Rights Offenses* (Durham, NC: Duke University Press, 2012); Vivian Lee, *Hong Kong Cinema since 1997: The Post-nostalgic Imagination* (London: Palgrave, 2009); Yau Ching, *Filming Margins: Tang Shu Shuen, a Forgotten Hong Kong Woman Director* (Hong Kong: Hong Kong University Press, 2004), and "Porn Power: Sexual and Gender Politics in Li Han-Hsiang's *Fengyue* Films," in *As Normal as Possible: Negotiating Sexuality and Gender in Mainland China and Hong Kong*, ed. Yau Ching (Hong Kong: Hong Kong University Press, 2010), 113–31; and Stephanie DeBoer, *Coproducing Asia: Locating Japanese-Chinese Regional Film and Media* (Minneapolis: University of Minnesota Press, 2014).

6. For just a sampling of the countless post-1997 film studies still focusing on action and crime films from the reunification era, despite different methodological approaches, see Meaghan Morris, Siu Leung Li, and Stephan Chan Ching-kiu, eds., *Hong Kong Connections: Transnational Imagination in Action* (Durham, NC: Duke University Press, 2005); Kin-yan Szeto, *The Martial Arts Cinema of the Chinese Diaspora: Ang Lee, John Woo and Jackie Chan in Hollywood* (Carbondale: Southern Illinois University Press, 2011); David Martin-Jones,

Deleuze, Cinema and National Identity: Narrative Time in National Contexts (Edinburgh: Edinburgh University Press, 2006), especially 188–95; David Desser, "Triads and Changing Times: The National Allegory of Hong Kong Cinema, 1996–2000," *Quarterly Review of Film and Video* 26 (2009): 179–93; Man-Fung Yip, "In the Realm of the Senses: Sensory Realism, Speed, and Hong Kong Martial Arts Cinema," *Cinema Journal* 53, no. 4 (2014): 76–97; Katherine Spring, "Sounding Glocal: Synthesizer Scores in Hong Kong Action Cinema," in *American and Chinese-Language Cinemas: Examining Cultural Flows*, ed. Lisa Funnell and Man-Fung Yip (New York: Routledge, 2015), 38–52; Andrew Grossman, "Homosexual Men (and Lesbian Men) in a Heterosexual Genre: Three Gangster Films from Hong Kong," in *Queer Asian Cinema: Shadows in the Shade*, ed. Andrew Grossman (New York: Harrington Park Press, 2000), 237–72; Leon Hunt, *Kung Fu Cult Masters* (London: Wallflower Press, 2003); Kwai-Cheung Lo, "A Borderline Case: Ethnic Politics and Gangster Films in Post-1997 Hong Kong," *Postcolonial Studies* 10, no. 4 (2007): 431–36; Stephen Teo, *Chinese Martial Arts Cinema: The* Wuxia *Tradition* (Edinburgh: Edinburgh University Press, 2009).

7. A backlash against anti-reflectionism can be found in Margaret Hillenbrand, "The National Allegory Revisited: Writing Private and Public in Contemporary Taiwan," *positions* 14, no. 3 (Winter 2006): 633–62; and Desser, "Triads and Changing Times."

8. Actually a homonym, the villain's given name "Peng" uses a different character (meaning "shack") than that of the Chinese premier (referencing a large bird) but, due to the similarity in sound, still recalls that historical figure.

9. Rey Chow, "King Kong in Hong Kong: Watching the 'Handover' from the U.S.A.," *Social Text* 55 (Summer 1998): 93–108.

10. Shu-mei Shih, "After National Allegory," in *Visuality and Identity: Sinophone Articulations across the Pacific* (Berkeley: University of California Press, 2007), 141–64, 142.

11. Daniel F. Vukovich, *China and Orientalism: Western Knowledge Production and the P.R.C.* (London: Routledge, 2012), 36, 119, 89.

12. Chi-Kwan Mark, *Hong Kong and the Cold War: Anglo-American Relations 1949–1957* (Oxford: Clarendon, 2004). See also Andrew J. Whitfield, *Hong Kong, Empire and the Anglo-American Alliance at War, 1941–45* (New York: Palgrave, 2001); and Johannes R. Lombardo, "Eisenhower, the British and the Security of Hong Kong, 1953–60," *Diplomacy & Statecraft* 9, no. 3 (1998): 143–53.

13. Poshek Fu, *Between Shanghai and Hong Kong: The Politics of Chinese Cinemas* (Stanford, CA: Stanford University Press, 2003).

14. See, e.g., Man-Fung Yip, "Closely Watched Films: Surveillance and Postwar Leftist Cinema," in *Surveillance in Asian Cinema: Under Eastern Eyes*, ed. Karen Fang (New York: Routledge, forthcoming); Wong Ain-ling, ed., *The Shaw Screen: A Preliminary Study* (Hong Kong: Hong Kong Film Archive, 2003).

15. Christina Klein, *Cold War Orientalism: Asia in the Middlebrow Imagina-*

tion, 1945–1961 (Berkeley: University of California Press, 2003); Gina Marchetti, *Romance and the "Yellow Peril": Race, Sex, and Discursive Strategies in Hollywood Fiction* (Berkeley: University of California Press, 1993).

16. Charles Leary, "The Most Careful Arrangements for a Careful Fiction: A Short History of Asia Pictures," *Inter-Asia Cultural Studies* 13, no. 4 (2012): 548–58. See also Sai-shing Yung, "Containment and Integration: A Preliminary Study of Asia Press and Asia Pictures Limited," in *The Cold War and Hong Kong Cinema*, ed. Wong Ain-ling and Lee Pui-tak (Hong Kong: Hong Kong Film Archive, 2009), 249–62 (in Chinese).

17. On *Air Hostess*, see Gary Needham, "Fashioning Modernity: Hollywood and the Hong Kong Musical 1957–64," and Charles Leary, "Electric Shadow of an Airplane: Hong Kong Cinema, World Cinema," both in *East Asian Cinemas: Exploring Transnational Connections on Film*, ed. Leon Hunt and Leung Wing-fai (London: I. B. Taurus, 2008), 41–56, 57–68, respectively.

18. Song Mu, "The Man Who Jumped Off the Connaught Centre," in *Hong Kong Collage: Contemporary Stories and Writing*, ed. Martha P. Y. Cheung (Hong Kong: Oxford University Press, 1998), 55–63. Written in 1984, the original story first appeared (in Chinese) in the *Sing Tao Evening Post* weekly magazine on September 25, 1985.

19. Eric Kit-wai Ma, "Outsiders on Television," in *Culture, Politics, and Television in Hong Kong* (New York: Routledge, 1999), 62–96. Also see Vivian Lee, "The Mainland 'Other' in the Hong Kong Commercial Mainstream: Political Change and Cultural Adaptation," in *How East Asian Films Are Reshaping National Identities*, ed. Andrew David Jackson, Michael Gibb, and David White (Lewiston, NY: Edwin Mellen Press, 2006), 155–56.

20. As explained in Karen Fang, *John Woo's* A Better Tomorrow (Hong Kong: Hong Kong University Press, 2004), both terms derive from *A Better Tomorrow*'s Chinese title, which loosely translates as "true colors of a hero." Local references to the cycle of movies spawned by *A Better Tomorrow*'s success picked up on this theme by calling them *yingxiong pian* (hero stories), while Western reception—which sometimes used the term "heroic bloodshed"—conjoined that attribute with an emphasis on violence that aligned the cycle with general global categories of action and crime.

21. The paramilitary strength of the prosperous colony portrayed in this scene would have been obvious to local residents, particularly those aware of the realism imparted by the film's scriptwriter. The helicopter portrayed in the scene is presumably one of the Wessex helicopters then operated by the British Royal Air Force on behalf of the local government.

22. For hospitals' social and political power throughout early Hong Kong, see the groundbreaking work of Hong Kong historian Elizabeth Sinn, *Power and Charity: A Chinese Merchant Elite in Colonial Hong Kong* (Hong Kong: Hong Kong University Press, 2003).

23. *Long Arm of the Law* opened in Hong Kong in July 1984. Although the Joint Declaration was not signed until December of that year, talks between Britain and China had begun by 1982, well before *Long Arm of the Law* was even made.

24. Yau, "Border Crossing," 188.

25. For post-Tiananmen critical studies of *Long Arm of the Law*, see Ying-chi Chu, *Hong Kong Cinema: Coloniser, Motherland and Self* (New York: Routledge, 2003), 104; and Emily Tsz Yan Fong, "Changing Intergroup Relations with Mainland Chinese: An Analysis of Changes in Hong Kong Movies as a Popular Cultural Discourse," *Multilingua* 29 (2010): 29–53.

26. See, e.g., Mike Davis, "Fortress L.A.," in *City of Quartz: Excavating the Future in Los Angeles* (New York: Vintage, 1992).

27. On the Hong Kong subway, see M. S. Gaylord and J. F. Galliher, "Riding the Underground Dragon," *British Journal of Criminology* 31, no. 1 (1991): 15–26.

28. See, e.g., Joelle Collier, "A Repetition Compulsion: Discontinuity Editing, Classical Chinese Aesthetics, and Hong Kong's Culture of Disappearance," *Asian Cinema* 10, no. 2 (1999): 67–79.

29. A. R. Cuthbert, "Ambiguous Space, Ambiguous Rights—Corporate Power and Social Control in Hong Kong," *Cities* 14, no. 5 (1997): 295–311; and Janet Ng, *Paradigm City: Space, Culture, and Capitalism in Hong Kong* (Albany: SUNY Press, 2009).

30. For critical observations of the surveillance themes in *Comrades, Almost a Love Story*, see Michael Hoover and Lisa Odham Stokes, "Hong Kong in New York: Global Connections, National Identity, and Filmic Representations," *New Political Science* 25, no. 4 (December 2003): 509–32. Also see Miriam Bratu Hansen, "Benjamin and Cinema: Not a One-Way Street," *Critical Inquiry* 25 (Winter 1999): 306–43, which specifically mentions the ATM POVs as a "running gag . . . which may or may not be that of an internal surveillance camera" (307n2).

31. See, e.g., Abbas, *Hong Kong*; Natalia Sui Hung Chan, "Rewriting History: Hong Kong Nostalgia Cinema and Its Social Practice," in *The Cinema of Hong Kong: History, Arts, Identity*, ed. Poshek Fu and David Desser (Cambridge: Cambridge University Press, 2000), 252–72.

32. On *Rouge* and *Centre Stage*, see Rey Chow, "A Souvenir of Love," in *At Full Speed: Hong Kong Cinema in a Borderless World*, ed. Esther Yau (Minneapolis: University of Minnesota Press, 2001), 209–29; and Abbas, *Hong Kong*, 39–47.

33. In the actual event that inspired Cheung's film, 105 cage dwellers were evicted from their eight hundred–square-foot home. "The Story behind *Cageman*," *Straits Times*, August 13, 1993; and Fionnuala Halligan, "*Cageman* Sweeps Local Film Awards," *South China Morning Post*, April 24, 1993, 1.

34. As is well known, the Tiananmen protests began with a student-

organized hunger strike. Also corroborating *Cageman*'s Tiananmen connotations is the fact that the actual tenement protest originally inspiring Cheung's film occurred in 1989, the same year as Tiananmen.

35. See, e.g., Siu-keung Cheung, "Speaking Out: Days in the Lives of Three Hong Kong Cage Dwellers," *positions* 8, no. 1 (2000): 235–62.

36. The Shaw version of *The House of 72 Tenants* further highlights the character's detailed mapping of his address by having the camera pan from each location as he names it.

37. On the perverse and infantilized nature of characters in Wong's films, see Ewa Mazierska and Laura Rascoli, "Trapped in the Present: Time in the Films of Wong Kar-wai," *Film Criticism* 25 no. 2 (2000/2001): 2–20; and Thorsten Botz-Bornstein, "Wong Kar-wai's Films and the Culture of the *Kawaii*," *SubStance* 37, no. 2 (2008): 94–109.

38. Before the widespread use of portable two-way radios, police call boxes were common throughout the Hong Kong urban landscape as an efficient means of registering beat information.

39. The films are loosely based on the notorious "Big Four," a group of ethnic Chinese police sergeants who in the 1950s and 1960s oversaw extensive extortion, kickback, and corruption schemes between police and organized crime. Somewhat related to this cycle of reunification-era police corruption movies is *The Tigers* (1991), an ensemble drama set in the contemporary period that is similarly sympathetic to corrupt officers.

CHAPTER THREE

1. See, e.g., Cheuk Pak-Tong, "The Beginnings of the Hong Kong New Wave: The Interactive Relationship between Television and the Film Industry," *Post Script* 19, no. 1 (1999): 10–27, and *Hong Kong New Wave Cinema (1978–2000)* (Chicago: Intellect Books, 2008); Law Kar, "The 'Shaolin Temple' of the New Hong Kong Cinema," and James Kung and Zhang Yucai, "Hong Kong Cinema and Television in the 1970s: A Perspective," both in *A Study of Hong Kong Cinema in the Seventies*, The Eighth Hong Kong International Film Festival Catalogue, 110–16, 10–17, respectively (Hong Kong: Hong Kong Urban Council, 1984).

2. The acronym refers to Criminal Investigation Department, the branch to which plainclothes detectives belong. Following the force's own institutional practice, in this chapter I use "RHKP" when specifically referring to the force during the years 1969–97, when "Royal" was part of its official title, and "HKP" when referring to the agency either before or after those years or without regard to a specific historical moment.

3. For ICAC history and powers, see Max J. Skidmore, "Promise and Peril in Combating Corruption: Hong Kong's ICAC," in *The Future of Hong Kong*, ed. Max J. Skidmore, Annals of the American Academy of Political and Social Science (Thousand Oaks: SAGE Periodicals Press, 1996), 118–30; Jeremiah K. H.

Wong, "The ICAC and Its Anti-corruption Measures," in *Corruption and Its Control in Hong Kong: Situations up to the Late Seventies*, ed. Rance P. L. Lee (Hong Kong: Chinese University Press, 1981), 45–74; and H. J. Lethbridge, "Corruption, White Collar Crime and the I.C.A.C," *Hong Kong Law Journal* 6, no. 2 (1976): 150–78. Despite renewed attention to the *ICAC* series around the time of its fortieth anniversary, there are still few critical and scholarly studies of the *CID* and *ICAC* television series. See Long Tin, "Grey in the Midst of White: Undercover Agents in ICAC Drama Series," trans. King-fai Tam, in *The Quiet Revolution: 40 Years of ICAC Drama Series*, ed. Li Cheuk-to and Keith Chan, with English editors Ken Smith, Joanna Lee, and Amory Hui (Hong Kong: Government of the Hong Kong Special Administration Region, 2014), 190–95. For industry recognition of the ICAC's continuing influence as a media producer throughout its forty-year history, see Karen Chu, "Hong Kong Film Fest to Screen Anti-corruption TV Movie 'Better Tomorrow,'" *Hollywood Reporter*, February 24, 2014, http://www.hollywoodreporter.com/news /hong-kong-film-fest-screen-682717.

4. David Bordwell, *Planet Hong Kong: Popular Cinema and the Art of Entertainment* (Cambridge, MA: Harvard University Press, 2000), 121.

5. Although I do not mean to be disingenuous about bureaucratic data suggesting public esteem for the HKP or to assume that professional respect conferred by governments or other police forces also reflects civilian feeling, the HKP's professional reputation is a tenet of both local and global history. Historians and official government statements alike invariably credit the HKP reforms and the anti-corruption culture inaugurated by the ICAC as a lodestone in the territory's stability and economic growth in the last quarter of the twentieth century. Within the profession itself, the HKP is frequently held up as a standard of urban policing, with other municipal and national police forces—including the HKP's own colonial model, the London Metropolitan Police—studying and adapting HKP practices. For HKP histories, see Kam C. Wong, *Policing in Hong Kong* (Burlington, VT: Ashgate, 2012); Kevin Sinclair, *Royal Hong Kong Police, 1844–1944: 150th Anniversary Commemorative Publication* (Hong Kong: Police Public Relations Bureau, 1994); Karen Fang, "Britain's Finest: The Royal Hong Kong Police," in *After the Imperial Turn: Thinking with and through the Nation*, ed. Antoinette Burton (Durham, NC: Duke University Press, 2003), 293–307; Jon Vagg, "Policing Hong Kong," *Policing and Society* 1 (1990): 235–47; Kevin Sinclair and Stephanie Holmes, *Asia's Finest: An Illustrated Account of the Royal Hong Kong Police* (Hong Kong: Unicorn, 1983); Allan Y. Jiao, *The Police in Hong Kong: A Contemporary View* (Lanham, MD: University Press of America, 2007); Harold Traver and Jon Vagg, eds., *Crime and Justice in Hong Kong* (Hong Kong: Oxford University Press, 1991); Colin Criswell and Mike Watson, *The Royal Hong Kong Police (1841–1945)* (Hong Kong: Macmillan, 1982). For policing studies that single out the HKP for praise, particularly among colonial forces, see Georgina Sinclair, *At the End of the Line: Colonial Policing and*

the Imperial Endgame, 1945–80 (Manchester, UK: Manchester University Press, 2006); David M. Anderson and David Killingray, *Policing the Empire: Government, Authority, and Control, 1830–1940* (Manchester, UK: Manchester University Press, 1991), and *Policing and Decolonization: Politics, Nationalism and the Police, 1917–1965* (Manchester, UK: Manchester University Press, 1992).

6. John Fiske, *Media Matters: Everyday Culture and Political Change* (Minneapolis: University of Minnesota Press, 1996); Christopher P. Wilson, *Cop Knowledge: Police Power and Cultural Narrative in Twentieth-Century America* (Chicago: University of Chicago Press, 2000). For similar intersections and collaborations between crime and law enforcement in a space outside the Global North, see Jonathan Smolin, *Moroccan Noir: Police, Crime, and Politics in Popular Culture* (Bloomington: Indiana University Press, 2013).

7. See, e.g., Yiu Kong Chu, *The Triads as Business* (London: Routledge, 2000); Frederic Dannen and Barry Long, *Hong Kong Babylon: An Insider's Guide to the Hollywood of the East* (New York: Hyperion, 1997); Sylvia J. Martin, "Of Ghosts and Gangsters: Capitalist Cultural Production and the Hong Kong Film Industry," *Visual Anthropology* 28, no. 1 (2012): 32–49.

8. February 1993 saw the arrival of two mainland officers in Hong Kong appointed for a one-year term as Chinese police liaisons within the colony; by the end of the year, China reciprocated, formally inviting HKP officers to visit China. S. Y. Yue, "Beijing Visit on the Cards for Police," *South China Morning Post*, November 29, 1993. Although the RHKP had already begun liaising with the Chinese Public Security Bureau as early as the late 1970s, the 1993 exchange was the first formal, publicized collaboration, effectively succeeding and replacing the force's decades-long regular exchange and training with British police.

9. As many viewers would have recognized about Li, the star was a Chinese celebrity even before he became a Hong Kong film star, having been a Chinese national youth martial arts champion who performed before Nixon during the US president's celebrated 1972 visit to China.

10. For a parallel example of Hong Kong cinema's tendency proliferate its already ubiquitous cop movies and subgenres, the mid-1980s launched a cycle of female-cop action films, including the *Yes, Madam!* (1985, 1987, 1988, 1989, 1993, 1995, 1996), *Royal Warriors* (1986, 1987), and *Inspector Wears Skirts* (1988, 1989, 1990, 1992) series, many starring Michelle Yeoh and made in response to the unexpected success of Yeoh's first *Yes, Madam!* and *Royal Warriors* movies.

11. Further illustrative of the film's comic allegory, *Combo Cops* encapsulates this political-cultural dichotomy in the characters' names. The British-trained Hong Kong cop is named "James Fok" and is several times described as "007"; the mainland cop is "Huang Fei," a tongue-in-cheek name clearly positioning the fictional officer as a modern-day incarnation of Chinese film icon and folk hero Wong Fei-hung.

12. Cheuk Pak Tong, "The Changing Image of Chinese Public Security Officer in Hong Kong Cinema in the Nineties," in *Hong Kong Film Genres*, ed. Law Kar, Ng Ho, and Cheuk Pak Tong (Hong Kong: Oxford University Press, 1997), 153–68 (in Chinese). For studies of the PSB, see Michael Dutton, *Policing Chinese Politics* (Durham, NC: Duke University Press, 2005), who transliterates the term as *gonganbu*; and John Byron and Robert Pack, *The Claws of the Dragon: Kang Sheng, the Evil Genius behind Mao—and His Legacy of Terror in People's China* (New York: Simon and Schuster, 1992).

13. *Hap zok* is the phrase most commonly used in films for "joint venture"; the term appears in *Her Fatal Ways*. For examples of the phrase within business and policy, see William W. L. Low, G. M. Naidu, and Richard C. M. Yam, "Dynamic and Responsive Firm Strategy: A Case Study of Hong Kong and China Collaborations in Pearl River Delta," *Journal of Global Marketing* 14, no. 4 (2001): 27–49; Yiu To and Ray Yep, "Global Capital and Media Control: A Case of Joint Venture in China's Media Market before WTO," *East Asia: An International Quarterly* 25, no. 2 (June 2008): 167–85.

14. Norman Miners, "The Localisation of the Hong Kong Police Force, 1842–1947," *Journal of Imperial and Commonwealth History* 18 (1990): 296–315. Also see Mathieu Deflem, Richard Featherstone, Yunqing Li, and Suzanne Sutphin, "Policing the Pearl: Historical Transformations of Law Enforcement in Hong Kong," *International Journal of Police Science and Management* 10, no. 3 (2007): 349–56.

15. Both the transformative impact of the 1967 riots and the role of the police in those events are an axiom of local culture. See, e.g., Robert Bickers and Ray Yep, eds., *May Days in Hong Kong: Riot and Emergency in 1967* (Hong Kong: Hong Kong University Press, 2009).

16. Mark S. Gaylord and Harold Traver, "Colonial Policing and the Demise of British Rule in Hong Kong," *International Journal of the Sociology of Law* 23 (1995): 23–43, 31, 33.

17. The term refers to Peter Fitzroy Godber, a former chief superintendent in the RHKP who was discovered to have a fortune in overseas accounts. Although Godber initially escaped apprehension and was hardly unique, his exposure came at a time of mounting public criticism of the force.

18. *Police Magazine* is in Cantonese, and *Police Report* is its shorter English-language version. The television programs have been in continuous production since the mid-1970s, making them among the territory's longest-running and most extensively recognized programs.

19. Although *The House of 72 Tenants*' relatively vague period setting does not specify the exact historical era it portrays, viewers knowledgeable about HKP history could have read in the debauched police superintendent a wry allusion to Charles May, a nineteenth-century captain superintendent who owned a number of brothels until he sold them as a result of government pres-

sure. See Criswell and Watson, *The Royal Hong Kong Police*; and Christopher Munn, *Anglo-China: Chinese People and British Rule in Hong Kong, 1841–1880* (Hong Kong: Hong Kong University Press, 2009).

20. *Mou seoi mou seoi* is a Cantonese pun, which plays on *seoi* to mean both "money" and "water." As Li Cheuk-to points out, the 1973 *House of 72 Tenants* also coincided with the controversial Hawkers Licensing Provision Act, whose mandated licensing fees for street vendors were widely regarded by locals as an imposition on the working poor and which the movie's corrupt police constable references with his constant demands for licenses and payments to overlook violations. Li Cheuk-to, "Postscript," in *A Study of Hong Kong Cinema in the Seventies*, The Eighth Hong Kong International Film Festival Catalogue (Hong Kong: Hong Kong Urban Council, 1984), 127–81, 127.

21. *Anti-Corruption* was released in late August 1975; the many "Get Godber" rallies organized by students and held in public parks began earlier that spring and were still active at the time of the film's release.

22. In his 1973 deposition, prosecuted RHKP superintendent Ernest P. M. Hunt claimed to have seen an expat officer burning an HK five hundred–dollar note; cited in Peter N. S. Lee, "The Causes and Effects of Police Corruption: A Case in Political Modernization," in *Corruption and Its Control in Hong Kong: Situations up to the Late Seventies*, ed. Rance Lee (Hong Kong: Chinese University Press, 1981), 167–98, 195.

23. The 1969 Granada television film about the Hong Kong drug trade, *A Case to Answer*, was first broadcast in Britain and rebroadcast only weeks later in Hong Kong through local English-language service Rediffusion. See Mark Hampton, "British Legal Culture and Colonial Governance: The Attack on Corruption in Hong Kong, 1968–1974," *Britain and the World* 5, no. 2 (2012): 223–39, 230.

24. To further underscore the debauched police superintendent as outdated, the character's immoral and outmoded behavior is signified not only by his age and ancient practice of concubinage but also by his traditional formal dress worn for the "wedding" ceremony, which is pointedly different from the police constable's official uniform and the modern, *cheongsam*-style dresses worn by a number of the film's female characters.

25. First established in 1948 as a special unit within CID, the HKP Anti-Corruption Branch was founded in conjunction with the 1948 Prevention of Corruption Ordinance. The branch was elevated to its own office in the initial anti-corruption reforms in 1971 but as a result of the Godber scandal was replaced in 1974 by the ICAC.

26. Later compiled and released as the second part of Cowell's trilogy film, *The Heroin Wars* (1996), a thirty-year study of narcotics production and trade in Southeast Asia's "Golden Triangle," the Hong Kong episode "Smack City" features the HKP's investigations into triad-controlled neighborhood drug distribution.

27. A nine-episode series that was shot in 1977 and aired in Britain and parts of the Commonwealth, *Hong Kong Beat* was one of several BBC documentaries about colonial policing made around the same time. *Hong Kong Beat* was not broadcast in Hong Kong itself.

28. See "60's Hong Kong Police Recruitment," YouTube, uploaded September 4, 2008, https://youtu.be/VHZa26jo62g?list=PL5B230mmb44n8F3fZvYWN oR_P-Jt1w5DZ. Although I have never been able to ascertain who oversaw the film's production, all scholars agree that the short likely appeared between 1973 and 1975, around the time of introduction of new financial incentives for recruitment and corruption prevention.

29. On Hui's ICAC employment (and subsequent self-reference in her semi-autobiographical film *Song of the Exile*), see Elaine Yee Lin Ho, "Women on the Edges of Hong Kong Modernity: The Films of Ann Hui," in *Spaces of Their Own: Women's Public Sphere in Transnational China*, ed. Mayfair Mei-hui Yang (Minneapolis: University of Minnesota Press, 1999), 162–87, 164–65. For an alternative account of the ICAC's influences over Hui, Leung Ping-kwan claims that the impressionist treatment of a real double homicide in *The Secret* (1979) reflects the director's artistic commitment to "provide an interpretation different from the police's official version." Leung Ping-kwan, "Urban Cinema and the Cultural Identity of Hong Kong," in *The Cinema of Hong Kong: History, Arts, Identity*, ed. Poshek Fu and David Desser (Cambridge: Cambridge University Press, 2000), 240.

30. *OffBeat*, the HKP's official magazine, is a professionally produced publication nominally intended for former officers and their families, but its high production values and extensive distribution throughout HKP public offices and government spaces in general suggest a desire to attract a more extensive audience. The Junior Police Call is an HKP-led youth organization designed both to disseminate HKP values and provide an alternative to triad-vulnerable youth; for many years, it has been one of the largest youth organizations in the world outside the Boy Scouts.

31. On temporal discontinuity in Hong Kong cinema (including Jackie Chan), see Joelle Collier, "A Repetition Compulsion: Discontinuity Editing, Classical Chinese Aesthetics, and Hong Kong's Culture of Disappearance," *Asian Cinema* 10, no. 2 (1999): 67–79.

32. See, e.g., Rance P. L. Lee, ed., *Corruption and Its Control in Hong Kong: Situtations up to the Late Seventies* (Hong Kong: Chinese University Press, 1981), 11. Universally known among local Chinese, the phrase gained further English-language exposure with the September 1973 publication of an official report by Sir Alastair Blair-Kerr, a government servant appointed by new governor Murray MacLehose to investigate the current HKP corruption scandal. See Robert Klitgaard, *Controlling Corruption* (Berkeley: University of California Press, 1991), 105–7. Perhaps equally evocative of HKP corruption history in this scene is the fact that the speeding vehicle specifically is a minibus, a pri-

vate and independently operated shared-ride passenger van distinct to Hong
Kong urban transport, whose vulnerability to local graft became an early site
of corruption exposure. See, e.g., Peter Harris, "The Bus and Its Riders: An Approach to the Problem of Corruption in Hong Kong," in *Hong Kong: A Study in
Bureaucratic Politics* (Hong Kong: Heinemann Asia, 1978), 140–61.

33. Beginning with *Winners and Sinners* (1983), the hugely popular *Lucky
Stars* series of ensemble action comedies featuring Sammo Hung, Richard Ng,
John Shum, Charlie Chin, and Stanley Fung included the sequels and spin-
offs *My Lucky Stars* (1985), *Twinkle Twinkle Lucky Stars* (1985), *Lucky Stars Go
Places* (1986), and the five-installment *Pom Pom* series (1984–92).

34. At one point in the film, the female rookie rationalizes her participation in the Miss Hong Kong pageant by arguing that "police are the citizen's
nanny" and that she has "duty to promote our image" by "bring[ing] citizens
closer to their uncle [the police]."

35. "Yingxiong gushi" or "Hero Story," *Police Story*'s theme song, anticipates the *yingxiong pian* themes that suffused local cinema with the release of
A Better Tomorrow in the following year.

36. See, e.g., Laikwan Pang, "Jackie Chan, Tourism, and the Performing
Agency," in *Hong Kong Film, Hollywood and the New Global Cinema: No Film Is
an Island*, ed. Gina Marchetti and Tan See Kam (New York: Routledge, 2007),
206–18.

37. See, e.g., Darren Goodsir, "Police Future up for Investigation," *South
China Morning Post*, November 26, 1994; Anthony G. O. Yeh, "Planning and
Management of Hong Kong's Border," in *From Colony to SAR: Hong Kong's
Challenges Ahead*, ed. Joseph Y. S. Cheng and Sonny S. H. Lo (Hong Kong: Chi-
nese University Press, 1995), 261–92.

38. See, e.g., "Changes Kept to a Minimum for Territory's Law Enforcers,"
South China Morning Post, February 24, 1997; Kevin Sinclair, "Safe in the Hands
of Asia's Finest," *South China Morning Post*, October 14, 1996, 19.

39. For the political symbolism of the police characters in *Her Fatal Ways III*
and *IV*, see Shu-Mei Shih's excellent discussion in *Visuality and Identity: Sinophone Articulations across the Pacific* (Berkeley: University of California Press,
2007), 108–13. The film is also discussed in Li-Mei Chang, "Whose Fatal Ways:
Mapping the Boundary and Consuming the Other in Border Crossing Films,"
in *Chinese Connections: Critical Perspectives on Film, Identity, and Diaspora*, ed.
Tan See-Kam, Peter X. Feng, and Gina Marchetti (Philadelphia: Temple University Press, 2009), 177–89.

40. Initially founded in 1938 as the Anti-Communist Squad, Special Branch
was disbanded in 1995. *Her Fatal Ways II* appeared in 1991.

41. The blue HKP uniform that in 1994 replaced the militarized olive-
green traditionally associated with the HKP *luk yee* was an adaptation of the
blue "winter" uniform customarily used by local police during the cooler seasons. By replacing the colonial uniform and removing its unfortunate resem-

blance with contemporary PLA dress, the new blue uniform dispelled strong associations with either state while maintaining some institutional continuity.

42. *Banana Cop* was released in April 1984, just as initial agreements about China's succession to Hong Kong sovereignty were being established.

43. On *The Longest Summer*, see Shih, *Visuality and Identity*, 150–57.

44. Winnie Chung, "Tasting the Bitter Fruit of Success," *South China Morning Post*, January 11, 1999.

45. On *The Final Night of the Royal Hong Kong Police*, see Cheuk Pak-Tong, *Hong Kong New Wave Cinema*, 214–15.

46. Although focused on law and the justice system rather than the police, Herman Yau's 2001 drama, *From the Queen to the Chief Executive*, also exemplifies the conflation of cinematic and institutional change in *The Final Night of the Royal Hong Kong Police*. Like Lau's film, Yau's movie focuses on the uncertain policies exposed by the shift in sovereignty (specifically, imprisoned youth), and similarly includes within its realistic, unglamorized depiction of Hong Kong life extensive scenes of pre-reunification civic protest.

47. See, e.g., Stephen Teo, *Director in Action: Johnnie To and the Hong Kong Action Film* (Hong Kong: Hong Kong University Press, 2007); Laikwan Pang, "Postcolonial Hong Kong Cinema: Utilitarianism and (Trans)Local," *Postcolonial Studies* 10, no. 4 (2007): 413–30.

48. Vivian Lee, "PTU: Re-mapping the Cosmopolitan Crime Zone," in *Chinese Films in Focus II*, ed. Chris Berry (London: BFI, 2008). Similarly, throughout the *Tactical Unit* series, HKP departments such as the PPRB and the Complaints Against Police Officers (CAPO)—another accountability branch introduced as part of the HKP reforms in the mid-1980s—play important roles in the plot, simultaneously continuing local cinema's long history of detailed representations of local policing while using those official agencies and the particularly cynical or disaffected ethos with which To portrays them as paradigms of civic alienation from the new political environment.

49. Although *Comrades in Arms* is, like the other *Tactical Unit* movies, a television movie produced by To but crediting a different director, I follow Stephen Teo (and general industry convention) in attributing to Johnnie To those productions he oversaw and that clearly bear the imprint of his interest and themes.

50. *Sparrow*'s place in local and global surveillance cinema traditions deserves more attention. Paying homage both to the French New Wave and a distinctly Hong Kong tradition of pickpocket movies, the film subverts mainland surveillance while promoting alternative surveillance regimes strongly identified with Western and capitalist culture.

51. The Water Police was established by the British navy soon after colonial annexation of the territory in 1841—three years before the founding of the land police in 1844. Due to its need for personnel familiar with local waters and the ethnic customs of local fishing populations, the Water Police

had already begun to demilitarize and enlist local recruits by the late nineteenth century. By the end of World War II—that is, decades before the HKP reform era of the 1970s—the Water Police had already undergone one name change and was in the process of restyling its uniform to suppress its naval origins, thereby positioning it as a prescient figure of postwar continuity (despite its actual, ongoing collaboration with the British navy). See Iain Ward, *Sui Geng: The Hong Kong Marine Police, 1841–1950* (Hong Kong: University of Hong Kong Press, 1991); P. J. Melson, ed., *White Ensign, Red Dragon: The History of the Royal Navy in Hong Kong, 1841–1941* (Hong Kong: Edinburgh Financial Publishing, 1997); and Kathleen Harland, *The Royal Navy in Hong Kong, since 1841* (Liskeard, Cornwall, UK: Maritime Books, 1991).

CHAPTER FOUR

1. First signed in 2003, the Closer Economic Partnership Agreement (CEPA) between Hong Kong and the mainland allows Hong Kong companies preferential access to the mainland market through cooperative trade and investments. For film, this mandates a minimum degree of mainland location, financing, talent, and crew, as well Putonghua (Mandarin) dialogue.

2. See, e.g., Louise Watt, "Co-productions; How to Grab Chinese and Western Audiences? Delicately," *Globe and Mail*, June 27, 2014, R2.

3. For coverage of Hollywood efforts to accommodate mainland policy, see Kyle Smith, "Shanghaied: Shocked That Hollywood Collaborated with the Nazis? It's Doing the Exact Same Thing Today with China," *New York Post*, August 4, 2013. Chinese characters were either added (*Iron Man 3*) or removed (*Men in Black 3*) when the originals were recut. *Red Dawn* was digitally reedited because the remake, originally shot in 2010, received vocal criticism from Chinese activists and protesters, eventually resulting in MGM's decision that all political and national references to China would in the Chinese release be digitally replaced with reference to North Korea.

4. The quoted regulations are from China's State Administration of Press, Publication, Radio, Film and Television, which oversees media operations in the country and implements censorship. See Zhiwei Xiao, "Prohibition, Politics, and Nation-Building: A History of Film Censorship in China," in *Silencing Cinema: Film Censorship around the World*, ed. Daniel Biltereyst and Roel Vande Winkel (New York: Palgrave, 2013), 109–30. For a similar reaction to the mainland version of *Lady Cop & Papa Crook* (2008), another movie closely associated with the *Infernal Affairs* creative team, see Rebecca Tsui, "Plot Spoiled by Red Tape," *South China Morning Post*, January 25, 2009.

5. For studies of censorship and the material effect of state surveillance on cinema, see Lee Grieveson, *Policing Cinema: Movies and Censorship in Early-Twentieth-Century America* (Berkeley: University of California Press, 2004); Christina Vatelescu, *Police Aesthetics: Literature, Film and the Secret Police in So-*

viet Times (Stanford, CA: Stanford University Press, 2010). For censorship and state intervention in Hong Kong film in particular, see Kristof Van den Troost, "Under Western Eyes? Colonial Bureaucracy, Surveillance and the Birth of the Hong Kong Crime Film," in *Surveillance in Asian Cinema: Under Eastern* Eyes, ed. Karen Fang (New York: Routledge, forthcoming); David Newman, "British Colonial Censorship Regimes: Hong Kong, Straits Settlements, and Shanghai International Settlement, 1916–1941," in *Silencing Cinema: Film Censorship around the World*, ed. Daniel Biltereyst and Roel Vande Winkel (New York: Palgrave, 2013), 167–90; and Yu-lai Lo, "Some Notes about Film Censorship in Hong Kong," in *21st Hong Kong International Film Festival Catalog* (Hong Kong: Hong Kong International Film Festival, 1997), 60–63.

6. On *dapian*, see Chris Berry, "What's Big about the Big Film? 'De-Westernizing' the Blockbuster in Korea and China," in *Movie Blockbusters*, ed. Julian Stringer (London: Routledge, 2003), 217–29.

7. David Desser, "Reclaiming a Legacy: The New-Style Martial Arts Saga and Globalized Entertainment," in *East Asian Cinema and Cultural Heritage*, ed. Kinnia Yau Shuk-ting (New York: Palgrave, 2011), 2–25, 2.

8. See, e.g., Robert Eng, "Is *Hero* a Paean to Authoritarianism?," *UCLA International Institute*, September 7, 2004, http://web.international.ucla.edu/institute /article/14371; J. Hoberman, "Man with No Name Tells a Story of Heroics, Color Coordination," *Village Voice*, August 17, 2004, http://www.villagevoice.com /film/man-with-no-name-tells-a-story-of-heroics-color-coordination-6406262.

9. Anthony Fung, *Global Capital, Local Culture: Transnational Media Corporations in China* (New York: Peter Lang, 2008). As many have noted, film director Zhang Yimou's expertise in orchestrating the opening ceremonies for the 2008 Beijing Olympics was a vivid illustration of the authoritarian spectacle Susan Sontag once called "fascinating fascism." See, e.g., Thomas J. Berghuis, "The World according to Beijing in 2008," *Modern China Studies*, 23 no. 1 (2016): 135–47.

10. Laikwan Pang, "Postcolonial Hong Kong Cinema: Utilitarianism and (Trans)Local," *Postcolonial Studies* 10, no. 4 (2007): 413–30; Mirana Szeto and Yun-chung Chen, "Mainlandization or Sinophone Translocality? Challenges for Hong Kong SAR New Wave Cinema," *Journal of Chinese Cinemas* 6, no. 2 (2012): 115–34, and "To Work or Not to Work: The Dilemma of Hong Kong Film Labor in the Age of Mainlandization," *Jump Cut* 55 (2013), http://ejumpcut.org /archive/jc55.2013/SzetoChenHongKong/.

11. Yiu-wai Chu, *Lost in Transition: Hong Kong Culture in the Age of China* (Albany: State University of New York Press, 2013); Stephanie DeBoer, *Coproducing Asia: Locating Japanese-Chinese Regional Film and Media* (Minneapolis: University of Minnesota Press, 2014).

12. Tony Rayns, "Deep Cover," *Sight and Sound* 14, no. 1 (2004): 26–29, 28; Law Wing-sang, "Hong Kong Undercover: An Approach to 'Collaborative Co-

lonialism,'" *Inter-Asia Cultural Studies* 9, no. 4 (2008): 522–42. On *Infernal Affairs'* "non-places," also see Gina Marchetti, *Andrew Lau and Alan Mak's* Infernal Affairs—the Trilogy (Hong Kong: Hong Kong University Press, 2007), 40–50.

13. David Martin-Jones, *Deleuze, Cinema and National Identity: Narrative Time in National Contexts* (Edinburgh: Edinburgh University Press, 2006).

14. Chu, *Lost in Transition*, 119, 118.

15. For *The Departed*'s borrowings from the Whitey Bulger case, see Lee Hammel, "Former State Police Detective from Worcester Lends a Hand to Scorsese's New Movie," *Sunday Telegram*, October 9, 2005, A1. For other analyses of *The Departed*'s relationship to *Infernal Affairs*, see Yiman Wang, *Remaking Chinese Cinema: Through the Prism of Shanghai, Hong Kong and Hollywood* (Honolulu: University of Hawai'i Press), 152–56.

16. On Thailand's symbolic importance in *Infernal Affairs*, see Marchetti, *Andrew Lau and Alan Mak's* Infernal Affairs, 55, 69.

17. For Hollywood Sinophobia, see Gina Marchetti, *Romance and the "Yellow Peril": Race, Sex, and Discursive Strategies in Hollywood Fiction* (Berkeley: University of California Press, 1993); Naomi Greene, *From Fu Manchu to Kung Fu Panda: Images of China in American Film* (Honolulu: University of Hawai'i Press, 2014).

18. As journalist and anti-surveillance activist Glenn Greenwald describes the geopolitics of Chinese surveillance, "Chinese routers and servers represent not only economic competition but also surveillance competition: when someone buys a Chinese device instead of an American one, the NSA loses a crucial means of spying on a great many communication activities." Glenn Greenwald, *No Place to Hide: Edward Snowden, the NSA, and the US Surveillance State* (New York: Metropolitan Books, 2014), 151. For a similar Sinophobia in contemporary American surveillance entertainment, see Lisa Nakamura, "Interfaces of Identity: Oriental Traitors and Telematic Profiling in 24," *Camera Obscura* 24, no. 1 70 (2009): 109–33.

19. *The Departed*'s casting of the Chinese buyers is further mystifying given rumors that Hong Kong megastar Andy Lau—star and producer of *Infernal Affairs*—wanted a cameo in the Hollywood adaptation. See Gary G. Xu, *Sinascape: Contemporary Chinese Cinema* (Lanham, MD: Rowman and Littlefield, 2007), 155.

20. Esther Yau, "Genre Study and Cold War Cinema: Comments on Spy Detection Films of the Seventeen Year Period," *Dangdai dianying/Contemporary Cinema* 3 (2006): 74–80; Xiaoning Lu, "*The Might of the People*: Counter-Espionage Films and Participatory Surveillance in the Early PRC," in *Surveillance in Asian Cinema: Under Eastern Eyes*, ed. Karen Fang (New York: Routledge, forthcoming) .

21. Leo Ou-Fan Lee, "Spying on the Spyring," in *Musings: Reading Hong Kong, China and the World* (Hong Kong: East Slope Publishing, 2011), 120–28.

22. Michael J. Shapiro, "Intercity Cinema: Hong Kong at the Berlinale,"

Journal for Cultural Research 12, no. 1 (2008): 99–119, 110. Further emphasizing the comparability of Hong Kong surveillance culture to that of other cities, Shapiro compares Hong Kong with Berlin.

23. Tara Loader Wilkinson, "New Dawn for Day Trading; Activity Surges with City's Army of Investors Opening Up More Trading Platforms," *South China Morning Post*, May 13, 2013, 5; Mukul Munish, "For Whom the Bells Toll; over a Third of the City's Adult Population Actively Trades in Stocks. What Do These People Spend Their Days Doing?," *South China Morning Post*, September 22, 2009, 34.

24. Rey Chow, "Things, Common/Places, Passages of the Port City: On Hong Kong and Hong Kong Author Leung Ping-kwan," *differences* 5, no. 3 (1993): 179–204; Aihwa Ong, "Flexible Citizenship among Chinese Cosmopolitans," in *Cosmopolitics: Thinking and Feeling beyond the Nation*, ed. Pheng Cheah and Bruce Robbins (Minneapolis: University of Minnesota Press, 1998), 134–62, and *Neoliberalism as Exception: Mutations in Citizenship and Sovereignty* (Durham, NC: Duke University Press, 2006).

25. Abid Rahman, "Jeff Robinov's Studio 8 to Remake Hong Kong Surveillance Thriller 'Overheard,'" *Hollywood Reporter*, November 27, 2014, http://www.hollywoodreporter.com/news/jeff-robinovs-studio-8-remake-752721.

26. Romance genres, of course, are hardly exclusive of surveillance themes, as readily apparent in local and global surveillance films such as *A Moment of Romance* (on which To served as producer) and *The Bodyguard*. Not surprisingly, To's signature interests surveillance and voyeurism are key aspects of *Don't Go Breaking My Heart*, as they are in many of To's commercial romances. A key aspect of the plot of *Don't Go Breaking My Heart* is the ability to monitor romantic interests through closely positioned office windows, and it recalls To's depiction of office gossip in the earlier 2000 office romance *Needing You*.

27. *Drug War* premiered at the Rome Film Festival in November 2012; its Hong Kong and China release was in April 2013. *Sparrow* premiered at the 2008 Berlin Film Festival, several months before its Hong Kong release.

28. Liz Shackleton, "South Korea to Remake Johnnie To's *Drug War*," *Screen Daily*, May 18, 2014, http://www.screendaily.com/territories/asia-pacific/south-korea-to-remake-drug-war/5072086.article.

29. See, e.g., Jason Anderson, "Police Thriller Evades Chinese Censors; Deft Plotting, Intriguing Action Makes *Drug War* One of To's Best," *Toronto Star*, August 9, 2013, E2.

CONCLUSION

1. See, e.g., Clifford Lo, "Octopus Gives Police Long Tentacles: Data Recorded on Cards Helps Officers Find and Track Suspects," *South China Morning Post*, March 1, 2010.

2. See, e.g., Phyllis Tang, "Privacy Law Changes to Be Put Forward; Data

Protection Rules Don't Meet Public's Expectations, Henry Tang Says after Oc-topus Row," *South China Morning Post*, August 21, 2010.

3. Chandak Sengoopta, *Imprint of the Raj* (London: Pan Macmillan, 2004).

4. Aaron Doyle, Randy Lippert, and David Lyon, eds., *Eyes Everywhere: The Global Growth of Camera Surveillance* (New York: Routledge, 2011); Çağatay To-pal, "Global Citizens and Local Powers: Surveillance in Turkey," *Social Text 83*, no. 2 (Summer 2005): 85–93.

5. See, e.g., Ranjani Mazumdar, "Terrorism, Conspiracy, and Surveillance in Bombay's Urban Cinema," *Social Research* 78, no. 1 (2011): 143–72; concerning *[REC]* and *Tesis*, see Garrett Stewart, *Closed Circuits: Screening Narrative Surveil-lance* (Chicago: University of Chicago Press, 2015).

6. See Kyung Hyun Kim, *Virtual Hallyu: Korean Cinema of the Global Era* (Durham, NC: Duke University Press, 2011).

7. See, e.g., Leon Hunt, *Kung Fu Cult Masters* (London: Wallflower Press, 2003); Peter X. Feng, "False Consciousness and Double Consciousness: Race, Virtual Reality, and the Assimilation of Hong Kong Action Cinema in *The Ma-trix*," in *Chinese Connections: Critical Perspectives on Film, Identity, and Diaspora*, ed. Tan See-Kam, Peter X. Feng, and Gina Marchetti (Philadephia: Temple University Press, 2007), 9–21.

8. Glenn Greenwald, Ewen MacAskill, and Laura Poitras, "Covert Surveil-lance: 'I Have No Intention of Hiding . . . I Have Done Nothing Wrong': Ed-ward Snowden, the Man Responsible for the Leaks of Secret Documents De-tailing the NSA's Widespread Phone and Internet Surveillance," *The Guardian*, June 10, 2013, 2.

9. See, e.g., Lana Lam, "Snowden's Legacy; Still Awaiting Answers on Spy-ing Claims, but Observers Say That by Standing Up to Washington It Proved It Is Not Just Another Chinese City," *South China Morning Post*, June 14, 2014.

10. See, e.g., Paul Mozur and Alan Wong, "Hong Kong Protestors Flock to Off-Grid Messaging App," *New York Times*, September 29, 2014; Paul Mozur, Alan Wong, and Andrew Jacobs, "Fake App Eavesdrops on Hong Kong Pro-testers' Phones," *New York Times*, October 2, 2014. Further underscoring the protests' global aspirations, contemporary journalism often characterized the Hong Kong events as the latest in a string of civic demonstrations by nonwhite populations since the 2011 "Arab Spring." The term "Umbrella movement" or "Umbrella revolution" condensed these references, invoking the umbrel-las Hong Kong protesters began to use as symbolic defense against pepper spray while aligning themselves with the majority demonstrations that had criticized government throughout the Arab World.

11. For more on 72 *Tenants of Prosperity*'s homage and references to local cinema history, see Vivian Lee, "Contested Heritage: Cinema, Collective Mem-ory, and the Politics of Local Heritage in Hong Kong," in *East Asian Cinema and Cultural Heritage: From China, Hong Kong, Taiwan to Japan and South Korea*, ed. Kinnia Yau Shuk-ting (New York: Palgrave, 2011), 53–79.

Abbas, Ackbar. *Hong Kong: Culture and the Politics of Disappearance*. Minneapolis: University of Minnesota Press, 1997.

Anderson, David M., and David Killingray. *Policing and Decolonization: Politics, Nationalism and the Police, 1917–1965*. Manchester, UK: Manchester University Press, 1992.

———. *Policing the Empire: Government, Authority, and Control, 1830–1940*. Manchester, UK: Manchester University Press, 1991.

Anderson, E. N., Jr. "Some Chinese Methods of Dealing with Crowding." *Urban Anthropology* 1, no. 2 (1972): 141–50.

Anderson, Jason. "Police Thriller Evades Chinese Censors; Deft Plotting, Intriguing Action Makes *Drug War* One of To's Best." *Toronto Star*, August 9, 2013, E2.

Andrejevic, Mark. *iSpy: Surveillance and Power in the Interactive Era*. Lawrence: University Press of Kansas, 2007.

Andrejevic, Mark, and Mark Burdon. "Defining the Sensor Society." *Television & New Media* 167, no. 1 (2015): 19–36.

Arnold, Wayne. "Military Hardware Is Adapted to Fight SARS." *New York Times*, May 12, 2003, C4.

Bamford, James. *The Shadow Factory: The NSA from 9/11 to the Eavesdropping on America*. New York: Anchor, 2009.

Barr, Michael. *Who's Afraid of China? The Challenge of Chinese Soft Power*. London: Zed Books, 2011.

Berghuis, Thomas J. "The World according to Beijing in 2008." *Modern China Studies* 23, no. 1 (2016): 135–47.

Berry, Chris. "What's Big about the Big Film? 'De-Westernizing' the Blockbuster in Korea and China." In *Movie Blockbusters*, edited by Julian Stringer, 217–29. London: Routledge, 2003.

Bickers, Robert, and Ray Yep, eds. *May Days in Hong Kong: Riot and Emergency in 1967*. Hong Kong: Hong Kong University Press, 2009.

Bordwell, David. "Aesthetics in Action: Kungfu, Gunplay, and Cinematic Expressivity." In *At Full Speed: Hong Kong Cinema in a Borderless World*, edited by Esther C. M. Yau, 73–93. Minneapolis: University of Minnesota Press, 2001.

———. *Planet Hong Kong: Popular Cinema and the Art of Entertainment*. Cambridge, MA: Harvard University Press, 2000.

Botz-Bornstein, Thorsten. "Wong Kar-wai's Films and the Culture of the *Kawaii*." *SubStance* 37, no. 2 (2008): 94–109.

Byron, John, and Robert Pack. *The Claws of the Dragon: Kang Sheng, the Evil Genius behind Mao—and His Legacy of Terror in People's China*. New York: Simon and Schuster, 1992.

Carroll, Noel. "Notes on the Sight Gag." In *Comedy/Cinema/Theory*, edited by Andrew S. Horton, 25–42. Berkeley: University of California Press, 1991.

Castells, Manuel, Lee Goh, and R. Yin-Wang Kwok. *The Shekkipmei Syndrome: Economic Development and Public Housing in Hong Kong and Singapore*. London: Pion, 1990.

Certeau, Michel de. *The Practice of Everyday Life*. Berkeley: University of California Press, 1984.

Chan, Brenda. "Gamblers and Trickers: The Forgotten Gambling Films of the 1970s." *Journal of Chinese Cinemas* 4, no. 2 (2010): 89–104.

———. "Identity and Politics in Hong Kong Gambling Films of the 1990s: *God of Gamblers III* and *God of Gambler's Return*." *New Cinemas: Journal of Contemporary Film* 9, no. 1 (2011): 35–48.

Chan, Natalia Sui Hung. "Rewriting History: Hong Kong Nostalgia Cinema and Its Social Practice." In *The Cinema of Hong Kong: History, Arts, Identity*, edited by Poshek Fu and David Desser, 252–72. Cambridge: Cambridge University Press, 2000.

Chang, Li-Mei. "Whose Fatal Ways: Mapping the Boundary and Consuming the Other in Border Crossing Films." In *Chinese Connections: Critical Perspectives on Film, Identity, and Diaspora*, edited by Tan See-Kam, Peter X. Feng, and Gina Marchetti, 177–89. Philadelphia: Temple University Press, 2009.

"Changes Kept to a Minimum for Territory's Law Enforcers." *South China Morning Post*, February 24, 1997, 3.

Cheuk Pak Tong. "The Beginnings of the Hong Kong New Wave: The Interactive Relationship between Television and the Film Industry." *Post Script* 19, no. 1 (1999): 10–27.

———. "The Changing Image of Chinese Public Security Officer in Hong Kong Cinema in the Nineties." In *Hong Kong Film Genres*, edited by Law

Kar, Ng Ho, and Cheuk Pak Tong, 153–68. Hong Kong : Oxford University Press, 1997 (in Chinese).

———. *Hong Kong New Wave Cinema (1978–2000)*. Chicago: Intellect Books, 2008.

Cheung, Siu-keung. "Speaking Out: Days in the Lives of Three Hong Kong Cage Dwellers." *positions* 8, no. 1 (2000): 235–62.

Chow, Rey. "From Biopower to Ethnic Difference." In *The Protestant Ethnic and the Spirit of Capitalism*, 1–17. New York: Columbia University Press, 2002.

———. "Introduction: On Chineseness as Theoretical Problem." *boundary 2* 25 (Fall 1988): 1–24.

———. "King Kong in Hong Kong: Watching the Handover from the U.S.A." *Social Text* 55 (Summer 1998): 93–108.

———. "Nostalgia of the New Wave: Structure in Wong Kar-Wai's *Happy Together*." *Camera Obscura* 14, no. 3 (1999): 30–49.

———. *The Protestant Ethnic and the Spirit of Capitalism*. New York: Columbia University Press, 2002.

———. "A Souvenir of Love." In *At Full Speed: Hong Kong Cinema in a Borderless World*, edited by Esther Yau, 209–29. Minneapolis: University of Minnesota Press, 2001.

———. "Things, Common/Places, Passages of the Port City: On Hong Kong and Hong Kong Author Leung Ping-kwan." *differences* 5, no. 3 (1993): 179–204.

———. *Writing Diaspora: Tactics of Intervention in Contemporary Cultural Studies*. Bloomington: Indiana University Press, 1993.

Chow, Yiu Fai. "The Inevitable III: Screens on Screens, an Artistic Attempt." *Situations* 7, no. 2 (Summer 2014): 89–106.

Chu, Karen. "Hong Kong Film Fest to Screen Anti-corruption TV Movie 'Better Tomorrow.'" *Hollywood Reporter*, February 24, 2014, http://www.hollywoodreporter.com/news/hong-kong-film-fest-screen-682717.

Chu, Yinghchi. *Hong Kong Cinema: Coloniser, Motherland and Self*. New York: Routledge, 2003.

Chu, Yiu Kong. *The Triads as Business*. London: Routledge, 2000.

Chu, Yiu-wai. *Lost in Transition: Hong Kong Culture in the Age of China*. Albany: State University of New York Press, 2013.

———. "The Rise of China and Its Soft Power: Chineseness Reconfigured in the Age of Global Modernity." In *Lost in Transition: Hong Kong Culture in the Age of China*, 19–41. Albany: State University of New York Press, 2013.

Chung, Winnie. "Tasting the Bitter Fruit of Success." *South China Morning Post*, January 11, 1999.

Collier, Joelle. "A Repetition Compulsion: Discontinuity Editing, Classical Chinese Aesthetics, and Hong Kong's Culture of Disappearance." *Asian Cinema* 10, no. 2 (1999): 67–79.

Criswell, Colin, and Mike Watson. *The Royal Hong Kong Police (1841–1945)*. Hong Kong: Macmillan, 1982.

Curtin, Michael. *Playing to the World's Biggest Audience: The Globalization of Chinese Film and TV*. Berkeley: University of California Press, 2007.

Cuthbert, A. R. "Ambiguous Space, Ambiguous Rights—Corporate Power and Social Control in Hong Kong." *Cities* 14, no. 5 (1997): 295–311.

———. "The Right to the City: Surveillance, Private Interest and the Public Domain in Hong Kong." *Cities* 12, no. 5 (1995): 293–310.

Dannen, Frederic, and Barry Long. *Hong Kong Babylon: An Insider's Guide to the Hollywood of the East*. New York: Hyperion, 1997.

Davis, Mike. "Fortress L.A." In *City of Quartz: Excavating the Future in Los Angeles*, 223–63. New York: Vintage, 1992.

DeBoer, Stephanie. *Coproducing Asia: Locating Japanese-Chinese Regional Film and Media*. Minneapolis: University of Minnesota Press, 2014.

Deflem, Mathieu, Richard Featherstone, Yunqing Li, and Suzanne Sutphin. "Policing the Pearl: Historical Transformations of Law Enforcement in Hong Kong." *International Journal of Police Science and Management* 10, no. 3 (2007): 349–56.

Deleuze, Gilles. "Postscript on the Societies of Control." *October* 59 (Winter 1992): 3–7.

Denzin, Norman K. *The Cinematic Society: The Voyeur's Gaze*. London: SAGE Publications, 1995.

Desser, David. "Reclaiming a Legacy: The New-Style Martial Arts Saga and Globalized Entertainment." In *East Asian Cinema and Cultural Heritage*, edited by Kinnia Yau Shuk-ting, 2–25. New York: Palgrave, 2011.

———. "Triads and Changing Times: The National Allegory of Hong Kong Cinema, 1996–2000." *Quarterly Review of Film and Video* 26 (2009): 179–93.

Desyllas, Jake, Philip Connoly, and Frank Hebbert. "Modelling Natural Surveillance." *Environment and Planning B: Planning and Design* 30 (2003): 643–55.

Ding, Sheng. *The Dragon's Hidden Wings: How China Rises with Its Soft Power*. Lanham, MD: Lexington Books, 2008.

Dixon, Wheeler Winston. *It Looks at You: The Returned Gaze of Cinema*. Albany: State University of New York Press, 1995.

Doyle, Aaron, Randy Lippert, and David Lyon, eds. *Eyes Everywhere: The Global Growth of Camera Surveillance*. New York: Routledge, 2011.

Dutton, Michael. *Policing Chinese Politics*. Durham, NC: Duke University Press, 2005.

Eng, Robert. "Is *Hero* a Paean to Authoritarianism?" *UCLA International Institute*, September 7, 2004, http://web.international.ucla.edu/institute/article/14371.

Fang, Karen. "'Absurdity of Life': An Interview with Michael Hui." In *Not Just a Laughing Matter: Interdisciplinary Approaches to Political Humor in China*, edited by Sharon Wesoky and King-fai Tam. New York: Springer, forthcoming.

———. "Britain's Finest: The Royal Hong Kong Police." In *After the Imperial Turn: Thinking with and through the Nation*, edited by Antoinette Burton, 293–307. Durham, NC: Duke University Press, 2003.

———. *John Woo's* A Better Tomorrow. Hong Kong: Hong Kong University Press, 2004.

Faure, David. "Paying for Convenience: An Aspect of Corruption That Arises from Revenue Spending." In *Corruption and Its Control in Hong Kong: Situations up to the Late Seventies*, edited by Rance P. L. Lee, 133–65. Hong Kong: Chinese University Press, 1981.

Feng, Peter X. "False Consciousness and Double Consciousness: Race, Virtual Reality, and the Assimilation of Hong Kong Action Cinema in *The Matrix*." In *Chinese Connections: Critical Perspectives on Film, Identity, and Diaspora*, edited by Tan See-Kam, Peter X. Feng, and Gina Marchetti, 9–21. Philadelphia: Temple University Press, 2009.

Fiske, John. *Media Matters: Everyday Culture and Political Change*. Minneapolis: University of Minnesota Press, 1996.

Fong, Emily Tsz Yan. "Changing Intergroup Relations with Mainland Chinese: An Analysis of Changes in Hong Kong Movies as a Popular Cultural Discourse." *Multilingua* 29 (2010): 29–53.

Fore, Steve. "Golden Harvest Films and the Hong Kong Movie Industry in the Realm of Globalization." *Velvet Light Trap* 34 (1994): 40–58.

14th Hong Kong International Film Festival. *The China Factor in Hong Kong Cinema*. Hong Kong: Urban Council, 1990.

Fu, Poshek. *Between Shanghai and Hong Kong: The Politics of Chinese Cinemas*. Stanford, CA: Stanford University Press, 2003.

———, ed. *China Forever: The Shaw Brothers and Diasporic Cinema*. Urbana: University of Illinois Press, 2008.

Fung, Anthony. *Global Capital, Local Culture: Transnational Media Corporations in China*. New York: Peter Lang, 2008.

Gad, Christopher, and Lone Koefed Hansen. "A Closed Circuit Technological Vision: On Minority Report, Event Detection and Enabling Technologies." *Surveillance & Society* 11, no. 1/2 (2013): 148–62.

Galuppo, Mia, and Chris Godley. "Surveillance Cinema: 14 Movies Featuring Big Brother." *Hollywood Reporter*, June 21, 2013, http://www.hollywood reporter.com/gallery/surveillance-cinema-14-movies-featuring-566300/1-v -for-vendetta.

Gaylord, Mark S., and Harold Traver. "Colonial Policing and the Demise of British Rule in Hong Kong." *International Journal of the Sociology of Law* 23 (1995): 23–43.

Gaylord, M. S., and J. F. Galliher. "Riding the Underground Dragon." *British Journal of Criminology* 31, no. 1 (1991): 15–26.

Golden Harvest: Leading Change in Changing Times. Hong Kong: Hong Kong Film Archive, 2013.

Goodsir, Darren. "Police Future up for Investigation." *South China Morning Post*, November 26, 1994, 19.

Goodstadt, Leo. *Uneasy Partners: The Conflict between Public Interest and Private Profit in Hong Kong*. Hong Kong: Hong Kong University Press, 2005.

Greene, Naomi. *From Fu Manchu to Kung Fu Panda: Images of China in American Film*. Honolulu: University of Hawai'i Press, 2014.

Greenwald, Glenn. *No Place to Hide: Edward Snowden, the NSA, and the U.S. Surveillance State*. New York: Metropolitan Books, 2014.

Greenwald, Glenn, Ewen MacAskill, and Laura Poitras. "Covert Surveillance: 'I Have No Intention of Hiding . . . I Have Done Nothing Wrong': Edward Snowden, the Man Responsible for the Leaks of Secret Documents Detailing the NSA's Widespread Phone and Internet Surveillance." *The Guardian*, June 10, 2013, 2.

Grieveson, Lee. *Policing Cinema: Movies and Censorship in Early-Twentieth-Century America*. Berkeley: University of California Press, 2004.

Grossman, Andrew. "Homosexual Men (and Lesbian Men) in a Heterosexual Genre: Three Gangster Films from Hong Kong." In *Queer Asian Cinema: Shadows in the Shade*, edited by Andrew Grossman, 237–72. New York: Harrington Park Press, 2000.

Gunning, Tom. *The Films of Fritz Lang: Allegories of Vision and Modernity*. London: BFI, 2000.

———. "Tracing the Individual Body: Photography, Detectives and Early Cinema." In *Cinema and the Invention of Modern Life*, edited by Leo Charney and Vanessa R. Schwartz, 15–45. Berkeley: University of California Press, 1996.

———. "What I Saw from the Rear Window of the Hotel des Folies-Dramatiques, or the Story Point of View Films Told." In *Ce que je vois de mon ciné: La représentation du regard dans le cinéma des premiers temps*, edited by André Gaudreault, 33–43. Paris: Merudiens Klincksieck, 1988.

Hager, Nicky. *Secret Power: New Zealand's Role in the International Spy Network*. Nelson, New Zealand: Craig Potton, 1996.

Haggerty, Kevin D., and Richard V. Ericson. "The Surveillant Assemblage." *British Journal of Sociology* 51, no. 4 (2000): 605–22.

Halligan, Fionnuala. "*Cageman* Sweeps Local Film Awards." *South China Morning Post*, April 24, 1993, 1.

Hammel, Lee. "Former State Police Detective from Worcester Lends a Hand to Scorsese's New Movie." *Sunday Telegram*, October 9, 2005, A1.

Hampton, Mark. "British Legal Culture and Colonial Governance: The Attack on Corruption in Hong Kong, 1968–1974." *Britain and the World* 5, no. 2 (2012): 223–39.

Hansen, Miriam Bratu. "Benjamin and Cinema: Not a One-Way Street." *Critical Inquiry* 25 (Winter 1999): 306–43.

———. "Fallen Women, Rising Stars, New Horizons: Shanghai Silent Film as Vernacular Modernism." *Film Quarterly* 54, no. 1 (2000): 10–22.

Harland, Kathleen. *The Royal Navy in Hong Kong, since 1841*. Liskeard, Cornwall, UK: Maritime Books, 1991.

Harris, Peter. "The Bus and Its Riders: An Approach to the Problem of Corruption in Hong Kong." In *Hong Kong: A Study in Bureaucratic Politics*, by Peter Harris, 140–61. Hong Kong: Heinemann Asia, 1978.

Hillenbrand, Margaret. "The National Allegory Revisited: Writing Private and Public in Contemporary Taiwan." *positions* 14, no. 3 (Winter 2006): 633–62.

Ho, Elaine Yee Lin. "Women on the Edges of Hong Kong Modernity: The Films of Ann Hui." In *Spaces of Their Own: Women's Public Sphere in Transnational China*, edited by Mayfair Mei-hui Yang, 162–87. Minneapolis: University of Minnesota Press, 1999.

Hoberman, J. "'Man with No Name' Tells a Story of Heroics, Color Coordination." *Village Voice*, August 17, 2004.

Hoover, Michael, and Lisa Odham Stokes. "Hong Kong in New York: Global Connections, National Identity, and Filmic Representations." *New Political Science* 25, no. 4 (December 2003): 509–32.

Hunt, Leon. *Kung Fu Cult Masters*. London: Wallflower Press, 2003.

"Il fait rire toute l'Asie." *Cahiers du Cinema*, September 1984, 36–38.

Jacobs, Jane. *The Death and Life of American Cities*. New York: Random House, 1961.

Jacobs, Katrien. *People's Pornography: Sex and Surveillance on the Chinese Internet*. Bristol, UK: Intellect, 2012.

Jarvie, Ian. *Window on Hong Kong: A Sociological Study of the Hong Kong Film Industry and Its Audience*. Hong Kong: Centre of Asian Studies, Hong Kong University, 1977.

Jiao, Allan Y. *The Police in Hong Kong: A Contemporary View*. Lanham, MD: University Press of America, 2007.

Kammerer, Dietmar. "Video Surveillance in Hollywood Movies. *Surveillance & Society* 2, no. 2/3 (2004): 464–73.

Kaufman, Michael T. "What Does the Pentagon See in 'Battle of Algiers'?" *New York Times*, September 7, 2003. Section 4, 3.

Kim, Kyung Hyun. *Virtual Hallyu: Korean Cinema of the Global Era*. Durham, NC: Duke University Press, 2011.

King, Ambrose. "Administrative Absorption of Politics in Hong Kong: Emphasis on the Grass Roots Level." *Asian Survey* 15 (1995): 422–39.

———. (as Jin Yaoji). "Zhongguo Ren Dui Siyinquan De Lijie." *Ming Pao Monthly*, February 1994, 56–62.

Klein, Christina. *Cold War Orientalism: Asia in the Middlebrow Imagination, 1945–1961*. Berkeley: University of California Press, 2003.

Kleinhans, Chuck. "Becoming Hollywood? Hong Kong Cinema in the New Century." In *Chinese Connections: Critical Perspectives on Film, Identity, and Diaspora*, edited by Tan See-Kam, Peter X. Feng, and Gina Marchetti, 109–21. Philadelphia: Temple University Press, 2009.

Klitgaard, Robert. *Controlling Corruption.* Berkeley: University of California Press, 1991.

Kracauer, Siegfried. *From Caligari to Hitler: A Psychological History of the German Film.* Princeton, NJ: Princeton University Press, 2004.

Kung, James, and Zhang Yucai. "Hong Kong Cinema and Television in the 1970s: A Perspective." In *A Study of Hong Kong Cinema in the Seventies,* The Eighth Hong Kong International Film Festival Catalogue, 10–17. Hong Kong: Urban Council, 1984.

Kurlantzick, Joshua. *Charm Offensive: How China's Soft Power Is Transforming the World.* New Haven, CT: Yale University Press, 2007.

Lam, Lana. "Snowden's Legacy; Still Awaiting Answers on Spying Claims, but Observers Say That by Standing Up to Washington It Proved It Is Not Just Another Chinese City." *South China Morning Post,* June 14, 2014.

Lau Siu-Kai. *Utilitarian Familiarism: An Inquiry into the Basis of Political Stability.* Hong Kong: Chinese University of Hong Kong Social Research Centre, 1977.

Lau Siu-kai and Kuan Hsin-chi. *The Ethos of the Hong Kong Chinese.* Hong Kong: Chinese University Press, 1988.

Lau, Jenny. "Besides Fists and Blood: Hong Kong Comedy and Its Master of the Eighties." *Cinema Journal* 37, no. 2 (1998): 18–34.

———. "A Cultural Interpretation of the Popular Cinema of China and Hong Kong." In *Perspectives on Chinese Cinema,* edited by Chris Berry, 166–74. London: British Film Institute, 1991.

Law Kar. "Michael Hui: A Decade of Sword Grinding." In *A Study of Hong Kong Cinema in the Seventies,* The Eighth Hong Kong International Film Festival Catalogue, 62–68. Hong Kong: Hong Kong Urban Council, 1984.

———. "The 'Shaolin Temple' of the New Hong Kong Cinema." In *A Study of Hong Kong Cinema in the Seventies,* The Eighth Hong Kong International Film Festival Catalogue, 110–16. Hong Kong: Hong Kong Urban Council, 1984.

Law Kar and Frank Bren. *Hong Kong Cinema: A Cross-cultural View.* Lanham, MD: Scarecrow Press, 2004.

Law, Wing-sang. "Hong Kong Undercover: An Approach to 'Collaborative Colonialism.'" *Inter-Asia Cultural Studies* 9, no. 4 (2008): 522–42.

———. "The Violence of Time and Memory Undercover: Hong Kong's *Infernal Affairs. Inter-Asia Cultural Studies* 7, no. 3 (2006): 383–402.

Leary, Charles. "Electric Shadow of an Airplane: Hong Kong Cinema, World Cinema." In *East Asian Cinemas: Exploring Transnational Connections on Film,* edited by Leon Hunt and Leung Wing-fai, 57–68. London: I. B. Taurus, 2008.

———. "The Most Careful Arrangements for a Careful Fiction: A Short History of Asia Pictures." *Inter-Asia Cultural Studies* 13, no. 4 (2012): 548–58.

Lee, Leo Ou-Fan. *Shanghai Modern: The Flowering of a New Urban Culture in China, 1930–1945.* Cambridge, MA: Harvard University Press, 1999.

———. "Spying on the Spyring." In *Musings: Reading Hong Kong, China and the World*, 120–28. Hong Kong, East Slope Publishing, 2011.

———. "Two Films from Hong Kong: Parody and Allegory." In *New Chinese Cinemas: Forms, Identities, Politics*, edited by Nick Browne, Paul G. Pickowicz, Vivian Sobchack, and Esther Yau, 202–16. Cambridge: Cambridge University Press, 1994.

Lee, Paul S. N. "The Absorption and Indigenization of Foreign Media Cultures: A Study on a Cultural Meeting Point of the East and West: Hong Kong." *Asian Journal of Communication* 1, no. 2 (1991): 52–72.

Lee, Peter N. S. "The Causes and Effects of Police Corruption: A Case in Political Modernization." In *Corruption and Its Control in Hong Kong: Situations up to the Late Seventies*, edited by Rance Lee, 167–98. Hong Kong: Chinese University Press, 1981.

Lee, Rance P. L. "Bureaucratic Corruption and Political Instability in Nineteenth-Century China." In *Corruption and Its Control in Hong Kong: Situations up to the Late Seventies*, edited by Rance P. L. Lee, 105–32. Hong Kong: Chinese University Press, 1981.

———, ed. *Corruption and Its Control in Hong Kong: Situtations up to the Late Seventies*. Hong Kong: Chinese University Press, 1981.

Lee, Vivian. "Contested Heritage: Cinema, Collective Memory, and the Politics of Local Heritage in Hong Kong." In *East Asian Cinema and Cultural Heritage: From China, Hong Kong, Taiwan to Japan and South Korea*, edited by Kinnia Yau Shuk-ting, 53–79. New York: Palgrave, 2011.

———. *Hong Kong Cinema since 1997: The Post-nostalgic Imagination*. London: Palgrave, 2009.

———. "The Mainland 'Other' in the Hong Kong Commercial Mainstream: Political Change and Cultural Adaptation." In *How East Asian Films Are Reshaping National Identities*, edited by Andrew David Jackson, Michael Gibb, and David White, 155–66. Lewiston, NY: Edwin Mellen Press, 2006.

———. "PTU: Re-mapping the Cosmopolitan Crime Zone." In *Chinese Films in Focus II*, edited by Chris Berry, 182–88. London: BFI, 2008.

Léfait, Sébastien. *Surveillance on Screen: Monitoring Contemporary Films and Television Programs*. Lanham, MD: Scarecrow Press, 2012.

Lethbridge, H. J. "Corruption, White Collar Crime and the I.C.A.C." *Hong Kong Law Journal* 6, no. 2 (1976): 150–78.

Leung Ping-kwan. "Urban Cinema and the Cultural Identity of Hong Kong." In *The Cinema of Hong Kong: History, Arts, Identity*, edited by Poshek Fu and David Desser, 227–51. Cambridge: Cambridge University Press, 2000.

Leung, Cheuk-fan. "The Lure of the Exotic: Hong Kong Cinema in Japan." In *Border Crossings in Hong Kong Cinema*, edited by Law Kar, 156–59. Hong Kong: Leisure and Cultural Services Department, 2000.

Levin, Thomas Y. "Rhetoric of the Temporal Index: Surveillant Narration and the Cinema of 'Real Time.'" In *Ctrl [Space]: Rhetorics of Surveillance from Ben-*

tham to Big Brother, edited by Thomas Y. Levin, Ursula Frohne, and Peter Weibel, 578–93. Cambridge, MA: MIT Press, 2002.

Li Cheuk-to. "Postscript." In *A Study of Hong Kong Cinema in the Seventies*, The Eighth Hong Kong International Film Festival Catalogue, 127–31. Hong Kong: Hong Kong Urban Council, 1984.

———. "The Return of the Father: Hong Kong New Wave and Its Chinese Context in the 1980s." In *New Chinese Cinemas: Forms, Identities, Politics*, edited by Nick Browne, Paul G. Pickowicz, Vivian Sobchak, and Esther Yau, 160–79. Cambridge: Cambridge University Press, 1994.

Lii, Ding-Tzann. "A Colonized Empire: Reflections on the Expansion of Hong Kong Films in Asian Countries." In *Trajectories: Inter-Asia Cultural Studies*, edited by Kuan-Hsing Chen, 122–41. New York: Routledge, 1998.

Lo, Clifford. "Octopus Gives Police Long Tentacles: Data Recorded on Cards Helps Officers Find and Track Suspects." *South China Morning Post*, March 1, 2010, 3.

Lo, Kwai-Cheung. "A Borderline Case: Ethnic Politics and Gangster Films in Post-1997 Hong Kong." *Postcolonial Studies* 10, no. 4 (2007): 431–46.

Lo, Kwai-Cheung, and Evan Man Kit-Wah. *Age of Hybridity: Cultural Identity, Gender, Everyday Life Practice and Hong Kong Cinema of the 1970s*. Hong Kong: Oxford University Press, 2005 (in Chinese).

Lo, Yu-lai. "Some Notes about Film Censorship in Hong Kong." In *21st Hong Kong International Film Festival Catalog*, 60–63. Hong Kong: Hong Kong International Film Festival, 1997.

Lombardo, Johannes R. "Eisenhower, the British and the Security of Hong Kong, 1953–60." *Diplomacy & Statecraft* 9, no. 3 (1998): 143–53.

Long Tin. "Grey in the Midst of White: Undercover Agents in ICAC Drama Series." Translated by King-fai Tam. In *The Quiet Revolution: 40 Years of ICAC Drama Series*, edited by Li Cheuk-to and Keith Chan, with English editors Ken Smith, Joanna Lee, and Amory Hui, 190–95. Hong Kong: Government of the Hong Kong Special Administration Region, 2014.

Low, William W. L., G. M. Naidu, and Richard C. M. Yam. "Dynamic and Responsive Firm Strategy: A Case Study of Hong Kong and China Collaborations in Pearl River Delta." *Journal of Global Marketing* 14, no. 4 (2001): 27–49.

Lu, Xiaoning. "*The Might of the People*: Counter-espionage Films and Participatory Surveillance in the Early PRC." In *Surveillance in Asian Cinema: Under Eastern Eyes*, edited by Karen Fang. New York: Routledge, forthcoming.

Lyon, David. *Surveillance Studies: An Overview*. Cambridge, UK: Polity, 2007.

Ma Ngok, *Political Development in Hong Kong: State, Political Stability, and Civil Society*. Hong Kong: Hong Kong University Press, 2007.

Ma, Eric Kit-wai. "Outsiders on Television." In *Culture, Politics, and Television in Hong Kong*, 62–96. New York: Routledge, 1999.

Malcolm, Derek. "The Blade Cuts Sharper." *The Guardian*, November 26, 1992.

Marchetti, Gina. *Andrew Lau and Alan Mak's* Infernal Affairs—*the Trilogy*. Hong Kong: Hong Kong University Press, 2007.

———. *Romance and the "Yellow Peril": Race, Sex, and Discursive Strategies in Hollywood Fiction*. Berkeley: University of California Press, 1993.

Marchetti, Gina, and Tan See Kam, eds. *Hong Kong Film, Hollywood and the New Global Cinema: No Film Is an Island*. New York: Routledge, 2007.

Mark, Chi-Kwan. *Hong Kong and the Cold War: Anglo-American Relations, 1949–1957*. Oxford: Clarendon, 2004.

Martin, Sylvia J. "Of Ghosts and Gangsters: Capitalist Cultural Production and the Hong Kong Film Industry." *Visual Anthropology* 28, no. 1 (2012): 32–49.

Martin-Jones, David. *Deleuze, Cinema and National Identity: Narrative Time in National Contexts*. Edinburgh: Edinburgh University Press, 2006.

Marx, Gary T. "The New Surveillance." In *Undercover: Police Surveillance in America*, by Gary T. Marx, 206–33. Berkeley: University of California Press, 1988.

Mathiesen, Thomas. "The Viewer Society: Michel Foucault's 'Panopticon' Revisited." *Theoretical Criminology* 1, no. 2 (1997): 215–34.

Maxwell, Richard. "Surveillance: Work, Myth, and Policy." *Social Text* 83, no. 2 (Summer 2005): 1–19.

Mazierska, Ewa, and Laura Rascoli. "Trapped in the Present: Time in the Films of Wong Kar-wai." *Film Criticism* 25, no. 2 (2000/2001): 2–20.

Mazumdar, Ranjani. "Terrorism, Conspiracy, and Surveillance in Bombay's Urban Cinema." *Social Research* 78, no. 1 (2011): 143–72.

Melson, P. J., ed. *White Ensign, Red Dragon: The History of the Royal Navy in Hong Kong, 1841–1941*. Hong Kong: Edinburgh Financial Publishing, 1997.

Miller, D. A. *The Novel and the Police*. Berkeley: University of California Press, 1989.

Miners, Norman. "The Localisation of the Hong Kong Police Force, 1842–1947." *Journal of Imperial and Commonwealth History* 18 (1990): 296–315.

Moretti, Franco. "Planet Hollywood." *New Left Review* 9 (2001): 90–101.

Morris, Meaghan. "Transnational Imagination in Action Cinema: Hong Kong and the Making of a Global Popular Culture." *Inter-Asia Cultural Studies*, 5, no. 2 (2004): 181–99.

Morris, Meaghan, Siu Leung Li, and Stephen Chan Ching-kiu, eds. *Hong Kong Connections: Transnational Imagination in Action Cinema*. Durham, NC: Duke University Press, 2005.

Mozur, Paul, and Alan Wong. "Hong Kong Protesters Flock to Off-Grid Messaging App." *New York Times*, September 29, 2014, http://sinosphere .blogs.nytimes.com/2014/09/29/hong-kong-protesters-flock-to-off-grid -messaging-app/?_r=0.

Mozur, Paul, Alan Wong, and Andrew Jacobs. "Fake App Eavesdrops on Hong Kong Protesters' Phones." *New York Times*, October 2, 2014, B4.

Munish, Mukul. "For Whom the Bells Toll; over a Third of the City's Adult Population Actively Trades in Stocks. What Do These People Spend Their Days Doing?" *South China Morning Post*, September 22, 2009, 34.

Munn, Christopher. *Anglo-China: Chinese People and British Rule in Hong Kong, 1841–1880*. Hong Kong: Hong Kong University Press, 2009.

Musser, Charles. "Work, Ideology and Chaplin's Tramp." *Radical History Review* 41 (1988): 36–66.

Nakamura, Lisa. "Interfaces of Identity: Oriental Traitors and Telematic Profiling in 24." *Camera Obscura* 24, no. 1 70 (2009): 109–33.

Needham, Gary. "Fashioning Modernity: Hollywood and the Hong Kong Musical, 1957–64." In *East Asian Cinemas: Exploring Transnational Connections on Film*, edited by Leon Hunt and Leung Wing-Fai, 41–56. London: I. B. Tauris, 2008.

Newman, David. "British Colonial Censorship Regimes: Hong Kong, Straits Settlements, and Shanghai International Settlement, 1916–1941." In *Silencing Cinema: Film Censorship around the World*, edited by Daniel Biltereyst and Roel Vande Winkel, 167–90. New York: Palgrave, 2013.

Ng Ho. "A Portrait of the Comedian as a Schizophreniac." In *A Study of Hong Kong Cinema in the Seventies*, The Eighth Hong Kong International Film Festival Catalogue, 69–72. Hong Kong: Hong Kong Urban Council, 1984.

Ng, Grace, ed. *One for All: The Union Film Spirit*. Hong Kong: Hong Kong Film Archive, 2011.

Ng, Janet. *Paradigm City: Space, Culture, and Capitalism in Hong Kong*. Albany: SUNY Press, 2009.

Nye, J. S., Jr. *Soft Power: The Means to Success in World Politics*. New York: PublicAffairs, 2004.

Nye, J. S., Jr., and W. Jisi. "Hard Decisions on Soft Power: Opportunities and Difficulties for Chinese Soft Power." *Harvard International Review* 31, no. 2 (Summer 2009): 18–22.

Ong, Aihwa. "Flexible Citizenship among Chinese Cosmopolitans." In *Cosmopolitics: Thinking and Feeling beyond the Nation*, edited by Pheng Cheah and Bruce Robbins, 134–62. Minneapolis: University of Minnesota Press, 1998.

———. *Neoliberalism as Exception: Mutations in Citizenship and Sovereignty*. Durham, NC: Duke University Press, 2006.

Pang, Laikwan. *Creativity and Its Discontents: China's Creative Industries and Intellectual Property Rights Offenses*. Durham, NC: Duke University Press, 2012.

———. *Cultural Control and Globalization in Asia: Copyright, Piracy, and Cinema*. New York: Routledge, 2006.

———. "Jackie Chan, Tourism, and the Performing Agency." In *Hong Kong Film, Hollywood and the New Global Cinema: No Film Is an Island*, edited by Gina Marchetti and Tan See-Kam, 206–18. New York: Routledge, 2007.

———. "Postcolonial Hong Kong Cinema: Utilitarianism and (Trans)Local." *Postcolonial Studies* 10, no. 4 (2007): 413–30.

Parenti, Christian. *The Soft Cage Surveillance in American from Slavery to the War on Terror.* New York: Basic Books, 2004.

Polan, Dana. *Power and Paranoia: History, Narrative, and the American Cinema, 1940–1950.* New York: Columbia University Press, 1986.

Rahman, Abid. "Jeff Robinov's Studio 8 to Remake Hong Kong Surveillance Thriller 'Overheard.'" *Hollywood Reporter*, November 27, 2014, http://www .hollywoodreporter.com/news/jeff-robinovs-studio-8-remake-752721.

Rayns, Tony. "Deep Cover." *Sight and Sound* 14, no. 1 (2004): 26–29.

Rodriguez, Hector. "The Emergence of the Hong Kong New Wave." In *At Full Speed: Hong Kong Cinema in a Borderless World*, edited by Esther Yau, 53–69. Minneapolis: University of Minnesota Press, 2001.

———. "The Fragmented Commonplace: Alternative Arts and Cosmopolitanism in Hong Kong." In *Multiple Modernities: Cinemas and Popular Media in Transcultural Asia*, edited by Jenny Kowk Wah Lau, 128–48. Philadelphia: Temple University Press, 2002.

———. "Organizational Hegemony in the Hong Kong Cinema." *Post Script* 19, no. 1 (Fall 1999): 107–19.

Rooney, Nuala. *At Home with Density.* Hong Kong: Hong Kong University Press, 2003.

Rule, James. *Privacy in Peril.* Oxford: Oxford University Press, 2007.

Sammon, Paul. *Future Noir: The Making of* Blade Runner. New York: Harper-Prism, 1996.

Sandell, Jillian. "Reinventing Masculinity: The Spectacle of Male Intimacy in the Films of John Woo." *Film Quarterly* 49, no. 4 (1996): 23–34.

Scocca, Tom. "Martin Scorsese, Now a Great Hong Kong Director." *New York Observer*, October 9, 2006, 8.

Scott, A. O. "The Leisure Class Bears Its Burden." *New York Times*, August 23, 2012, C1.

Sek Kei. "The Vicissitudes of Golden Studios: From Factory-Oriented Production to Star System and Satellite Operation." In *Golden Harvest: Leading Change in Changing Times*, 26–33. Hong Kong: Hong Kong Film Archive, 2013.

Sengoopta, Chandak. *Imprint of the Raj.* London: Pan Macmillan, 2004.

Shackleton, Liz. "South Korea to Remake Johnnie To's *Drug War*," *Screen Daily*, May 18, 2014, http://www.screendaily.com/territories/asia-pacific/south -korea-to-remake-drug-war/5072086.article.

Shapiro, Michael J. "Every Move You Make: Bodies, Surveillance, and Media." *Social Text* 83, no. 2 (2005): 21–34.

———. "Intercity Cinema: Hong Kong at the Berlinale." *Journal for Cultural Research* 12, no. 1 (2008): 99–119.

Shearing, Clifford, and Philip Stenning. "Modern Private Security: Its Growth and Implications." *Crime and Justice* 3 (1981): 193–245.

Shih, Shu-mei. "After National Allegory." In *Visuality and Identity: Sinophone Articulations across the Pacific*, 1401–64. Berkeley: University of California Press, 2007.

——. *Visuality and Identity: Sinophone Articulations across the Pacific*. Berkeley: University of California Press, 2007.

Sinclair, Georgina. *At the End of the Line: Colonial Policing and the Imperial Endgame, 1945–80*. Manchester, UK: Manchester University Press, 2006.

Sinclair, Kevin. *Royal Hong Kong Police, 1844–1944: 150th Anniversary Commemorative Publication*. Hong Kong: Police Public Relations Bureau, 1994.

——. "Safe in the Hands of Asia's Finest." *South China Morning Post*, October 14, 1996, 19.

Sinclair, Kevin, and Stephanie Holmes. *Asia's Finest: An Illustrated Account of the Royal Hong Kong Police*. Hong Kong: Unicorn, 1983.

Sinn, Elizabeth. *Power and Charity: A Chinese Merchant Elite in Colonial Hong Kong*. Hong Kong: Hong Kong University Press, 2003.

Skidmore, Max J. "Promise and Peril in Combating Corruption: Hong Kong's ICAC." In *The Future of Hong Kong*, edited by Max J. Skidmore, Annals of the American Academy of Political and Social Science, 118–30. Thousand Oaks: SAGE Periodicals Press, 1996.

Slotkin, Richard. *Gunfighter Nation: The Myth of the Frontier in Twentieth-Century America*. New York: Atheneum, 1992.

Smart, Alan. *The Shek Kip Mei Myth: Squatters, Fires and Colonial Rulers in Hong Kong, 1950–1963*. Hong Kong: Hong Kong University Press, 2006.

Smith, Kyle. "Shanghaied: Shocked That Hollywood Collaborated with the Nazis? It's Doing the Exact Same Thing Today with China." *New York Post*, August 4, 2013, 23.

Smolin, Jonathan. *Moroccan Noir: Police, Crime, and Politics in Popular Culture*. Bloomington: Indiana University Press, 2013.

Song Mu. "The Man Who Jumped off the Connaught Centre." Translated by Jane C. C. Lai. In *Hong Kong Collage: Contemporary Stories and Writing*, edited by Martha P. Y. Cheung, 55–63. Hong Kong: Oxford University Press, 1998.

Spring, Katherine. "Sounding Glocal: Synthesizer Scores in Hong Kong Action Cinema." In *American and Chinese-Language Cinemas: Examining Cultural Flows*, edited by Lisa Funnell and Man-Fung Yip, 38–52. New York: Routledge, 2015.

Stewart, Garrett. *Closed Circuits: Screening Narrative Surveillance*. Chicago: University of Chicago Press, 2015.

——. "Modern Hard Times: Chaplin and the Cinema of Self-Reflection." *Critical Inquiry* 3, no. 2 (1976): 295–314.

——. "Surveillance Cinema." *Film Quarterly* 66, no. 2 (Winter 2012): 5–15.

Stokes, Lisa Odham, and Michael Hoover. *City on Fire: Hong Kong Cinema.* London: Verso, 1999.

"The Story behind *Cageman.*" *Straits Times,* August 13, 1993, 2.

Stringer, Julian. "'Your Tender Smiles Give Me Strength': Paradigms of Masculinity in John Woo's *A Better Tomorrow* and *The Killer.*" *Screen* 38, no. 1 (1997): 25–41.

Szeto, Kin-yan. *The Martial Arts Cinema of the Chinese Diaspora: Ang Lee, John Woo and Jackie Chan in Hollywood.* Carbondale: Southern Illinois University Press, 2011.

Szeto, Mirana, and Yun-chung Chen. "Mainlandization or Sinophone Translocality? Challenges for Hong Kong SAR New Wave Cinema." *Journal of Chinese Cinemas* 6, no. 2 (2012): 115–34.

———. "To Work or Not to Work: The Dilemma of Hong Kong Film Labor in the Age of Mainlandization." *Jump Cut* 55 (2013), http://ejumpcut.org/archive/jc55.2013/SzetoChenHongKong/.

Tang, Phyllis. "Privacy Law Changes to be Put Forward; Data Protection Rules Don't Meet Public's Expectations, Henry Tang Says after Octopus Row." *South China Morning Post,* August 21, 2010.

Tavernise, Sabrina. "Newly Vigilant, U.S. Will Screen Fliers for Ebola." *New York Times,* October 9, 2014, 1.

Teo, Stephen. *Chinese Martial Arts Cinema: The* Wuxia *Tradition.* Edinburgh: Edinburgh University Press, 2009.

———. *Director in Action: Johnnie To and the Hong Kong Action Film.* Hong Kong: Hong Kong University Press, 2007.

———. *Hong Kong Cinema: The Extra Dimensions.* London: British Film Institute, 1997.

———. "The 1970s: Movement and Transition." In *The Cinema of Hong Kong: History, Arts, Identity,* edited by Poshek Fu and David Desser, 90–110. Cambridge: Cambridge University Press, 2000.

Teo, Stephen, and Vivian Lee. "Placing Value in the Missing and the Lost." *Journal of Chinese Cinemas* 4, no. 2 (2010): 83–87.

To, Yiu, and Ray Yep. "Global Capital and Media Control: A Case of Joint Venture in China's Media Market before WTO." *East Asia: An International Quarterly* 25, no. 2 (June 2008): 167–85.

Topal, Çağatay. "Global Citizens and Local Powers: Surveillance in Turkey." *Social Text* 83, no. 2 (Summer 2005): 85–93.

Traver, Harold. "Orientations toward Privacy in Hong Kong." *Perceptual and Motor Skills* 59 no. 2 (1984): 635–44.

Traver, Harold, and Jon Vagg, eds. *Crime and Justice in Hong Kong.* Hong Kong: Oxford University Press, 1991.

Tsang, Steve. *A Modern History of Hong Kong.* London: I. B. Tauris, 2004.

Tsui, Curtis K. "Subjective Culture and History: The Ethnographic Cinema of Wong Kar-wai." *Asian Cinema* 7, no. 2 (Winter 1995): 93–124.

Tsui, Rebecca. "Plot Spoiled by Red Tape." *South China Morning Post*, January 25, 2009, 12.

Turner, John S. "Collapsing the Interior/Exterior Distinction: Surveillance, Spectacle, and Suspense in Popular Cinema." *Wide Angle* 20, no. 4 (1998): 93–123.

Turner, Matthew. "60s/90s: Dissolving the People." In *Hong Kong Sixties: Designing Identity*, edited by Matthew Turner and Irene Ngan, 13–36. Hong Kong: Hong Kong Arts Centre, 1995.

24th Hong Kong International Film Festival. Hong Kong: Urban Council, 2000.

Vagg, Jon. "Policing Hong Kong." *Policing and Society* 1 (1990): 235–47.

Van den Troost, Kristof. "Under Western Eyes? Colonial Bureaucracy, Surveillance and the Birth of the Hong Kong Crime Film." In *Surveillance in Asian Cinema: Under Eastern Eyes*, edited by Karen Fang. New York: Routledge, forthcoming.

Vatelescu, Christina. *Police Aesthetics: Literature, Film and the Secret Police in Soviet Times.* Stanford, CA: Stanford University Press, 2010.

Virilio, Paul. *War and Cinema: The Logistics of Perception.* London: Verso, 1989.

Vukovich, Daniel F. *China and Orientalism: Western Knowledge Production and the P.R.C.* London: Routledge, 2012.

Wakefield, Alison. *Selling Security: The Private Policing of Public Space.* Portland, OR: Willan Publishing, 2003.

Walsh, Mike. "Hong Kong Goes International: The Case of Golden Harvest." In *Hong Kong Film, Hollywood and the New Global Cinema: No Film Is an Island*, edited by Gina Marchetti and Tan See-Kam, 167–76. New York: Routledge, 2007.

Wang, Yiman. *Remaking Chinese Cinema: Through the Prism of Shanghai, Hong Kong, and Hollywood.* Honolulu: University of Hawai'i Press, 2013.

Ward, Iain. *Sui Geng: The Hong Kong Marine Police, 1841–1950.* Hong Kong: University of Hong Kong Press, 1991.

Watt, Louise. "Co-productions; How to Grab Chinese and Western Audiences? Delicately." *Globe and Mail*, June 27, 2014, R2.

Whitfield, Andrew J. *Hong Kong, Empire and the Anglo-American Alliance at War, 1941–45.* New York: Palgrave, 2001.

Wilkinson, Tara Loader. "New Dawn for Day Trading; Activity Surges with City's Army of Investors Opening Up More Trading Platforms." *South China Morning Post*, May 13, 2013, 5.

Williams, Tony. "Space, Place, and Spectacle: The Crisis Cinema of John Woo." *Cinema Journal* 36, no. 2 (1997): 67–84.

Wilson, Christopher P. *Cop Knowledge: Police Power and Cultural Narrative in Twentieth-Century America.* Chicago: University of Chicago Press, 2000.

Wing-fai, Leung. "Multi-media Stardom, Performance and Theme Songs in Hong Kong Cinema." *Canadian Journal of Film Studies* 20, no. 1 (2011): 41–60.

Wong Ain-ling, ed. *The Shaw Screen: A Preliminary Study.* Hong Kong: Hong Kong Film Archive, 2003.

Wong, Edward. "Hong Kong's Final Cut?" *Los Angeles Times,* June 15, 1997, 1.

Wong, Jeremiah K. H. "The ICAC and Its Anti-corruption Measures." In *Corruption and Its Control in Hong Kong: Situations up to the Late Seventies,* edited by Rance P. L. Lee, 45–74. Hong Kong: Chinese University Press, 1981.

Wong, Kam C. *Policing in Hong Kong.* Burlington, VT: Ashgate, 2012.

Xiao, Zhiwei. "Prohibition, Politics, and Nation-Building: A History of Film Censorship in China." In *Silencing Cinema: Film Censorship around the World,* edited by Daniel Bilteyrest and Roel Vande Winkel, 109–30. New York: Palgrave, 2013.

Xu, Gary G. *Sinascape: Contemporary Chinese Cinema.* Lanham, MD: Rowman and Littlefield, 2007.

Yau Ching. *Filming Margins: Tang Shu Shuen, a Forgotten Hong Kong Woman Director.* Hong Kong: Hong Kong University Press, 2004.

———. "Porn Power: Sexual and Gender Politics in Li Han-Hsiang's *Fengyue* Films." In *As Normal as Possible: Negotiating Sexuality and Gender in Mainland China and Hong Kong,* edited by Yau Ching, 113–31. Hong Kong: Hong Kong University Press, 2010.

Yau Shuk-ting, Kinnia. "From Shaw Brothers to Golden Harvest: Raymond Chow and Japan." In *Golden Harvest: Leading Change in Changing Times,* 43–49. Hong Kong: Hong Kong Film Archive, 2013.

Yau, Esther. "Border Crossing: Mainland China's Presence in Hong Kong Cinema." In *New Chinese Cinemas: Forms, Identities, Politics,* edited by Nick Browne, Paul G. Pickowicz, Vivian Sobchak, and Esther Yau, 180–201. Cambridge: Cambridge University Press, 1994.

———. "Genre Study and Cold War Cinema: Comments on Spy Detection Films of the Seventeen Year Period." *Dangdai dianying/Contemporary Cinema* 3 (2006): 74–80.

Yeh, Anthony G. O. "Planning and Management of Hong Kong's Border." In *From Colony to SAR: Hong Kong's Challenges Ahead,* edited by Joseph Y. S. Cheng and Sonny S. H. Lo, 261–91. Hong Kong: Chinese University Press, 1995.

Yeung, Frederick. "Industry Remembers Those Classic Adverts." *South China Morning Post,* May 30, 2007, 4.

Yip, Man-Fung. "Closely Watched Films: Surveillance and Postwar Leftist Cinema." In *Surveillance in Asian Cinema: Under Eastern Eyes,* edited by Karen Fang. New York: Routledge, forthcoming.

———. "In the Realm of the Senses: Sensory Realism, Speed, and Hong Kong Martial Arts Cinema." *Cinema Journal* 53, no. 4 (2014): 76–97.

Yue, S. Y. "Beijing Visit on the Cards for Police." *South China Morning Post,* November 29, 1993, 2.

Yung, Sai-shing. "Containment and Integration: A Preliminary Study of Asia Press and Asia Pictures Limited." In *The Cold War and Hong Kong Cinema*, edited by Wong Ain-ling and Lee Pui-tak, 249–62. Hong Kong: Hong Kong Film Archive, 2009.

Zimmer, Catherine. *Surveillance Cinema*. New York: NYU Press, 2015.

———. "Surveillance Cinema: Narrative between Technology and Politics." *Surveillance & Society* 8, no. 4 (2011): 427–40.

Page numbers followed by f indicate material in figures.